From War to Peace

Altered Strategic Landscapes
in the Twentieth Century

Edited by Paul Kennedy
and William I. Hitchcock

Yale University Press
New Haven and London

Published with assistance from the foundation established in memory of
Philip Hamilton McMillan of the Class of 1894, Yale College.

Set in Melior type by Binghamton Valley Composition. Printed in the
United States of America by Vail-Ballou Press, Binghamton, New York.

Library of Congress Cataloging-in-Publication Data

From war to peace : altered strategic landscapes in the twentieth century /
edited by Paul Kennedy and William I. Hitchcock.
    p.   cm.
Includes bibliographical references and index.
ISBN 0-300-08010-7 (cloth : alk. paper)
1. World politics—20th century.   2. Nationalism—History—20th
century.   3. Racism—History—20th century.   I. Kennedy, Paul.
II. Hitchcock, William I.

D443 .F77 2000
909.82—dc21   00-031035

A catalog record for this book is available from the British Library.

The paper in this book meets the guidelines for permanence and durability
of the Committee on Production Guidelines for Book Longevity of the
Council on Library Resources.

10 9 8 7 6 5 4 3 2 1

Contents

YAP 12/20/00

Contents

Acknowledgments

These essays were first presented to a conference at Yale University in June 1996. The sponsor was International Security Studies, a research program at Yale that promotes the study of strategy, diplomacy, and international affairs in a historical context. The conference was made possible by the generous support of the Smith Richardson Foundation, and we would like to express our deep thanks to the officers of the foundation, especially its president, Peter Richardson. The staff of ISS, especially Ann Carter-Drier, Susan Hennigan, and Rose Pawlikowski, also deserve our warm thanks for assisting both with the conference itself and with the subsequent preparation of this book. We wish to thank Charles Hill for his valuable insight along the way, and William G. Gray for editorial assistance.

Introduction

Paul Kennedy and
William I. Hitchcock

"Bliss was it in that dawn to be alive," wrote Wordsworth about the last days of the revolutionary eighteenth century. So, too, might one have thought as the 1980s drew to a close. In just a few years—the blink of an eye in historical terms—a breathtaking series of transformations to a long-established international order occurred, apparently without warning, and still more astonishing, without violence or war. In 1989–91, the Cold War came to an end, the Germans tore down the Berlin Wall and reunited their nation, the Soviet empire imploded, Eastern Europe shook off its totalitarian shackles, and American power stood supreme above any challengers. Saddam Hussein discovered how well prepared and willing the United States was to exercise its newfound role as global hegemon when, in 1990, he invaded Kuwait, only to be expelled by a U.S.-led international coalition. In those heady days, even the United Nations appeared to have found a new role as a world arbiter, an actor in world affairs that possessed credibility, resolve, and purpose. It seemed perfectly reasonable that U.S. president George Bush should have spoken of a "new world order."

The post–Cold War world has disappointed us. The clarity of 1989 has been blurred by new and unforeseen international problems, from nuclear proliferation, ethnic conflict, and transnational economic instability to environmental degradation, demographic explosion, and resource depletion. Each calls for immediate action, but the tools, and the strategic thinking to deploy them, appear to be lacking. This book was conceived, then, at a time of international fluidity and "strategic drift." It is not our purpose to propose solutions or offer a new paradigm for the present circumstances. Rather, these essays seek to place contemporary debates about the international order in historical perspective. We invited some of the leading historians of twentieth-century international relations to analyze the process by which planners and peacemakers in the years immediately following 1918, 1945, and 1989 attempted to craft a viable postwar order. The authors pay particular attention both to the objectives of the planners and to the obstacles that faced them. Reviewing the history of postwar settlements, we may draw some comfort from the fact that ours is not the first generation to have struggled with the challenge of creating a lasting international order in the wake of war. European and American leaders in 1918 and 1945 believed they, too, had an opportunity and an obligation to create a new international system that would insure peace and stability. The efforts of the first generation proved a dismal failure; the efforts of the second an incomplete success. The jury is still out on our own.

The Shadow of the Past

At the risk of oversimplification, we can impose a narrative upon the postwar settlements that concern us here, and draw out three important themes that emerge from each. Perhaps the most evident feature in all three periods is what Arno Mayer called, in another context, "the persistence of the old regime."

That is, in framing a postwar order, policymakers and strategists quite naturally seek to address the causes of the war from which they have just emerged. Yet in resolving problems of the past, planners tend to overlook or underestimate the transformations brought on by the conflict itself. In 1919, as Carole Fink's essay discusses, the four Allied leaders at Versailles sought to rectify the problems that had led to war five years earlier. German power had to be reduced; secret alliances had to be repudiated; and militarism had to be extirpated. Thus, the powers at Versailles demanded reparations from Germany and a breakup of its empire, its monarchy, and its army. Diplomacy would be carried on in public, to preclude the secret and binding commitments that had appeared to predetermine the July crisis of 1914; and a policy of multilateral disarmament would prevent a renewed arms race.

Yet the Versailles settlement did not solve the underlying elements of instability that had been either exacerbated or in fact brought into existence by the war itself. In breaking up Germany and Austria-Hungary, Versailles promoted ethnonationalism in Eastern Europe, a poor foundation for order, and a factor easily exploited by the Nazis, as the Sudeten crisis of 1938 revealed. In imposing harsh economic penalties on Germany, Versailles weakened the international economic fabric that had tied states together before the war. In stripping Germany of its monarchy, army, navy, and colonies, yet failing to foster an alternative German civic culture that championed democracy, the planners at Versailles gave Germans reason for humiliation but not the means to bear it. Finally, in placing their trust in the power of international opinion and institutions to enforce the peace, the Versailles powers stripped themselves of the elements of coercion that a viable peace settlement requires. In fact, the successor states to the Austro-Hungarian Empire were weak and unsteady, and offered little counterweight to any long-term German revival. Trying to solve old problems, the peacemakers at Versailles created a host of new ones.

A similar pattern can be discerned in the post–World War II settlement. Melvyn Leffler's chapter shows that from the start of the war, the United States took the lead in designing a postwar order that would address the causes of the war then raging. These were thought to include, once again, concentrated German power, economic autarky, and indeed the Versailles settlement itself, which had been too harsh on Germany and yet too weak to enforce its provisions. Thus, any postwar settlement would have to concede an important role to the great powers and their spheres of influence, in which they would be encouraged to enforce stability and order. The pursuit of order, however, had to be a common objective of the powers, who would work within an international body, the United Nations: a neat blend of Wilson's idealism with Roosevelt's canny sense for the art of the possible. At the same time, FDR and his successor Harry S. Truman also sought to avoid the debilitating policy of reparations that had crippled Germany and disrupted Europe's economy. Instead, they believed, productivity and international trade must be quickly revived so as to buttress the political settlement. Finally, German power would be contained through a complete social, political, and institutional restructuring of the country that would require an extended occupation by the victorious powers. Here was the remedy for the ills of Versailles: eliminating the harshness of the settlement while giving the powers more means to enforce it.

Post–World War II planners had learned from the experience of Versailles that economic integration and multilateralism were critical foundations for political stability. They also understood that the United States must take a major role in the postwar period, as it had been unwilling to do after 1919. As Randall Woods demonstrates, the Bretton Woods agreements reflected America's commitment to Western European economic recovery, and offers vivid testimony to the possibilities of creative leadership in fostering international stability.

At the same time, these successes were tempered by the failure to anticipate the impact of two new factors that the war itself had brought sharply to the forefront of international relations: atomic weapons and ideology. The American possession of the atomic bomb, and the unwillingness of the Americans to share their knowledge, immediately skewed the international power balance, making the hopeful, cooperative idea of Roosevelt's "four policemen" appear quite naive, and in any case disingenuous from the Soviet point of view. Furthermore, the Soviets saw America's atomic monopoly as one element in a much broader, carefully scripted American plan to coerce Russia into a subservient and marginal role in world affairs. Meanwhile, Americans read Soviet unwillingness to accept the American design for a balanced, largely democratic and interdependent world as a sign of truculence, hostility, and mistrust. In the eighteen months following the end of the war, disputes in Germany, the Near East, and the Mediterranean convinced Americans of the aggressive nature of Soviet policy in Europe. This strategic conflict was fed by ideology. One legacy of the war was that both Soviet and American leaders had come to believe that their respective political systems—which at heart were diametrically opposed— were not only viable but had been the crucial element in defeating Hitler. It was natural that they would now draw upon their enhanced ideological consciousness to shape a peace consistent with the lessons of the war as they understood them. Here was an insoluble problem that shattered FDR's hope for a world order upheld by four great-power partners. The settlement of 1945 was, therefore, an incomplete one. The period of rapid economic growth and integration among the Western market economies emerged within a larger context of ideological rivalry and nuclear threat.

The disappointing consequences of the 1945 settlement explain the euphoria felt all across the West at the fall of the Berlin Wall in November 1989. Within two years, the Soviet empire collapsed and half a century of repression in Eastern Europe was finally brought to a close. Still, the "peacemakers" who came together in 1990–91 to craft a new international order were in fact simply taking care of unfinished business. Philip Zelikow and Gregory Flynn take us through the process by which American and European leaders agreed to settle the German problem by unifying that country. This task was handled with skill and tact, and the degree of strategic and diplomatic partnership between the former rival superpowers led all the participants to assume that a new era of cooperation and stability had dawned.

Yet no sooner was the German problem settled—the great conundrum that had defeated planners in 1919 and 1945—than the focus of strategic affairs quickly shifted to other complex problems that had lain dormant in the Cold War. Scarcely able to enjoy the fruits of their labors in Germany, statesmen were called on to grapple with the collapse of the Russian economy and state institutions—a collapse that was made all but inevitable once the coercive communist regime was abandoned. Indeed, the series of global economic crises that have erupted in the 1990s from Russia to Mexico to Asia appear stubbornly impervious to the tried-and-true solutions offered by the International Monetary Fund; as Diane Kunz shows, states find themselves less and less able to guide global economic activity and are ever more subject to its vagaries. At the same time, governments face such post–Cold War problems as the proliferation of nuclear technology, whose impact on the strategic balance is still unknown.

The end of the Cold War lifted the lid from numerous long-simmering ethnic rivalries, both within Europe and beyond, and so new was this kind of conflict that the major powers had no sense for how to handle it. Indeed, neither the U.N. Charter nor international law provides clear authorization for intervention in matters once considered the "internal affairs" of states, even when these matters have clear regional security implications. The civil war in the Balkans, for example, has been contained chiefly through the use of air power by the NATO alliance, while the United Nations has been marginalized: precisely the opposite of what was once considered so promising about the "new world order."

And planners have been forced to grapple with other challenges that transcend the Cold War and its legacy, such as the rise of Islamic fundamentalism as an international political force; or the advent of "soft" security issues such as environmental degradation. The essay by Paul Kennedy suggests that only a settlement that is able to incorporate strategies for dealing with both state-to-state relations and new transnational security issues will truly be enduring. As in the past, so in our own time, we have worked to solve the causes of the previous crisis but have been less well prepared to adapt to a new and uncharted postwar strategic landscape.

Generating Consensus for Order

A second feature common to each postwar period treated in this volume is the search by each generation of planners for international and domestic consensus in support of the postwar order. A settlement cannot long survive if its chief guarantors do not find reason to uphold it. There are always revisionist powers somewhere on the international horizon; but when these states become capable of unilaterally challenging the international system, an organized multilateral response must emerge to resist it, or the system will collapse. The challenge of mobilizing states to act also has a domestic dimension, as Charles Maier's analysis here points out: if the public, or civic institutions, can be mobilized to support international order or to fend off a challenge to it, the settlement is likely to endure. When public opinion rejects a given system or shows no interest in its survival, states will risk few resources to maintain it.

The failure to generate broad international or domestic support for the Versailles settlement hobbled it from the very start. Wilson's vision was undermined by a complete lack of interest in European affairs on the part of the U.S. Congress and the American public. Britain, too, failed to engage its prestige or its resources in ensuring a Franco-German balance of power in Europe, due to its far greater imperial commitments than continental ones. France was an active upholder of the Versailles system but found willing supporters only in the weak, newly minted states of Eastern Europe. France alone could not uphold an international order that was despised by Germany and vilified by a still dormant but simmering Soviet Union. No enduring international consensus for the Versailles settlement was ever generated among the great powers.

The failure of domestic, civic, and non-governmental organizations to build consensus also shortened the life of the Versailles settlement. For a brief shining moment, self-determination, liberalism, respect for minority rights, and the promise of social reform held sway in the rhetoric of the postwar planners. These were domestic corollaries to the high-minded universalism of the League of Nations. But there was an inherent contradiction between self-determination and ethnonationalism on one hand and internationalism on the other. The local forces of particularism, encouraged by the breakup of old empires and the lofty language of self-determination, undercut a normative international structure that impinged upon the prerogatives of the nation-state. The principles that had led to the championing of national and minority rights could easily be, and were, extended in an argument against any restraining or coercive international order. Nationalism was a powerful bonding agent within the states of Europe; it also served to weaken fatally the fragile international structures that had been hopefully advanced at Versailles.

States proved better at creating consensus in favor of the post–World War II settlement. Though the United States, the Soviet Union, and most of their European partners expressed dissatisfaction with the division of Europe and the creation of two rival blocs, in fact both superpowers found that the Cold War division served them well. It offered a recognized structure that over time—perhaps by 1955, certainly by 1963—had settled into a code of conduct for the two sides that neither was eager to challenge. Crafting this peace was not an easy or inevitable process, as Marc Trachtenberg argues. It required vigilance and intense negotiation, as well as the restraint of second-tier allies. The system that emerged pushed ideological conflict to the periphery of the international order where, as Tony Smith shows, the stakes were lower and the weapons were conventional. For the United States and Western Europeans, this international consensus was buttressed by affluence and by transnational cultural and economic integration that served to diminish nationalist particularities. On the other side of the Iron Curtain, the imperial structure of Soviet rule in Eastern Europe precluded the question of manufacturing domestic consent. This "negative" dimension of the Cold War settlement of course served international stability, but at a high price for half of Europe, and at the cost of constant tension between the two sides.

In this sense, the 1945 settlement bears some resemblance to the order framed by the Congress of Vienna in 1815. Then, the major powers agreed on who was to be seated at the conference table; they agreed on how the international system was to be governed; and they shared basic assumptions about what kind of domestic order—autocratic and conservative—they wished to uphold. This settlement weathered the storm of 1848 intact, and the Crimean War of 1854–56 sent only minor tremors through the international landscape. The advent of the German Empire in 1871 was a rude challenge, of course; yet the Concert of Europe still managed to contain Germany's ambitions for another thirty years after the German "revolution." The parallels are instructive, if sobering: the endurance of the 1815 and 1945 settlements depended not only on great-power consensus about the "rules of the game" but also on some degree of internal coercion, strong enough in any case to contain dynamic internal challenges to state authority.

In our own time, crafting consensus has proved enormously difficult. Part of the problem is the difficulty in establishing who must be a party to it. Which are the great powers that will underpin a new international order? In all the previous periods we have discussed, there was no difficulty in naming them. Today, a list of great powers would certainly include China, but what about Russia? If nuclear weapons alone elevate a state to great-power status, the field is getting crowded: Israel, India, Pakistan, North Korea, Ukraine, among others. Or should population be a determining factor? If so, Indonesia, India, and Brazil, along with China, will hold sway at the conference table, displacing puny

Britain and France. Of course, economic power still determines great-power status, but this means that Japan and Germany must be included among the powers. Thus, merely identifying the states that might be future guarantors of order opens up difficult debates about who is a member of the great-power club.

If for the sake of convenience we look to the Permanent Five of the U.N. Security Council—United States, Russia, China, Britain, and France—we find little consensus on what the elements of international order should be. Should order be based on the transforming power of the marketplace, the promise of economic development for all, the hope of democratic governance? Or should it be based on regional hegemons, each free to govern its own country and perhaps its own region through local settlements that reflect regional power structures? Are spheres of influence valid as means of ensuring order, or can the powers agree on certain universal norms of international and domestic behavior that they are willing to sustain? Is globalization a force of creative and productive change, or a destructive, threatening force that will trigger regional resentment and backlash? Even to raise these questions is to reveal profound divergences among the major powers on what constitutes a basis for order. Here we are back to 1919; the model does not bode well for the future.

The Moral Imperative

Each of our three periods also reveals a tension between idealism and realism, between an international order in which power is the servant of principle and one in which ideals are simply used to justify a policy based on power. This is a problem peculiar to the twentieth century, in which public opinion and foreign policy are often intertwined; it is a dilemma that would have been quite as foreign to Lord Salisbury in the late Victorian period as to the conferees who crafted the Peace of Westphalia in 1648. In our own century, ideals matter; but what importance must they be accorded in the making of international order?

Woodrow Wilson believed that states could construct an international order upon a moral foundation, and in so doing would serve their collective interests. Wilson's vision assumed, however, that most states would be content with the status quo as ordered by Versailles, and that they would defend that order from the few who weren't. This hope proved badly misguided. The "settlement" of 1919–23 left various powerful states, notably Germany, Japan, and the Soviet Union, deeply dissatisfied. It also failed to place real power in the hands of the international organ that was charged with enforcing the peace: the League of Nations. Power was never mobilized to serve morals; the dream of a moral international order was never realized.

After 1945, the relation between morality and power was inverted. Peace required, and was premised upon, a preponderance of American power. Without it, any hope for pursuing a democratic and capitalist Europe would have been doomed to failure. At the same time, however, states had to mobilize public opinion in favor of the policy of containment, and this required clothing power politics in the cheerful bunting of high principle. The Truman Doctrine of 1947, which publicly announced the brass-knuckle policy of containment, had to be softened by the more reasoned appeals to economic well-being inherent in the Marshall Plan. In the late 1940s, it was still plausible to explain to the American public that feeding the hungry and restarting factories would help defend liberty and advance American ideals. However, the considerable reserve of good will and trust that the American government built up among its citizens and abroad was drawn upon rather heavily in subsequent years. In Asia, Africa, and Latin America, the United States paradoxically believed it had to support anti-democratic regimes in the interests of a democratic world order, thereby provoking deep cynicism among later generations about the legitimacy of any U.S.-led effort to promote its own ideals overseas.

The lesson of 1919 seemed to be that moralism in politics breeds weakness; the lesson of the Cold War seemed to be that realism estranged the country from its moral foundations. Since the end of the Cold War, there have been laudable efforts to restore a moral compass to the making of foreign policy, and an equal insistence on avoiding the pitfalls of naïveté. This at first appears to be a welcome blend of realpolitik and idealism. Yet what results has this stance yielded? In 1991, the United States successfully led a war to oust Iraqi forces from occupied Kuwait by combining three unusual elements: cooperation between Washington and Moscow, the active participation of the U.N. Security Council, and an international coalition of states. The outcome of Desert Storm led many to believe that this model might serve as a foundation for a post–Cold War settlement. But the major conflicts of the 1990s proved to be internal, and it quickly became evident that neither the United States nor the United Nations had any clear ideas about how to deal with them. United Nations troops in Bosnia proved woefully inadequate in bringing the warring parties to heel between 1991 and 1995. The United States sent its own troops into Somalia in 1993 in the interests of quelling civil war and feeding a famine-afflicted population. After the deaths there of eighteen U.S. Rangers in October 1993, the United States quickly withdrew its forces. The trauma of Somalia made the American public highly unwilling to intervene in the civil war in Rwanda, where in 1994 genocide raged unchecked.

There were cases in which the United States felt it necessary to act. In the former Yugoslavia, the Serbian-backed genocide against Bosnian Muslims provided shocking evidence that Europe was not free of the ethnic and religious hatred so frequently visible in the Third World. Genocide alone, however, did not mobilize the U.S. government to act. The war in the Balkans threatened to destabilize the region while weakening the European Union and the NATO alliance by showing their impotence. In 1995, after years of inaction, the United States compelled its still-reluctant NATO allies to undertake a massive bombing campaign against Serb forces in Bosnia, thereby bringing the Serbian, Muslim, and Croatian combatants to the bargaining table. Here was a welcome sight: muscular realism in the service of peacemaking. On the other hand, this policy antagonized Russia, which opposed air assaults against the Serbs; and the United States was obliged to circumvent the United Nations, whose Security Council could not be galvanized into action. In 1998, the United States led a massive seventy-eight-day air campaign against Serbia, this time in an effort to force Serbian withdrawal from the Yugoslav province of Kosovo. The cause was a noble one—the Serbs had begun a coordinated effort to deport all the ethnic Albanians from the province, triggering a refugee crisis of epic proportions. But the Americans led the operation from start to finish and supplied the great majority of air and naval power. Growling from the Russians went unheeded; the European Union was shown up as a toothless talking shop; and the United Nations was quite simply ignored.

At the same time, the United States undertook new initiatives in foreign policy that implied a broadening of American national interests. The United States pressed ahead with expanding NATO, thereby committing itself to a defense of Poland's eastern border with Belarus and Ukraine, and announced its intentions to bring the independent Baltic republics into the fold as well. This policy of course antagonized Russia, but it was undertaken in the interests of integrating Central Europe into the West—a policy the wealthy Western European states could now quietly abandon in the European Union. At the same time, the United States continued to pursue a policy of containment of Iraq, arguing that it threatened the Middle East and Persian Gulf, where a group of weak and fragile kingdoms were ill prepared to defend themselves from a regional threat. A new domino theory was proposed, only this time the threat was not communism but Islam: containing Iraq served to keep intact pliable and moderate Middle Eastern regimes; whereas a broader regional conflict would lead to destabilization, economic chaos, and a breeding ground for Islamic revolution.

The United States has adopted, then, a unilateral and global approach to world affairs. Is this stance consistent with the "new world order" that Americans had hoped to create? Clearly not. Rather, the United States has circumvented and weakened the

United Nations, on which a cooperative, Wilsonian vision might be based. Yet it has also failed to build a viable, Kissingerian balance-of-power order that rests on the shared interests of China, Russia, and the European Union. Instead, the current order appears reliant on American global hegemony, undergirded by market forces.

Successful foreign policy is predicated upon establishing priorities based on a careful assessment of national interests. The challenge is to define these interests and then to pursue them consistently, if possible in conjunction with other like-minded states. The reason for the failure of the Versailles settlement, it has often been noted, lay not in the treaty itself but in that it was never applied. The settlement of 1945, by contrast, endured as long as it did—and perhaps far too long—because of the rigidity of the great powers and their unwillingness to allow any flexibility in the system at all. The settlement of 1945 was, after all, responsible for a cold war. Our own time may be perilously suspended between the two. We would like to be guided by Wilson's vision of a world order premised on our own values; yet we also seem, as after 1945, to be committing ourselves to a costly policy of global proportions that will surely overcommit our resources and, in lean times, will be impossible to maintain. In the meantime, we have worsened relations with the "coming" power, China, while ignoring the potential value of cooperation with a weakened but still powerful Russia. All this seems to suggest that we are far from a coherent and stable post–Cold War "settlement." Given the flaws in previous attempts to order the international system, this willingness to ignore system-building, and to address international crises on an ad hoc basis, may have some merit. But would it not be ironic if, at the zenith of American power in the twentieth century, the United States proved unable to build a lasting international order consistent with its own interests and values? Would it not be still more ironic if the United States never even tried?

Reordering Europe After World War I

Part

The Great Powers and the New International System, 1919–1923

1

Carole Fink

Almost sixty years ago, on the eve of World War II, one of Britain's sagest historians analyzed the origins of the "twenty-years' crisis" as a conflict between two powerful impulses in international affairs. On one side were the utopians, the spiritual heirs of Rousseau, Kant, and Bentham, who believed in the ideal of achieving a harmony of global political and economic interests. On the other were the realists, whose robust ancestors, the realpolitikers, the determinists, the relativists, and the proponents of national interest, had preached not only that states, like human beings, inevitably failed to live up to their ideals but that all political principles were merely functions of time, space, and power. If utopians risk the dangers of naïveté, inflexibility, and hypocrisy, E. H. Carr reminded us that realists generally lack a moral spark and a basis for mobilizing the masses.[1] Like all antinomies, each requires the other's existence. Because neither can vanquish the other, international history derives much of its fascination, complexity, and tragedy from the interplay between these two symbiotic forces.[2]

Carr's is still a useful framework to analyze the peace settlement after World War I, the much-maligned "Versailles" and all the subsequent treaties and arrangements that established a well-defined, endlessly disputed, and ultimately failed system of European and global pacification.[3] Certainly the peacemakers, who had just directed the most destructive war in modern history— with almost ten million dead, twenty million suffering war-related injuries, and direct and indirect war costs exceeding $300 billion—were cognizant of the huge gap between ideals and practicality.[4] Unlike their more fortunate forebears in 1814–15, 1856, and 1878, the victors assembled in Paris against a background of disease, starvation, and enormous material and human disruption. They arrived in the wake of four years of total mobilization, unrelenting propaganda, and intemperate war aims, the abrupt collapse of four empires, and the eruption of violence and bloodshed within and among all the successor states.[5] Forced to balance their sudden, still recent triumph against the atmosphere of "anger and revolt . . . from one end of Europe to the other," the Allies wavered between a longing to restore (albeit with limited improvements) prewar conditions and the necessity of confronting revolutionary power realities.[6] The victors failed to comprehend that the legendary "normality" before 1914 had been the breeding ground for four years of slaughter, and they only dimly grasped the new challenges. Out of the ambiguous military verdict of November 1918 they imagined a *Stunde Null* without recognizing the still-powerful remnants of the past.[7]

The key figure who attempted to resolve this dilemma was President Woodrow Wilson. Between 1917 and 1919, he responded to the challenges of war and revolution with his unique formulation of a liberal capitalist internationalism, which linked America's main national interests—its anti-imperialism and anti-communism—with the creation of a just and stable world order. Freely borrowing from such European internationalists as Robert Cecil, Wilsonianism seized the moral and practical initiative from America's beleaguered Old World colleagues and appeared to provide the Central Powers with a sheet anchor against total defeat, and the dispossessed with hope against new forms of repression. As historian N. Gordon Levin has written, "Wilsonian America was to be the historical agent of the world's transformation from chaos and imperialism to orderly liberal rationality."[8]

Wilsonianism aimed at transforming world politics, first by committing America's considerable economic and military power to the Allied cause in order to defeat Imperial Germany, then by using that unequaled might to forge a just and durable peace, the centerpiece of which would be the League of Nations. The specifics of Wilsonianism, however, were, and still are, problematic. It was a dual system combining internationalism and national interests. Wilsonianism juxtaposed its author's power and prestige against the hopes and fears of an exigent public within a swiftly changing global environment. The compelling liberal slogans of 1917 and 1918 were, not unexpectedly, to be tarnished and diminished by their elaboration and contestation at the Paris Peace Conference.[9]

Pitted against Wilson were unavoidable political realities. The Republican victory in the midterm elections in the United States reduced his room for maneuver despite his efforts to ignore the consequences. In the exhausted but still truculent seventy-eight-year-old French premier Georges Clemenceau, and the vigorous and mercurial fifty-six-year-old British prime minister David Lloyd George, Wilson faced two formidable negotiating partners. They were leaders of the world's two largest empires, which had only recently patched up their ancient quarrels to become wary war partners and whose citizens had registered strong nationalist signals in the November 1918 elections. The American president also confronted the demands of numerous supplicants, the scrutiny of the internationalists, the suspicion of the neutrals, and the growing rage of the defeated.[10]

The victors had at their disposal a large group of talented experts who, late in the war, had begun to prepare for the peace. In the foreign and defense ministries and the ad hoc appointed commissions they gathered masses of documentation from geographers and geologists, historians and ethnologists, economists and military analysts, to lay before the peace conference. There was, however, meager coordination among governmental agencies and virtually none among the Allies. Almost nothing filtered up to Wilson, Lloyd George, and Clemenceau, who all took pride in their political acumen and historical judgment.[11]

Few at the time, or since, have deemed the Paris Peace Conference an auspicious forum for settling the problems of European, if not global, security. It was a poorly chosen site, still seething with wartime passions. Under the glare of the world press, scores of delegates, experts, and lobbyists descended in 1919 on the inadequately prepared French capital, which became a magnet for the world's claimants and intriguers, a noisebox of rumor and vilification, and a prodigal producer of maps, statistics, and propaganda tracts.[12] After the glittering opening session on January 18, "public diplomacy" was quickly replaced by the domination of the Supreme Allied Council whose twelve million soldiers, Clemenceau bluntly told the protesting small powers, had been decisive to victory. Acting in the utmost secrecy and often in the most haphazard manner, the Supreme Council not only controlled the peace deliberations but also served as an emergency government for large areas of Europe and claimed authority over vast colonial regions abroad. Thus, while hearing the claims of Poles and Czechs, Serbs and Romanians, Albanians and Greeks, Arabs and Jews—and ignoring scores of unofficial supplicants—the Allies oversaw military, economic, and political relations with Germany and the former Russian Empire, and attempted to mediate among the warring parties of east-central and southeastern Europe.[13]

By March 1919 the Council of Ten (including two representatives each from the United States, Great Britain, France, Japan, and Italy) had devolved into the Council of Five Foreign Ministers and the virtually omnipotent Council of Four, in which Wilson, Lloyd George, and Clemenceau—with the intermittent, largely ineffectual participation of Vittorio Orlando—shaped the postwar world.¹⁴ Meeting more than two hundred times over three months, in total secrecy and without formal agendas, in brief or long, continuous or interrupted sessions, in a chaos of overlapping and disconnected decision making that alarmed professional diplomats, three determined, harried, and often weary politicians established the main aspects of a modern "new diplomacy," navigating between a punitive peace and a peace of justice, between security and equity, between force and freedom.¹⁵

This "new diplomacy" introduced several innovations, including the unprecedented, lengthy, and potent presence—as well as the month-long absence—of a U.S. president; the exclusion of the defeated; and the enormous formal power of the host government. The exactions and exits of Italy and Japan undoubtedly caused greater damage than had previous disputes within victorious coalitions. Public opinion, although stifled by secrecy and censorship, was not entirely excluded. The Big Three received distorted, sanitized, and chaotic bits of "information" from the streets and pubs, the press and parliament, from a world increasingly distant from their private chambers where they spied on each other and bantered and argued over the fate of millions. From this hothouse of largely uncoordinated, asymmetrical, and hasty procedures came the three distinctive features of the "new diplomacy": a League of Nations; the doctrine of self-determination; and the attempt to forge a new economic order.¹⁶

The League of Nations

The last, and most cherished, of Wilson's Fourteen Points called for the establishment of a "general association of nations . . . formed under specific covenants for the purpose of affording mutual guarantees of political independence and territorial integrity to great and small states alike." This idea emerged from three nineteenth-century foundations: the venerable, if underutilized, Concert of Europe; the numerous international legal conventions pertaining to disarmament and arbitration; and the radical anti-war, anti-imperialist programs of pacifist, feminist, and socialist organizations.[17]

After World War I reached a brutal stalemate, the idea of a League of Nations attracted increasing support among Britons and Americans. The Bolshevik seizure of power, followed by the publication of all the secret treaties, forced the Allies to "cleanse their peace propositions of all imperialism."[18] Three days before Wilson's historic address to Congress, Lloyd George told the Trades Union Congress that he supported the creation of an international organization as a means of settling international disputes.[19]

The Big Three held different views on the nature and purpose of the proposed League. While all were opposed to any form of world government, Britain favored a loose structure of sovereign states; the United States, compulsory and binding arbitration and sanctions against recalcitrant powers; and France, judicial handling of all disputes along with an international army to enforce League decisions.[20]

The drafting of the Covenant of the League of Nations was the achievement of two committed Anglo-American jurists, Cecil Hurst and David Hunter Miller. The essential features included: (1) the establishment of a universal assembly, a Great-Power Council, and a permanent court of international justice; (2) the bestowal of territorial guarantees to all member states and the provision for sanctions against aggressors; (3) the establishment of a mandate system for the colonial territories of the defeated powers; and (4) the expression of the League's support of universal disarmament, the equitable treatment of labor, and fair trade practices among members. This was the Anglo-American vision of a "new diplomacy," which both gave lip service to universalism and enshrined the distinction between great powers and small; it made a slight advance on the principle of collective security and also acknowledged anti-militarist, anti-imperialist, and humanitarian sentiments.[21]

Wilson, who chaired almost every session of the nineteen-member League of Nations Commission, banned the recording of official minutes, which opened the floodgates to some very frank, even explosive exchanges.[22] The small powers, supported by France and Italy, overcame American and British objections to expanding the Council's membership with four elected members.[23] The British failed to persuade Wilson to reduce the scope of the League's collective guarantee but did succeed in inserting a revision clause giving the Assembly the right "to advise the reconsideration . . . of treaties which have become inapplicable, and of . . . conditions . . . which may endanger the peace of the world." The anxious victims of 1914 tried to plug the wide security gap, but the Belgians were defeated on compulsory arbitration and automatic sanctions and the French over their demands for a League army.

The covenant was adopted by a plenary session on April 28, 1919.[24] It was, according to Wilson, a "living thing," with the capacity to arbitrate, correct mistakes, and provide a measure of security to an unsettled continent and world.[25] History's first international organization was an undoubted accomplishment for the U.S. president, Cecil, and their adherents. Article 10, the League's collective guarantee of its members' territorial integrity and political independence, became the icon and demon of the "new diplomacy." Article 11 proclaimed the revolutionary gospel that peace in the twentieth century would be indivisible, and that any threat, anywhere on the globe, was of concern to the League. Cecil and Wilson counted on the benign influence of national and international opinion as well as the fledgling League machinery to stave off another 1914 firestorm.[26]

The critics were less sanguine. Clemenceau, with a different memory of 1914, bristled at France's failure to provide the League with a military arm and ridiculed Wilson and Cecil's confidence in "public opinion."[27] The Italians resented the exclusion of guarantees on access to trade and raw materials, and the Japanese of their clause promoting racial equality. Many British, Dominion, and American politicians disliked the threat of Article 10 to their national sovereignty. And the Germans were predictably bitter over Wilson's insistence on their "probationary" exclusion. Because of a fateful Allied political decision, also imposed by Wilson, the League began its life as the first twenty-six articles of all the treaties with the Central Powers, not as an independent part of the peace settlement. Thus, in German, Soviet, and other eyes, the League of Nations was an instrument of Allied victory and domination, not a herald of "new diplomacy" or internationalism.[28]

Wilson's newborn grew rapidly. The peace conference gave it control over mandates, the Saar and Danzig, disarmament and minority rights. But the League was deliberately excluded from such great-power prerogatives as "freedom of the seas" and naval disarmament, the Monroe Doctrine and the internal affairs of the French and British empires, and inter-Allied debts and German reparations, not to mention the Allied intervention and the settlement of borders with Soviet Russia.[29]

Were there alternatives? Probably not, under the conditions of 1919. Wilson had insisted, "If it won't work, it must be made to work," which was either a prescription for disaster or an argument for realism.[30] Without Wilson *and* Lloyd George there could be no League of Nations; with them, the institution had to conform to their political visions, their power to persuade and coerce, and their nations' inherent disinclination to make concrete and lasting military commitments. But there was never a true Anglo-American bloc. Wilson's revolutionary conception of the League as a solid replacement for a corrupt alliance system, a guardian of international order, and a protector of small states contradicted Lloyd George's desire for a cheap, self-enforcing peace, such as had been maintained by the old and more fluid Concert of Europe.[31]

The great gap between expectation and reality haunted the League's history.[32] The League's Secretariat became a core of budding if frustrated internationalism. Some of its members strove to improve its machinery and close the gaps in the covenant by establishing automatic sanctions or an absolute prohibition on war. Some strove to elevate the stature of the democratic Assembly over the ruling Council. But a more activist League conformed neither to Wilson's idealized vision of a world organization nor to the goals of his British and French partners.[33]

Without U.S. membership, Britain soon became disenchanted with Geneva; and with Germany excluded until 1926 and Soviet Russia until 1934, the League became a minor site of internationalism, totally dependent on the cooperation of its members, an artisan of small good deeds, and remote from the rough and tough realities of European and world politics.[34]

Regarded by some historians as a monument to a noble purpose, by others as the germ of a future "liberal international order," and by others as one of the "dangerously misleading illusions of the peace," the League was a product of the "new diplomacy," whose hopes, failures, and alleged lessons continue to spark debate in the continuing search for a more just and more effective international order.[35]

Self-Determination

Although by no means a Wilsonian invention, the principle of self-determination has largely been associated with Wilson, and for most of this century he has reaped both praise and censure for its application and violation.[36] Combining the principles of democracy and popular sovereignty, Wilson established the American experience as the norm for the world. He envisaged the nation as an "organic community" with a common historical experience, some semblance of political capacity, and a civic consciousness that would prepare it for democratic self-government. Wilson's definition, which favored historical, political, and cultural factors over such specifics as race, religion, ethnicity, and language and was both revolutionary and conservative, precise and ambiguous, contained the seeds of misunderstanding and distortion by the author and his audience.[37]

The historian-politician Wilson had never expected to apply the principle of self-determination to east-central and southern Europe. Point 10 had advocated neither the dissolution of the

Habsburg empire nor independence for its subjects.[38] But by 1918, when cautious slogans were overtaken by imperial collapse, revolutions, and internecine wars, Wilson, as reluctantly as Lloyd George and Clemenceau, acquiesced in the emergence and expansion of its successor states. But the president never claimed that the two hybrid creations, Czechoslovakia and Yugoslavia, satisfied his criteria for national self-determination.[39]

The Russian Revolution posed a more serious challenge to Wilsonianism. Viewing Lenin's minions as anti-democratic usurpers and tools of the Central Powers, as well as a potentially powerful force of international subversion, Wilson not only authorized a limited U.S. military intervention in the conflict but also insisted on the territorial integrity of the former czarist empire. Disingenuously, he pronounced his solidarity with the Russian people in their effort to achieve self-determination against the common enemies, the Germans and the Bolsheviks; and he showed little sympathy with the Baltic peoples' struggle for freedom.[40]

As the promise of self-determination, now freed from Wilson's qualifications, stirred peoples all over the world, from Ireland to Ukraine, from Palestine to the Sudetenland, the U.S. secretary of state, Robert Lansing, complained that Wilson had risked "peace and stability" by elevating a volatile concept and appealing to all sorts of undefined groups.[41]

Wilson nevertheless maintained his conservative stance with his reluctance to redraw the map of Europe, alter historical boundaries, and give "our enemies even the impression of injustice."[42] His Allied partners, on the other hand, adopted a simpler guideline, which was to define nations in largely *ethnic* terms, as a mélange of language, culture, race, and religion. Their advisers pored over census data and "ethnic maps," consulted geographers and demographers, to learn the arcane population details of such heavily mixed ethnic regions as Marienwerder, Teschen, and Silesia.[43]

The experts and politicians immediately realized that the putative Wilsonianism of ethnically pure states would be impossible to achieve.[44] In awarding a river bank, a railroad line, a mountain frontier, or an extended piece of territory to create a contiguous boundary with an ally, ethnographic criteria had to be violated. Each breach—and there were many—was justified by new code words, such as "historical units," "economic bases," and "strategic necessities."[45]

The Allies' treatment of Germany stretched every version of self-determination. Contrary to the Germans' expectations, Wilson was far more committed to European pacification and democratization than to ensuring that a postwar Germany include *all* the German people, however evolved their historical, national, and political consciousness might be.[46] In the Fourteen Points, he had already authorized cessions of Reich territory without plebiscites. He also insisted on maintaining the old frontier between Germany and the former Habsburg monarchy and barred an *Anschluss* with rump Austria.[47]

In the West, except for the cession of Alsace-Lorraine, the loss of Eupen-Malmédy, and the plebiscite in Schleswig, Germany's borders remained intact. Wilson vetoed Clemenceau's bid for the Saar and Lloyd George's Saar ministate.[48] On the more significant Rhineland issue, Wilson and Lloyd George wielded the doctrine of self-determination against Clemenceau's historical, religious, ethnic, economic, and strategic claims, agreeing only to a fifteen-year Allied occupation and a soon-to-be defunct security guarantee.[49]

It was the German-Polish border settlement that tested the Allies' cohesiveness, stamina, and ingenuity. Point 13 stated that the new Poland was to be inhabited by an "indisputably Polish population," have "free and secure access to the sea," *and* be guaranteed its political and economic independence by international covenant. France supported Warsaw's maximum territorial claims, which included most of Upper Silesia, Danzig, and an "expanded" corridor that included both major railways and placed some two million Germans under Polish control. The Anglo-Americans, woefully ignorant of Eastern European geography, pursued separate tactics. Wilson, who feared displacing "too many" Germans, nevertheless sympathized with the Poles.

Lloyd George, opposing a weak, bloated Poland, fought to make Danzig a free city and won plebiscites in Marienwerder, Allenstein, and Upper Silesia. The British premier recognized this crucial fault line in the new Europe. Since neither Wilson's League nor Britain's anodyne Article 19 could prevent German irredentism, the new borders had to be just or defendable—preferably both.[50] Lloyd George taunted, to great effect: Would the Allies make war for Danzig?[51]

Another dilemma was the minority question: how to secure protection for those peoples about to be "denied self determination" and turned over to an alien, even hostile sovereignty; how to discourage irredentism cloaked as a defense of minority rights; and how to enable the new and enlarged states between Germany and Bolshevik Russia to enjoy their new power and freedom without oppressing others. No sooner had the war ended in November 1918 than pogroms against Jews and other minorities erupted throughout Eastern Europe.[52]

Wilson viewed minority questions from an American perspective: the ultimate goal was assimilation.[53] But the new Eastern Europe, with its long imperial heritage and historic separation of national groups and religions, was an unlikely environment for assimilation. Neither the Allies nor the new states were prepared to grant any form of cultural or political autonomy, to create "states within states," kindle separatist sentiments, and set unwelcome examples for Western governments and empires.[54]

Moreover, Wilson and his colleagues were reluctant to interfere too strongly in the internal affairs of Poland and the other Eastern European states. Past efforts to write minority clauses at the congresses of Vienna, Paris, and Berlin had produced only empty promises, disappointed minorities, and an embarrassment to passive great powers. Wilson's original solution was to insert a very general statement in favor of religious freedom in the League of Nations Covenant modeled on the U.S. Constitution; when the Japanese demanded a guarantee of racial equality, he had to withdraw.[55]

On May 1, 1919, on Wilson's urging, the Big Three set up a

special committee to draw up a minority treaty with Poland, which became the model for all the new and enlarged Eastern European states.[56] Meeting almost daily and in secret, the committee conferred with Jewish leaders and Eastern European statesmen and produced a document and doctrine that changed the history of minority rights.[57]

The minority states strongly protested against the Allies' high-handedness and hypocrisy. Wilson responded: "We cannot afford to guarantee territorial settlements which [we] do not believe to be right, [or] leave elements of disturbance unremoved which . . . will disturb the peace of the world."[58] Abandoning the egalitarianism of his wartime pronouncements, Wilson insisted on the Allies' *right* to dictate rules of political conduct, despite their minimal political and military presence in Eastern Europe, and their *responsibility* to police this turbulent region.[59]

Nevertheless, the new states' objections could not be ignored because their compliance was essential for the new minorities system.[60] Thus the Big Three backed down in substantial ways. The Polish Minority Treaty, which was signed at Versailles minutes after the German treaty, contained basic guarantees of political, religious, and personal freedom, and some minimal protection for language, education, and culture, but withheld any recognition of national groups as political entities. The treaty was placed under the guarantee of the new League of Nations; but only Council members could enforce its clauses, and minorities were excluded from direct protests.[61]

The new minority system established at Versailles represented Wilsonianism at its best and its worst. The treaties were an undoubted advance, both practical and idealistic, designed to reassure threatened minorities, discourage irredentism, and help consolidate the new states. But given the conditions of violence, poverty, political radicalism, and intolerance in postwar Eastern Europe, the treaties' enforcement depended on the questionable premises of an activist League, cooperative governments, concerned great powers, and restrained defenders—none of which materialized. The League's cautious, cumbersome procedures left (minorities relatively unprotected, encouraged radical, revisionist solutions, and stiffened the minority states against concessions.[62]

The principle of self-determination adumbrated by Wilson opened a Pandora's box of confusion and contention in Central and Eastern Europe that persists today. Having conflated two separate concepts, national self-determination and popular sovereignty, Wilson alone was surprised at the chaotic results of his utterances. Although Wilson and his colleagues were not the parents of ethnonationalism, they were certainly midwives to the new order of ethnically heterogeneous nation-states in Central and Eastern Europe, all of which contained an explosive combination of triumphant and defeated self-determination that, to an alarming extent, persists today.[63]

The New Economic Order

In confronting the huge material costs of World War I —the ruined farmlands, flooded mines, destroyed transportation and communication systems, and depleted industries—the peacemakers and their publicists created a powerful and mystical concept: economic reconstruction. Lacking both factual and theoretical understanding, as well as political courage, the Europeans directed their gaze backward to a pre-1914 world that now seemed so orderly, so prosperous, before the catastrophe of war had disturbed it. They also seized upon the tempting prospect that "les boches paiera," that war debts would be forgotten, and that the American wealth and production that had fueled and funded the war would remain mobilized to fill the needs of peace.[64]

Among the invisible, long-term consequences of the war were the enormous demographic losses, the shifts in raw-material production, and the losses of old markets and old production sites. The extended isolation of the Central Powers created serious restraints on the revival of European trade. A prolonged inflation had spread over the entire European continent, eroding confidence and threatening the return to stability. Britain, France, and

Italy, but also Germany and Russia and the small powers, faced huge budget deficits, debts, and trade imbalances. While America had reaped the war's economic benefits, most of Europe, particularly the successor states, urgently needed credits not only for reconstruction but also to purchase food, raw materials, and machine tools to revive production.[65]

The partisans of reconstruction imagined that the circuits cut in 1914 and all the distortions that developed between 1914 and 1918 could be reconnected and corrected. They failed to comprehend the barriers that had been erected between victors and vanquished, between Bolsheviks and capitalists, between Europe and the rest of the world, and among all the newly emancipated peoples in Eastern Europe. Moreover, Europe's prewar dynamism was largely based on Britain's banking and financial system and Germany's industrial and commercial production. Restoration could not be accomplished without taking account of the American colossus and the needs of a devastated France, nor without a leadership able to comprehend the latent and visible, the long and short term, the political and the social, to redeem the war's suffering with real instead of symbolic actions. John Maynard Keynes and Etienne Mantoux agreed that the peacemakers had incorrectly given priority to *political* over economic problems.[66]

The central question of who would pay for the war's enormous destruction was reduced to the highly contentious issue of German reparations. The Allies' deliberations were complicated by a lack of precedents, a deficiency of accurate statistics, and especially by fundamental disagreement over how much Germany could, and should, be forced to pay. There were no "moderates."[67] In their often shabby, heated debates the French sought to cripple Germany, the British to double their claims by adding pensions and allowances, and the United States, wavering between realism and retribution, lacked the will and means to temper its partners' demands without reducing war debts. The victors separated without agreement because their disagreements were so profound.[68]

According to Keynes and many others as well, the Allies surrendered their high moral ground as victims of deliberate damage and destruction to become great extorters of Germany's wealth. Those magic German billions bandied about, which would restore devastated lives and lands and fuel prosperity and security, but were unconnected to the problems of transfer or to the economic impact on the receiver countries, gave the Germans a fine propaganda weapon. Article 231, for all its legal finesse and historical verisimilitude, was so unfortunately phrased as to give the Germans a powerful club to attack reparations and force the Allies to defend German war guilt as the principal foundation of the peace settlement.[69]

The Anglo-American proposal to delay a final reparations figure and schedule for two full years was an ostensibly practical effort to cool domestic tempers, obtain precise figures, and win a breathing space before serious negotiations. But this hiatus also prolonged and heightened international tensions, since the uncertainty served as a brake against Germany and Europe's economic recovery. Until a reparations figure was established and Germany actually began to pay, it was impossible to mobilize investment capital from the United States, Britain, or the neutrals to help rebuild Europe. The delay encouraged Germany's resentment and defiance, spread its misery abroad, and bolstered the Allies' disunity and the venom of their critics.[70]

In a final, futile gesture for European reconstruction, on April 23, 1919, Lloyd George sent Keynes's daring and elaborate plan to Wilson. It involved the mobilization of the Central Powers' reparations payments and tying them to inter-Allied debts to raise development capital for Central and Eastern Europe.[71] With it came another dire warning of the Bolshevik danger if no bold action were undertaken. Two weeks later, Wilson rejected the Keynes Plan as unsound. The United States, committed to a thorough return to economic liberalism *and* to the open door, shrank from any form of governmental intervention, coordination, and guarantees, refused to link reparations and war debts, castigated its European partners for their colonial greed and military profligacy, and fled from the shadow of inflation.[72]

The peacemakers parted unamicably at the end of June 1919, leaving reparations, debts, and reconstruction unsolved and Europe arguably worse off for their failed efforts. Keynes continued to lambaste the Big Three, and there was a dreary series of conferences throughout the 1920s over reparations, debts, and European reconstruction. The League tried its hand at promoting trade and economic recovery; but the crash of 1929 exposed the fragility of the new economic order.

In 1919, the peacemakers battled the Bolsheviks, their beaten enemies, their contentious small allies, and one another. Blending power, principle, and vast doses of inconsistency, Wilson, Lloyd George, and Clemenceau were openly competing against Lenin's call for world revolution, for the hearts of the masses longing for redemption from the long nightmare of battle and sacrifice. The three democratic leaders have been faulted for deciding almost everything among themselves, violating history, justice, and good sense, leaving too many revisionists, and thus creating a "twenty-year truce" until round two in the struggle for world power. If their panaceas fell short of justice and realism, this was due to the suddenness and paradoxes of their victory, the vast responsibilities they had inherited, and the flawed structure of the peace conference.

The "new diplomacy" of 1919, with its elements of virtue, realism, and confusion, nevertheless left its mark on the whole twentieth century in three of its still-contested legacies. First, a new international organization was created, and despite its undistinguished interwar record it was revived in 1945. The United States, after ignoring the League of Nations for more than two decades, championed the founding of the United Nations, whose Security Council possessed far greater power than its predecessor. To be sure, for the next half century the United Nations played a minor role in the bipolarized world of the Cold War.[73] The great powers, which did their own peacemaking, foisted on an ill-equipped, underfunded United Nations the most intractable problems of Asia, Africa, and the Middle East.[74]

Since the end of the Cold War, the U.N.'s role has vastly increased but has also become controversial.[75] While the great powers continue to police their own "near abroads," the proliferation of blue helmets from Haiti to the Balkans, Somalia to Cambodia, has produced mixed results. The United Nations cannot force combatants to the peace table or make them sign and comply. Reflecting the ambivalence of its progenitors, it remains a family of nations and an aspiring world government, a forum for international diplomacy and one of its secondary actors, not yet an "it" and primarily a "they," whose officials, except for such activists as Dag Hammarskjöld and Boutros Boutros-Ghali, dread antagonizing the great powers.[76] Idealists have advocated a stronger world organization endowed with its own troops to enforce Security Council resolutions.[77] Realists, noting the disasters in the Balkans and Africa as well as the U.N.'s own human rights abuses abroad, seek to limit its activities to humanitarian work.[78] Those in the middle have proposed a semi-activist United Nations assigned specific tasks, ranging from intelligence gathering to being the "trustee of failed states," a stand-in for a world community yet to be born. If Wilson and Cecil's heirs have accepted limits, the severest critics of the United Nations have come to recognize its ability—in spite of an unwieldy structure and its dependency on great-power paymasters and cooperation—to ameliorate the current international anarchy.

A second legacy of the League is that the principle of national self-determination has remained one of world's most powerful and contested ideologies. In the Atlantic Charter of 1941, Churchill and Roosevelt pledged to apply Wilsonian principles to any postwar territorial changes; but they were overruled by Stalin, who established borders and governments in Eastern Europe based on Soviet security needs and "solved" the minority problems in Eastern Europe with massive expulsions and resettlement. During the long Cold War, the self-determination applied to the former colonial world generally followed a similar surgical pattern with regard to religious and ethnic minorities.[79]

With the fall of the wall and Germany's reunification came a belated reckoning with the "Versailles system," leading to the peaceful partition of multinational Czechoslovakia and the violent disintegration of Yugoslavia along with the dissolution of the Soviet Union itself. The ferocious struggles in Bosnia and Northern Ireland have cast doubt over the viability of multinational entities, prompting idealists to advance supranational and local solutions and realists to pronounce the death knell of Wilson's vague and noble principle.[80]

Third, the economic lessons of 1919 and 1929 were fully recognized after World War II, but they were also treated in the context of the Cold War. Thus, the United States generously restored Western Europe under the banner of Bretton Woods and free trade while the Soviet Union dominated the finances and economies of its realm in Eastern Europe. Despite the pressures in the 1960s of mounting military commitments and consumer demand, the two rival systems competed for another quarter of a century until the West's mastery of guns and butter forced the Marxist command economies to collapse.[81]

The fall of communism, followed by a flurry of reconstruction schemes, brought neither substantial and coordinated outside aid nor significant cooperation among the post-communist states of Eastern Europe.[82] On the other hand, the feared mass westward exodus failed to materialize, and some shock therapy has worked. The triumph of global capitalism, which has brought Europe increased unemployment and political tension, has revived the old debate between the Keynesian planner-spenders and the free-marketeers.[83]

As in 1919, America's vision of world order, democracy, and capitalism has posed a model and a challenge to a still divided Europe; in a vastly more complex and dangerous world, utopians and realists continue to argue the principles and practice of internationalism, self-determination, and economic cooperation.

2

International Associationalism: The Social and Political Premises of Peacemaking After 1917 and 1945

Charles S. Maier

The scale, duration, and ferocity of World War I ensured that leaders of the combatant nations would seek to justify their struggle in terms not of realpolitik but of lofty values and ideology. Although the premier of Italy might cite national interest as a reason for fighting, even he qualified the cause as "sacred," or *sacro egoismo*. But American intervention and the importance of the United States in eventually helping to break the long stalemate made it certain that the architecture of the postwar settlement would include at least some of Woodrow Wilson's concepts. Wilsonianism involved an effort to institutionalize an international order based not on mere equilibrium but on democracy and social reform. This ambition meant that the arrangements of domestic politics and social institutions must interact with international security arrangements in new and explicit ways. Peace would rest on liberal democracies.

This chapter explores the post-1919 relationship of domestic politics, especially the thrust toward social reform, to international security arrangements; but it also compares the post–

World War I settlement with that fashioned after 1945. My intention is not to provide detailed coverage of two eras on which so much good recent scholarship has appeared but to think about the relationship between organizing domestic stability and producing international order as a sort of collective good. Since 1989, when the idea of "civil society" seemed powerful enough to challenge the party-states of Eastern Europe, observers have focused on its alternative to authoritarian governance. The logical next step is to reflect on the possibilities of civil society as an alternative to international anarchy or destructive national rivalries.

Without resolving in which direction the lines of causal influence flow, I am convinced that international orders—or even strategic landscapes—have domestic sociopolitical corollaries. These are often implicit and less visible than the provisions for disarmament or frontier changes that peace treaties directly stipulate. Nonetheless they remain important. The settlement after World War I was certainly not the first to be embedded in concepts about the social and political order among the countries making the peace. Indeed, my starting point is that ambitious efforts to assure stabilization, such as the peace settlements after great wars, either implicitly or explicitly build upon domestic arrangements within participating countries, as well as upon the specific agreements negotiated between them. But the settlement that concluded World War I enshrined certain political principles more explicitly than earlier treaty orders and made them appear essential to international security. Moreover, while the politicians, academics, advocates for religious and ethnic groups, bankers, and labor leaders who worked to construct and to maintain international stability envisaged a settlement resting on democratic nation-states, they relied further on a new fabric of complementary transnational associations. In this regard the international settlement shared the "associationalism" or reliance on group self-administration that characterized so much of American and European politics in the 1920s.

Political scientists have now devoted sustained attention to one aspect of the interaction between domestic and international systems, namely the relationship of regime type to international conflict. Different theorists have claimed weaker or stronger, less or more encompassing, versions of that relationship. The null hypothesis was that there was no determinate relationship between regime type and international conflict. Thus neo-realist doctrine essentially envisages states as black boxes, fated to rivalry no matter what their domestic institutions, simply by virtue of the Hobbesian nature of the international system. In contrast, it has become an article of faith among neo-liberal political scientists that democratic states do not readily go to war with each other. Recent decades have generated an ample literature that has claimed, then contested, then defended this proposition, which received its most celebrated early formulation in Immanuel Kant's essay "On Perpetual Peace." There Kant wrote that the first rule for perpetual peace was that the international order comprise republican polities. Kant's was one of the early formulations that linked the nature of the international order to the domestic arrangements prevailing within the states of an international system.[1]

There is now a large literature that attempts to test Kant's rule. While it is hard to find democracies that have gone to war with each other, that fact alone does not prove very much. What are the hallmarks of democracy for the law to count: plebiscitary institutions or parliamentary influence over strategic and foreign policy? Then, too, unless the states have real potential conflicts of interest the finding may be rather trivial. And of course, even if the proposition is confirmed, it does not imply that peaceful relations cannot pertain between democratic and non-democratic regimes. The Soviet Union and the United States avoided direct armed conflict for half a century: does that weaken the rule, or does the high level of rivalry short of war confirm it? Imperial Russia and the United States never went to war; the Third Republic and the tsar's monarchy were major allies.

Still, for all the questions that persist about the relationship of internal politics and international relations, most statesmen have long believed that some law of congruence pertains. To establish or ensure peace among states, diplomats have usually appealed to common values, whether a commitment to Christianity, an allegiance to a sort of European commonwealth, or a shared acceptance of some imperial suzerainty. Peace may be the absence of war, but it rests upon transnational values and morals. Conversely, governments that reject such value systems at home are likely to run amok abroad. The architects of the Vienna system remained convinced, not without good evidence, that a revolutionary power meant international instability, and they designed the Concert of Europe to eliminate that domestic source of conflict.[2] After World War I, political liberalism and national self-determination appeared to be the common principles that would facilitate international stability through collective security.

Woodrow Wilson made the Kantian connection between domestic and international politics quite plain when he exchanged possible conditions for an armistice with the German government in October 1918. No government, he asserted, that was built on authoritarian structures and in which foreign policy was not subject to parliamentary scrutiny could be relied on to make a lasting peace. In effect he introduced neo-Kantianism into the peace process, and his observations precipitated an abdication crisis in Berlin that quickly led to the flight of the emperor. Indirectly, the whole peace settlement was predicated on a vision of democratic states linked together in an overarching collective security framework. In effect the emerging settlement was built upon what might be thought of as the Wilsonian center. Excluded on the left was the Leninist regime, embroiled in a civil war supported by the major victorious powers at the peace conference; excluded on the right, by the force of historical change, were the imperial institutions that disappeared between 1917 and 1922.

Although, if we adopt Arno Mayer's perspective, the Clemenceau and Orlando governments might be designated advocates of the so-called forces of order, in fact, neither one represented a right-wing regime or reactionary values.[3] The former Central Powers that signed the European peace treaties were new republics that had allegedly transformed their institutions. No matter how imperfectly realized, the prevailing principle of nation-state construction was ethnic and plebiscitary. The reconstruction of Poland and the partial uniting of irredenta with national homelands after their removal from now defunct empires lay at the heart of the peacemaking process. These outcomes are familiar enough that I do not have to specify them here. Guaranteeing the new European order was the League of Nations, an association that was to unite democratic states committed to collective security. Both in terms of those inside the new Geneva framework and those unhappy and undemocratic regimes outside, the new international settlement grouped democracies committed allegedly to ethnic self-determination and to collective security. Eventually it would include all countries that seemed prepared to embrace the new ideals, including the German Republic, and even the Soviet Union. But it was one thing to admit the new countries of Europe to the democratic club; it was another to preserve them as democratic states.

The rigors of the international settlement worked to weaken the democratic order on which it implicitly rested. Even before the Great Depression struck, Spain, Italy, Hungary, and Poland had abandoned parliamentary democracy. The contradictory security provisions with which the Versailles powers sought to deal with a defeated but still ambitious Germany handicapped the democratic centrists in the Weimar Republic. Similarly the post-1918 settlement incorporated approaches to international political economy that further burdened fragile democratic institutions. The commitment of the international financial community to the gold-exchange standard and the de facto connection between German reparations and Allied war debts intensified economic hardship and undermined liberal-democratic coalitions. Since preserving peace in Europe would be a much chancier proposition were Germany to abandon parliamentary institutions, the social and economic corollaries of the Versailles settlement had very serious consequences.

When it comes to the reparation issue we are all familiar with the difficulties that emerged. But more than reparations was at stake. We sometimes forget how ambitious the Versailles order really was. The new settlement involved incentives for regime transformations, but it also encompassed an effort to construct what we might call today an international civil society. This is, I believe, one of the most interesting aspects of the peace that was negotiated, and it deserves our attention. Let me signal three aspects: the International Labor Organization (ILO), the minorities treaties signed with the states of Eastern Europe, and, a few years later, the intervention of financial experts and bankers in reconstructing currencies and adjusting debts.

Consider, first, the ILO, which was outlined in the labor clauses under Section 13 of the Versailles Treaty. The ILO arose out of the aspirations of the reformist working-class movements of the United States and Europe. Without the pressure of the emerging Third International and the Bolshevik seizure of power in Russia, it is doubtful that labor delegates could have inscribed such a commitment to an international organization, first in the Versailles Treaty and then in the League Charter. Nonetheless, the international organization also obeyed the logic of labor collaboration with business and the state that wartime production had cemented. It wrote into international law the corporatist collaboration that would become the most successful strategy for postwar stabilization.

Before World War I, in fact, governments had consented to a series of international conventions concerning women's and child labor and safety provisions, just as they had endeavored to control white slavery or prostitution. As early as 1914, Samuel Gompers of the American Federation of Labor had called for a world labor congress, a demand soon seconded by the French labor federation, the Confédération Générale du Travail (CGT). By 1916 labor delegates among the Allied powers convened in Paris, on the initiative of the CGT's Léon Jouhaux and William Appleton of the British General Federation of Trade Unions. Learning of the Paris meeting, Gompers protested; he was told by the British labor delegates that the European unionists did not wish to wait for a peace conference; moreover, they would not be ready to admit German delegates. Indeed much of the impulse in Britain derived from the shared desire of reformists and civil servants to keep the Labour Party left far away from any influence over the peace settlement. Nonetheless, by 1918, the Labour Party had managed to capture a role in shaping the international labor agenda. Similarly, Clemenceau worked to enhance the influence of the moderate Jouhaux, while limiting that of his more radical rival Albert Thomas. There is no scope here to trace the rivalries, not only the well-known ideological ones between Majoritarians and Minoritarians, but the personal and organizational ones as well. The AFL remained the privileged interlocutor of the American delegation, and Washington was chosen as the site of the constitutive meeting of the organization that would include representatives of labor and employers. In effect, the ILO resulted as much from the mutual suspicions and vetoes of contending labor leaders and wary government officials as from any shared vision of a working-class future. Nonetheless, it established a significant addition to the fabric of international organization; for it meant that labor delegates from individual countries could appeal domestic labor conditions to a League of Nations agency. Throughout the 1920s the ILO continued to function. Obviously it could not protect labor unions from the coercion of authoritarian governments, but it established a structure of institutional public opinion in which working-class interests found official recognition.[4]

The famous minority treaties served a similar purpose. Whether or not the treaties were useful or counterproductive remains subject to sharp debate. Once again the demand arose from the non-state sector: in this case Louis Brandeis and the American Jewish community that sought Wilson's help in protecting the status of the Jews in reconstituted Poland. Indeed religious guarantees had been written into peace treaties since Westphalia, but the application was now vastly expanded to enshrine the collective rights of the approximately twenty-five million citizens of ethnic minorities who were stranded inside the new national states of Eastern Europe. The provisions of these treaties, following the Polish paradigm, provided that the new nations had to guarantee the rights of political organization and representation, the use of minority-group languages in courtrooms, compensation for land transfers, and a fair share of school budgets. Alleged violations could be brought to the League Council and the International Court of Justice; what is more, such suits could be brought by parties outside the national territory, such that Hungary might sue on behalf of Magyars in Slovakia, or Germans on behalf of the Sudetens.[5]

What were the advantages and disadvantages of this ambitious effort to inscribe group guarantees into international law? Not surprisingly the new states resisted the obligation; they resented being singled out as potential persecutors, they complained about the infringement on sovereignty. Since the United States had resisted the Japanese demand for a clause about racial equality, it seemed hypocritical to enforce tolerance on small states in Europe. The Romanians—who after all were not emerging as a new state—protested loudest of all, but Clemenceau told Prime Minister Ionel Brătianu that since Romania was doubling its size by virtue of the settlement it would have to accept the terms. Considering that Romanian statesmen openly bragged about evading the guarantees for its Jewish minority, which the Congress of Berlin had sought to institute in 1878, it was hardly to be expected that it would become a land of racial tolerance. Ironically, in view of later developments, no treaty was imposed on the German Republic. Perhaps most seriously, by identifying minorities as privileged segments of the population with a special right of appeal to the League, the treaties may have contributed to the xenophobic resentments they were designed to control. Nonetheless, for a decade there was an active jurisprudence under the treaties: Germans in western Poland and the Sudetenland protested land confiscation, Hungarians in Slovakia and Romania were most sedulous about seeking their school rights. The regime of the treaties in fact threatened to become just a sort of instrument for ethnic interest-group politics. Indeed if minority claims could have been successfully transformed into the quest for patronage that ethnic groups successfully press in the United States (and which ethnic minorities had manipulated in the Habsburg domains), the minorities problem might have been durably transformed from irreconcilable questions of identity to negotiable issues of subventions. But the financial constraints in Eastern Europe, the ravages of the world economic crisis, and the rise of Hitler as a highly successful racialist demagogue doomed any such trajectory.

The minorities treaties and the ILO were both efforts to endow social groups with a status in international law that offered protection no matter what the attitude of the respective national governments. They established a juridical status for collective identities that transcended individual citizenship. In this respect they embodied the associational and functional approach to the representation of interests that characterized interwar democracies [6] International order was envisaged not merely as the result of a strategic balance that the more famous disarmament and occupation clauses also endeavored to enforce. In effect international order was to be built on the fabric of collective groups that claimed an international citizenship guaranteed by the League. The difficulty, however, was that the guarantees thereby provided were highly fragile. Consequently after World War II, such an approach was largely superseded. In the disillusion with the minorities treaties, the United Nations would focus on the enforcement of individual rights. The U.N. Declaration of Human Rights, the conventions on genocide, indeed the prosecution of war criminals, emphasized individual protection and individual transgression. Only recently, with the Copenhagen elaboration of the Helsinki process talks, has the potential for guaranteeing group rights (including that of claiming autonomy within a national territory) been revived.[7] The emphasis on non-governmental organizations in helping to structure the milieu of rights and guarantees within particular states also returns to a vision of international or transnational associations that the architects of the 1920s began to experiment with. The question remains whether such institutions can really secure the protection of group interests.

Certainly the ILO and the minorities treaties and other associational efforts could not mitigate the ravages of the depression, which arose in part precisely out of an effort to reestablish the international financial system independent of national governments. The Dawes Committee, followed by the diverse committees put together to stabilize national currencies in Eastern Europe and make conditions safe for private finance, was a major feature of the stabilization achieved in the second half of the 1920s. Such stabilization usually involved diminishing the claims of national sovereignty, removing control of the money supply from the hands of finance ministers, and in general seeking to enforce the controls if not of international public opinion at least of international capital. It mobilized private bankers, such as Eugene Mayer and Thomas Lamont, who worked in tandem with international agencies. And by helping prepare national economies for participation in the gold-exchange standard, it helped to liquidate the accumulated debts of the war and move the international monetary system from its reliance on inflation to convertibility. But the bankers' agreements also imposed a deflationary bias to the world economy that made each society more vulnerable to unemployment. In short, even as minorities spokesmen endeavored to weave a fabric of associations for an international civil society, the market forces they sought to restore undermined this very effort.[8]

Sketching in this landscape of international institution building means revisiting, as it were, the structures of stabilization that I wrote about at the national level in *Recasting Bourgeois Europe: Stabilization in France, Germany, and Italy in the Decade After World War I,* but now from the international or transnational level. Not surprisingly, given what I have said about attempted settlements, a certain congruence marked the principles that were supposed to govern national and international stabilization. There was a common reliance on associationalism or corporatism, that is, the endowment of interest groups with public-law rights, both within national political systems and in the treaty system and League of Nations. Second, there was a common effort to build these national and transnational associations on the political constituencies first of the center-left, then of the center-right. Most of these corporatist ventures—transnational and domestic—were intended to exclude the threats from political extremes—either that of the Third International on the left (hence the buttressing of the ILO) or of nationalist racism on the right (hence the minorities treaties). As it turned out, the forces of the left could be successfully quarantined, but the forces of the right were not to be so successfully mastered. While exponents of the center-left remained resolute (at least before the era of the Popular Front) in opposition to communist appeals, the leaders of the center-right were often more willing to make alliances of expedience with military saviors or fascist parties. Both the institutions of democracy in the new states of east-central Europe and the new efforts to institutionalize international civil society proved too frail to survive the depression and the run-up to the Second World War. No fabric of associationalism could stand up to the nasty reassertions of sovereignty and then hegemony in the interwar period. Indeed the accomplishments in practical terms were slight enough that they seemed to fall into oblivion.

On both the national and international level of politics, the attempts to build consensus on associational or civil-society approaches were disabled by serious contradictions. Underlying the social fabric of the peace settlement were two conflicting visions, both of which were implicit in Wilsonianism and the institutional approaches of the 1920s. The first vision was that of the democratic nation-state as the fundamental constituent of the international order. Wilsonianism, and perforce the consensus of Allied war aims by 1918, celebrated the nation-state as the appropriate framework for enacting democratic rights and participation. The "old diplomacy" that was so roundly condemned was the work of empires; thus the destruction of the archaic landed empires was eventually welcomed (the decision about Austria-Hungary came only in late spring 1918), and the colonial empires, which as Allied possessions could not be slated for dissolution, at least had to be moralized and made high-minded. The nation-state was to emerge democratized, enhanced, and legitimated within the League of Nations. Reformed Germany and resurrected Poland were major monuments to the nation-state. The Wilsonian moment, in effect, was the Mazzinian moment updated.

At the same time, however, Allied statesmen, including Wilson himself, and the domestic groups contending for influence in the wartime nations also seemed to believe that nation-states no longer provided an adequate basis for assuring the new world order that was sought after the Great War. If empires were no longer to be entrusted with stabilization, then a fabric of associations, based on ethnic or economic interest, had to be woven together in the very League structure designed to guarantee national security. The peace settlement was an effort to enhance both transnational associationalism and national self-sufficiency. Unfortunately these two contending principles of organization were at war with each other; and in the Great Depression the new, still fragile structures of minority and labor guarantees and even international capital flows fell victim to nationalist instincts.

Indeed it was often the very transnational and associationalist aspects of the settlement that most offended national sentiments. Employers who resented the ILO, nationalists who resented the protection of minorities, hard-pressed farmers and middle-class merchants, who stood to lose from the credit restrictions that attended monetary stabilization, all found the international civil society that emanated from the settlement especially destructive. If Wilsonianism was a wager on the complementarity of transnational approaches and democratic nationalism, the wager collapsed due to the inherent tension between these approaches. Wilsonian attitudes and subsequent American policy in the 1920s were self-defeating in another respect as well. Even as they emphasized the role of new nations and of national self-determination in general, Americans were reluctant to ease in any radical manner the burdens of international debt that so constrained economic policymaking within the nation-state. American policy in the 1920s was partially responsible at least for afflicting the national units that it wished to prosper with a continuing burden of international debt. United States policy after the Second World War largely overcame these disabling contradictions. It opted for nation-state agencies and subordinated private finance to public budgets. And despite the reticences of the Treasury, it subordinated fiscal orthodoxy to accommodationist policies. Looking at the anger of territorial populists today, whether Pat Buchanans or Jörg Haiders, and the discontent mobilized against the so-called forces of globalization, or trilateralism, NAFTA or the Maastricht criteria for European monetary union, it is easy to see that the contradictions involved in the 1919 approach are still with us.

It is revealing to compare the implicit principles of international society after 1919 with the premises of settlement after 1945. Once again the major political actors among the Allies, including leaders of the Resistance as well as the British and American governments, envisaged a social as well as political reconstruction: the Beveridge Plan, the charters of the Resistance, Roosevelt's principle of Freedom from Want, stipulated plans for economic reform and postwar welfare entitlements. The ILO remained in being; the incipient United Nations was to include UNESCO (the U.N. Educational, Scientific, and Cultural Organization) and for a while UNRRA (the U.N. Relief and Rehabilitation Administration). Nonetheless, the post-1918 innovation of according juridical status to collective actors went into retreat, to be superseded by an emphasis on individual rights. A High Commissioner for Refugees was established, but it was not an institution to which refugees had rights of corporate appeal: the refugee was the individual displaced person or family. If Jewish rights were supposed to have been protected by minorities treaties after World War I, they were to be safeguarded by recognition of the state of Israel after World War II. The difference was indicative. Individual rights and sovereign states were seen as more reliable principles and agents. In this respect, the international jurisprudence of the second postwar era can be interpreted as less ambitious after World War II, just as some of the far left's aspirations—abandoning as they did concepts of Council democracy—were also less ambitious. We can make one significant exception: war crimes trials, so frustrated by German resistance after World War I, became a major post-1945 development and indeed bequeathed a new legal order for crimes against humanity.

Another major difference from the 1920s involved the agents of international financial reconstruction. In conjunction (and in fact in partial competition) with Great Britain, the United States had begun to reorganize these during the war. By rejecting Keynes's concepts of penalizing creditor countries as well as debtor nations in the new International Monetary Fund, Washington's Treasury officials assured that they would control the terms of financial stabilization after the war. American policymakers of the postwar years divided between those at the U.S. Treasury and delegated to the IMF who sought to impose financial orthodoxy on Europe as the price of foreign assistance, and the more accommodationist forces in the Marshall Plan agencies. The split reflected the ambiguities of the Truman administration, which was divided between older New Dealers and advocates of more orthodox economic approaches, such as Treasury Secretary John Snyder. Despite these differences in American policymaking circles, few of the major political actors in the United States or abroad were willing to endow private and central bankers with the same prerogatives they had enjoyed in the 1920s. The Belgian financial establishment remained in the early postwar years the major archaic exception to the animus against central bank prerogatives.

Whereas United States financial circles had helped cover Europe's balance of payments in the 1920s through alliances of private banks, loosely supervised by the Treasury, in the 1940s and 1950s the United States government stepped in directly, through UNRRA, Government Aid and Relief in Occupied Areas, the European Recovery Program, and finally the Mutual Security Agency, to provide the liquidity needed for postwar finance. This assured the continuous flow of dollar assistance to Europe. Under the aegis of the Marshall Plan, American postwar leaders again urged Europeans away from a postwar inflationary accommodation toward monetary stabilization. This time, however, London no longer took the lead in such a readjustment, but rather tended to resist it. Restoration of currency convertibility through the step-by-step procedures of the European Payments Union, and pressure on other countries to choose a sustainable exchange rate for their currencies (which culminated with the devaluation of the pound sterling in 1949), paralleled the stabilization operations undertaken by commissions of bankers during the 1920s. But the difference of agents was critical. It was the U.S. Treasury, acting through such new intergovernmental institutions as the IMF, or Washington's own agencies for distributing foreign assistance such as the Economic Cooperation Administration, that executed policies. If the first postwar settlement had experimented with an international associationalism, the post-1945 settlement rested on an American-sponsored intergovernmentalism.

The post-1945 principles of settlement proved a more robust structure than those of 1919. We can suggest several reasons for this difference, but it is difficult to assign primacy to one, since they all interact. Given so-called bipartisanship in foreign policy, government supervision of international financial assistance proved steadier than did the bankers' initiatives of the 1920s. Bipartisanship rested in turn upon perception of the Soviet threat. Had communism appeared more of a menace to Western Europe in the 1920s, perhaps the United States would have adopted a more resolute public policy. Conversely, while the forces of aggrieved nationalism were strong at the end of the 1920s and eventually overpowered the associationalist initiatives of international civil society, in the post–World War II era the far right was discredited by fascism and suppressed outright in Eastern Europe. The center held after 1945, whereas it did not after World War I.

Perhaps it held because policymakers during and after World War II addressed not just the issues arising out of war—indeed these they divided over—but the legacy of the great interwar depression. The postwar planners strove as much to eliminate the causes of economic crisis as they did international conflict. Indeed they tended to see fascism, Nazism, and war as consequences of the Great Depression. After 1919, the vision of restoring a pre-1914 financial order hovered before London and Washington, for the world had fallen from the prosperity of 1913 into the waste and wreckage of war. But no equivalent dream of restoration blinded policymakers in Britain and the United States during World War II (perhaps Churchill excepted). The approaches of the 1920s, such as simple financial restoration or reliance on private and central bankers, were perceived as major causes of the world economic crisis. A bold and coherent national policy—indeed after 1945 an imperial policy—together with the coordination of policies of other states promised to avoid depression. Wilsonian political leaders in World War I had made the connection between political democracy and a peaceful international order, but not between a democracy and an international economic order free of deflationary pressures. The political leadership of World War II understood the second connection as well and thus achieved a more robust settlement.

By way of conclusion, it may be instructive to cast a quick glance at the present situation. For in many ways we have come full circle and have returned to the premises of the post-Versailles era, not those of Bretton Woods and the United Nations. We are intrigued once again by the promise of an international civil society, by the role that NGOs can play in knitting together a peaceful international order. The vision is captivating, but are these institutions really sufficient to preclude international conflict and forestall right-wing reaction? As in the settlement of the 1920s, we combine this reliance on associationalism with a rehabilitated economic orthodoxy that insists on monetary stabilization, budget cutting, and the virtues of central bankers. In short we welcome the modernizing force of international capitalism and try to tame its effects with the frail restraints of collective action. And once again we risk conjuring up a massive and ugly political reaction that celebrates ethnic nationalism and populism. One fault of the Versailles order may indeed have been that it was "trop doux pour ce qu'il avait de dur": too soft for the harshness it contained. Another was probably that its social guarantees were too feeble for the economic rigor it demanded. Sometimes I feel as if we are trying to rerun the experiment of the late 1920s, which is interesting for the historian, but disquieting for the citizen.

From World War
to Cold War

Part II

American Grand Strategy from World War to Cold War, 1940–1950

3

Melvyn P. Leffler

The events of 1940–41 transformed the way American officials thought about U.S. national security. With the Axis powers on the verge of gaining preponderance over the resources and industrial infrastructure of most of Eurasia, American policymakers resolved that such control jeopardized U.S. vital interests and could not be tolerated. While heretofore determined to remain aloof from an inevitable European conflict that they hoped would not affect their security, they now realized that their nation's well-being was inextricably tied to the configuration of power across the seas. President Franklin D. Roosevelt may still have harbored some hopes that the British and then the Russians might contain and perhaps defeat the Germans, but he no longer had any doubts that American interests were vitally engaged.[1]

Nor did many of his advisers doubt that long-term American interests required a world more open to the free flow of goods and capital. Quantitative restrictions, imperial preferences, exchange controls, and autarchical economic arrangements restricted trade, had prolonged the Great Depression, and bred jealousy and aggression.² Worse yet, Germany and Japan used such practices to tie other nations into their economic orbits and to bolster their strength artificially. Nazi Germany, Assistant Secretary of State Dean G. Acheson subsequently testified, organized a system that turned Europe inward upon itself "and with perfectly amazing skill had made that system work so effectively that the Germans were able to fight all the rest of the world and support reasonably well the peoples of Europe."³ The State Department officials who began planning for the postwar world as early as 1940 considered an open international system based on multilateral commercial and financial arrangements "indispensable to postwar security." The unrestricted flow of capital and goods would tend to bind other nations to the United States and discourage trade alliances that could endanger U.S. security.⁴

The two enduring ingredients of American grand strategy were fashioned on the eve of U.S. entry into World War II. Never again could the United States permit an adversary or coalition of adversaries to gain control of the preponderant resources of Europe and Asia; never again could the United States allow the world economy to be constricted and distorted by artificial restraints and discriminatory practices. American grand strategy was composed of geopolitical and economic strands. These strands were not cohesively integrated. Nor did they lead to clear sets of policies. Policy would be contingent on changing circumstances abroad as well as the evolution of political and economic conditions at home. But these notions, vague as they were, constituted the foundation for all American thinking about the postwar order. The strategic landscape in Europe and Asia would be transformed by the war itself, but the fundamentals of American thinking were largely in place before formal U.S. entry into the world conflagration.

Most of the men—George C. Marshall, Henry L. Stimson, Dean G. Acheson, Robert Lovett, W. Averell Harriman, John J. McCloy, James V. Forrestal, and Paul H. Nitze—who designed America's Cold War strategies first gathered around Roosevelt in 1939 and 1940. Their wartime tasks focused on mobilization, procurement, lend-lease, and economic warfare. They observed how industrial strength bestowed military power, how geographical conquest enhanced military capabilities. According to Acheson, the Nazi New Order and the Japanese Co-Prosperity Sphere "meant that the resources and population of neighboring countries had been turned entirely to the ends of the enemy and have been spent with utter ruthlessness."[5]

In 1940 these men and many of their colleagues in the Department of State as well as many of their business and banking associates in the Council on Foreign Relations went to work studying how U.S. economic and political interests could be protected if Eurasia were dominated by the Axis powers. The American economy, they concluded, might adjust. But the American free enterprise system would be altered radically; the political economy would be transformed; the role of government would become omnipresent; and political freedoms would be jeopardized.[6]

Nazi domination of the European marketplace afforded Germany great leverage over parts of South America, especially those nations that traditionally sold their grain, meat, and raw materials to the Old World. Germany's blitz through the Low Countries and defeat of France now meant that Argentina, Chile, Brazil, and Uruguay might easily fall prey to Nazi pressure. Given Germany's capacity to organize much of the world through its economic leverage and given the Nazi record of regulating trade for political and strategic purposes, Roosevelt's advisers and leading American businessmen grasped that the U.S. government itself might have to take over the export sector of the American economy and organize the producers of the Western Hemisphere and the British Empire (if it survived) into powerful cartels capable of negotiating on equal terms with their Axis counterparts.[7]

Roosevelt abhorred these ideas. They would, he said, "subject our producers, consumers, and foreign traders, and ultimately the entire nation, to the regimentation of a totalitarian system. For it is naive to imagine that we could adopt a totalitarian control of our foreign trade and at the same time escape totalitarian regimentation of our internal economy." We must not become, said Roosevelt, "a lone island in a world dominated by the philosophy of force. Such an island represents to me—the nightmare of a people lodged in prison, handcuffed, hungry, and fed through the bars from day to day by the contemptuous, unpitying masters of other continents." At stake was an entire way of life— the core values on which the entire American experiment was founded. We must defend, said Roosevelt, "a way of life which has given more freedom to the soul and body of man than has ever been realized in the world before."[8]

American grand strategy, in other words, was directly correlated with the protection not simply of U.S. land and territory, not simply with the promotion of U.S. economic interests, but with the preservation of its organizing ideology, its system of democratic capitalism. Faced with the prospect of the Axis countries' domination of Eurasia and the extension of their trading methods to the New World, the geopolitical configuration of the Eurasian land mass and the organization of the world trading system became matters of absolutely vital concern to the United States. In the wake of such developments, regardless of whether or not an attack on the Western Hemisphere was impending, the United States might have to cast aside its free political and economic institutions and become a garrison state.[9]

These notions would survive the war and become the central rationale for the Cold War strategy of the United States. The overriding purpose of U.S. foreign policy, Dean Acheson liked to say, was "to foster an international environment in which our national life and individual freedom can survive and prosper."[10] The strategic landscape would change after World War II, but the concern with the core values of democratic capitalism would persist. Should we lose the free countries of Europe and Asia, warned President Harry S. Truman, "then we would be isolated from our sources of supply and detached from our friends. Then we would have to take defense measures which might bankrupt our economy, and change our way of life so that we couldn't recognize it as American any longer." The U.S. government would have to restructure the nation's domestic economy, regiment its foreign trade, and monitor its domestic foes. "It would require," stressed Truman, "a stringent and comprehensive system of allocation and rationing in order to husband our smaller resources. It would require us to become a garrison state, and to impose upon ourselves a system of centralized regimentation unlike anything we have ever known."[11]

The essentials of American grand strategy called for a Eurasian land mass free from the the domination of a single hostile power (or coalition of adversaries) and a world trading system hospitable to the unrestricted movement of goods and capital. These essentials were reflected in the evolution of U.S. strategy during 1940 and 1941 when the defeat of Germany became the focal point of the Roosevelt administration's war plans. During the 1920s military planners had elaborated contingency plans for defeating the Japanese in the Pacific or for waging war against the British. During the 1930s, under the financial exigencies of the Great Depression and the pressures of isolationist sentiment, the strategic focus shifted to hemispheric defense. But the events of 1940 drastically altered American military thinking about the locus of U.S. vital interests and the means for achieving them. The United States and its institutions could not be safe unless the Nazis were contained and defeated.[12]

The grand strategy was encapsulated in noble rhetoric in the Atlantic Charter signed by Roosevelt and Prime Minister Winston Churchill in August 1941. The charter called for the restoration of sovereign states, the renunciation of territorial aggrandizement, the affirmation of basic freedoms, the opening of markets and raw materials, the desirability of international economic cooperation to improve living standards, and the disavowal of armaments pending the organization of a more permanent system of general security. National self-determination meant the obliteration of the Japanese and Nazi empires and envisioned the liberation of Europe and Asia from the control of formidable adversaries. The open door for trade and investment, although phrased cautiously to accommodate British sensibilities over their imperial preference system, nonetheless beckoned for a more open international economic order.[13]

That commitment to an open international order was reiterated time and again during the war as U.S. officials negotiated and then renegotiated the lend-lease agreements offering wartime aid to their allies. Testifying frequently before Congress, Acheson stressed the importance of lower tariffs, increased trade, and non-discriminatory treatment.[14] As he tried to educate legislators, Acheson's colleagues in the State and Treasury Departments spent countless hours laying plans for the establishment of the International Monetary Fund, the World Bank, and the General Agreement on Tariffs and Trade. Specialized studies have illuminated the bureaucratic conflicts, Anglophobic sentiments, and anti-Soviet attitudes that infused the debates over postwar economic and commercial policy. But if we dwell too heavily on these matters, we lose sight of the larger truth about the direction of U.S. grand strategy: the insistence that the postwar international economic environment be hospitable to the free flow of goods and capital. Lower tariffs, U.S. loans, and stable exchange rates were deemed the prerequisites to peace and prosperity in the postwar world as well as for safeguarding the security of the United States.[15]

Some critics have charged that U.S. officials spent too much time on the economic and financial bases of the postwar order. They believe that Roosevelt and his advisers disregarded geopolitical and strategic imperatives. The president, it is said, mistakenly demanded the unconditional surrender of Germany and Japan and assigned too much importance to the United Nations. He erred by talking about the rapid withdrawal of U.S. troops from Europe after the war and by seeking to win the good will of the Soviets. Such policies, critics insist, reflected a woeful disregard of geopolitical realities, Soviet ideological predilections, and U.S. national security interests.[16]

But such criticisms seem wide of the mark. Roosevelt's sphere of influence framework did acknowledge the reality of Soviet power in Eastern Europe and did concede that region to Soviet control, but only because Roosevelt believed such an arrangement was essential for organizing the peace, which, in part, meant satiating the Kremlin and discouraging it from additional aggrandizement. By cooperating with Stalin and satisfying Soviet Russia's security requirements, Roosevelt hoped to contain the Kremlin's ambitions. The spheres of influence policy, in other words, placed limits on Soviet advancement. Moreover, Roosevelt's conception of appropriate spheres accorded the British control over Western Europe and the Middle East. Both by limiting the Soviet sphere to Eastern Europe and by allocating critical areas in Western Europe and the Middle East to British oversight, Roosevelt was designing policies that comported with America's grand strategy: precluding any future adversary from gaining control of Europe and Asia.[17]

Roosevelt was willing to compromise the principles of self-determination and sovereign equality and he was inclined to withdraw from European political affairs, but he did not disregard U.S. security interests. During the war the Joint Chiefs of Staff drew up contingency plans for a rapid Anglo-American advance into Central Europe should Nazi forces on the Eastern front collapse and the Russians make a dash for Western Europe.[18] During the war, too, Roosevelt approved plans to create an elaborate overseas base system that was designed to defend the United States in depth and thereby avert another Pearl Harbor. The system also was conceived to facilitate the projection of U.S. power into Europe and Asia should it be necessary to do so.[19]

Because Wilsonian rhetoric resonated with the American people, the commitment to the United Nations and the rhetorical flourishes that went along with that commitment were essential to sustain the nation's overall involvement in international affairs. But the United Nations was to be organized in ways that safeguarded the vital interests of the United States and that institutionalized its domination, or at least partial domination, through the Security Council.[20] And although Roosevelt sincerely sought to cooperate with the Kremlin and thereby to contain its expansion through a collaborative approach, he deferred to Churchill's desire to withhold information about the atomic bomb. The British prime minister thought the new technology accorded the Americans "the power to mould the world." Roosevelt may have had his doubts about this, as John Harper recently argued, but nonetheless he did defer to Churchill's wishes, although knowing full well that the denial of information would fuel Stalin's suspicions.[21]

The important point to remember is that the desire to get along with the Soviets never reflected any ambivalence about the importance of safeguarding Europe and Asia from the control of a future enemy. In early 1945 several of the nation's most prominent experts on international relations wrote a study entitled "A Security Policy for America." Frederick S. Dunn, Edward M. Earle, William T. R. Fox, David N. Rowe, Harold Sprout, and Arnold Wolfers emphasized that it was imperative to prevent any one power or coalition of powers from gaining control of Eurasia. "Soviet Russia," they stressed, "is a power whose good intentions must be assumed until there is incontrovertible evidence to the contrary, but its intentions are sufficiently unclear so that the United States must in no case place sole reliance for its security on Soviet good intentions. . . . In all the world only Soviet Russia and the ex-enemy powers are capable of forming nuclei around which an anti-American coalition could form to threaten the security of the United States."[22]

The chiefs of staff of the armed services deemed the study so prescient that they adopted it as a formal paper of their own.[23] This did not mean that the chiefs wanted a showdown with the Kremlin; they did not. They hoped for good relations. But they also perceived the altered strategic landscape. Writing in May 1944, Admiral William Leahy, acting as the equivalent of today's chairman of the Joint Chiefs of Staff, wrote: "the outstanding fact to be noted is the recent phenomenal development of heretofore latent Russian military and economic strength—a development which seems certain to prove epochal in its bearing on future politico-military international relationships, and which has yet to reach the full scope attainable with Russian resources."[24]

Although most U.S. officials were reluctant to regard the Soviet Union as a future adversary in 1945, they nevertheless were keenly attuned to containing the advance of Soviet influence and power beyond the areas occupied at the end of the war. American decisions to occupy southern Korea, monopolize control of postwar Japan, and deploy two divisions of marines to China illustrated U.S. concerns about containing the expansion of Soviet influence in Asia. The preparations for and negotiations at Potsdam revealed the determination of almost all U.S. military and civilian officials to block Soviet inroads into Western Europe and the Middle East.[25] The Joint Chiefs of Staff and the Department of State, for example, agreed that the Soviets must not be allowed to participate in any schemes for the internationalization of the coal-rich Ruhr valley in western Germany. Russia, said the Joint Strategic Survey Committee, has already been "left as the sole great power on the Continent—a position unique in modern history." "Under present circumstances," admonished the Department of State, "the extension of Soviet power and influence into the heart of Western Europe through the device of [international] trusteeship would manifestly be open to grave doubt."[26] And anticipating Soviet requests for bases in the Dardanelles, U.S. officials determined that they must be rebuffed:

> To argue that it is necessary to preserve a unilateral military control by the U.S. or Britain over Panama or Gibraltar and yet deny a similar control to Russia at the Dardanelles may seem open to the criticism of being illogical. It is however, a logical illogicality. Neither the United States nor the British Empire can by the greatest stretch of imagination be accused of expansionist or aggressive ambitions. . . . Russia, however, has not as yet proven that she is entirely without expansionist ambitions. . . . She is inextricably, almost mystically, related to the ideology of Communism which superficially at least can be associated with a rising tide all over the world wherein the common man aspires to higher and

wider horizons. Russia must be sorely tempted to combine her strength with her ideology to expand her influence over the earth. Her actions in the past few years
give us no assured bases for supposing she has not
flirted with the thought.[27]

The desire to get along with the Soviets and to pursue his domestic agenda initially constrained the foreign policy initiatives
of President Harry S. Truman. In fact, the new chief executive
preferred to concentrate on domestic priorities and to leave matters of diplomacy to his chosen secretary of state, James F. Byrnes.
Truman, a former senator, was keenly attuned to the parochial,
nationalistic, isolationist predilections of many of his contemporaries. When the war ended he insisted on terminating lend-
lease and exacting tough terms from the British in the negotiations over a large postwar loan. Approaching the reparations
question at Potsdam, the new president insisted that the United
States not become Europe's Santa Claus. Aware of the public's
desire for lower taxes and its outrage over escalating prices, Truman sought to contain occupation costs and reduce military expenditures to a bare minimum. Most of all, he knew he had to
bring American boys home from Europe and Asia. Some officials
lamented the erosion of U.S. military strength, but political and
fiscal considerations dictated no other course.[28]

Truman and his advisers hoped to achieve their overriding
strategic objectives—a Eurasian land mass free of great-power
domination and an open-door world—without incurring large
expenditures and without assuming large commitments. But as
they observed the evolution of the social, economic, and political
landscape in 1945 and 1946, they grasped the new threats to their
grand strategy. Although they remonstrated vociferously against
Soviet repression in Eastern Europe, they were most concerned
about the dire conditions in Germany and in southern and western Europe. Assistant Secretary of War John McCloy traveled to
Germany in April 1945 and reported to Stimson that "there is a
complete economic, social, and political collapse going on in

Central Europe, the extent of which is unparalleled in history."
Stimson, in turn, warned the president on May 16, 1945, that
there will be "pestilence and famine in Central Europe next
winter. This is likely to be followed by political revolution and
Communist infiltration." A month later Undersecretary of State
Joseph Grew handed the president a long report on the international communist movement. "Europe today," the report concluded, constitutes a breeding ground for "spontaneous class hatred to be channeled by a skillful agitator." Speaking to the heads
of U.S. war agencies, Truman declared that "the future permanent peace of Europe depends upon the restoration of the economy of these liberated countries. . . . A chaotic and hungry Europe is not a fertile ground in which stable, democratic, and
friendly governments can be reared."[29]

Officials in the U.S. government accurately understood the
changed strategic landscape. In the aftermath of war, only one
other nation possessed the ability to gain control over large parts
of Europe and Asia. The Kremlin's latent strength stemmed not
so much from its military capabilities as from its capacity to cap-
italize on the widespread unrest, the yearnings for social and
economic reform, and the appeal and popularity of Communist
parties, especially in France, Italy, and Greece. Should these parties capture power, they might sign bilateral trade treaties with
the Soviet Union, or offer it highly coveted bases that might enhance the overall power of the Soviet Union.

American policymakers believed that prevailing economic and
commercial conditions played into the hands of local Communist
parties. In 1947, nearly two-thirds of Western Europe's trade was
organized bilaterally, particularly through exchange controls,
quantitative restrictions, and barter agreements. Faced with a severe shortage of dollars, European governments controlled their
imports, discriminated against countries whose currencies they
did not possess, and partially regimented their domestic economies in order to conserve scarce resources. Communist parties,
U.S. officials believed, felt most comfortable with domestic regimes that set priorities, regimented trade, and controlled eco-

nomic transactions. Internal price controls and state economic planning, for example, might allow wage hikes and enlarged social welfare programs without exposing home markets and local producers to international competition. Exchange controls, state planning, and communist popularity seemed to go hand in hand and constituted an interrelated threat leading either to the gradual aggrandizement of Soviet influence or the spread of autarchical arrangements that conflicted with the open world order that U.S. officials deemed requisite to American well-being and national security.[30]

The other part of the strategic landscape that so alarmed U.S. officials in the aftermath of World War II was the vacuum of power in Germany and Japan. In 1947, when the Joint Chiefs of Staff first grappled with defining overall priorities, they concluded that nothing could be more detrimental to U.S. security than the conquest or communization of Britain or France. But these nations could not be protected without the assistance of Germany. "The complete resurgence of German industry, particularly coal mining, is essential for the economic recovery of France—whose security is inseparable from the combined security of the United States, Canada, and Great Britain. The economic revival of Germany is therefore of primary importance from the viewpoint of U.S. security."[31] In their emphasis on co-opting German power for the West, the chiefs of staff sounded much like George F. Kennan, who was then organizing the Policy Planning Staff in the State Department. "The only really dangerous thing in my mind," said Kennan, "is the possibility that the technical skills of the Germans might be combined with the physical resources of Russia." Kennan did not think such a combination was likely to arise, but if it did, "then there would have come into existence an aggregate of economic and military industrial power which ought to make every one of us sit up and take notice damn fast."[32]

When U.S. officials began paying serious attention to designing a peace treaty with Japan, they immediately expressed similar fears. Japan, concluded Kennan's Policy Planning Staff in 1947, "cannot possess an independent destiny. It can function only as an American or Soviet satellite." By the late 1940s, when it was clear that the communists would triumph in China, all U.S. officials became convinced that Japan was the key to Asia's future. Long-term U.S. security interests, said the Central Intelligence Agency, required "the denial of Japan's capacity, both economic and military, to USSR exploitation." Our primary goal in Asia, Kennan emphasized, was perfectly clear: "The security of the United States must never again be threatened by the mobilization against us of the complete industrial area there as it was during the Second World War."[33]

When U.S. officials assessed the strategic landscape in the late 1940s, they did not so much fear Soviet military power as they worried about the prospects of the Kremlin luring Japan or Germany into its orbit or capitalizing on the strength of Communist parties or profiting from the spread of revolutionary nationalism in the underdeveloped world. The Soviets, according to Washington policymakers, had the capacity to gain control over key parts of Europe and Asia, but were unlikely to do so through the use of military force. George Kennan, of course, believed this more strongly than anyone else in policymaking circles. But even Russophobes like Secretary of Defense James Forrestal grasped that America's strategic superiority, atomic monopoly, warmaking capabilities, and naval power deterred the Kremlin from engaging in military aggression. "As long as we can outproduce the world, can control the seas and can strike inland with the atomic bomb," he noted in his diary in 1947, "we can assume certain risks otherwise unacceptable."[34]

Understanding their nation's superior strength and the Soviets' reluctance to wage war with the United States afforded American policymakers the time and the confidence to concentrate on co-opting and rebuilding West German and Japanese power, expediting the recovery and integration of Western Europe, and bolstering middle-of-the-road governments in those countries. The decisions to focus on these areas did not come without careful examination of threats, goals, tactics, and U.S. capabilities. After announcing the Truman Doctrine in March 1947 and embarking on a program of military aid to Greece and Turkey, the State Department, the Joint Chiefs of Staff, and a host of interdepartmental committees engaged in comprehensive assessments of U.S. priorities. They agreed to focus on western Germany, Western Europe, and Japan. They also agreed that economic aid needed to take precedence over military assistance. "In the necessary delicate apportioning of our available resources," wrote Assistant Secretary of War Howard Petersen, "the time element permits emphasis on strengthening the economic dikes against Soviet communism rather than upon preparing a possible eventual, but not yet inevitable war."[35]

The Marshall Plan was the cornerstone of U.S. policy. Its purposes were to alleviate the dollar gap, contain the spread of exchange controls and bilateral agreements, foster economic recovery, and erode the appeal of local Communist parties. If the European economy was not propped up, explained the Harriman Committee on the European Recovery Program, European countries would have to "resort to trade by government monopoly—not only for economic but for political ends. The United States would almost inevitably have to follow suit. The resulting system of state controls, at first relating to foreign trade, would soon have to be extended to the domestic economy to an extent that would endanger the survival of the American system of free enterprise." Likewise, if recovery was not expedited, "the countries of middle-western and Mediterranean Europe [would] sink under the burden of despair and become Communist." Scandinavia and North Africa would follow. "This transfer of Western Europe, the second greatest industrial area in the world, and of the essential regions which must inevitably follow such a lead, would radically change the American position. If it should prove that a weakened United Kingdom could not resist so powerful a current, the shift would be cataclysmic." The national security of the United States would be endangered and a "swift and complete conversion to a military footing" would have to occur. New constraints, concluded the Harriman Committee, would have to

be placed on "our economic and political life, perhaps extending
to our very form of government."[36]

The Marshall Plan was designed to achieve America's grand
strategy, that is, to promote a multilateral world order and to ensure that the Soviets would not indirectly gain control over the
critical resources and infrastructure of Western Europe. Although
U.S. officials often were not able to compel the French, Italian,
and other governments to do their bidding, and although the Marshall Plan cast aside the immediate goals of convertibility and
multilateral trade, nonetheless the key American objectives were
brilliantly achieved. Counterpart funds, says Chiarella Esposito,
were not able to influence the domestic economic policies of either France or Italy. But the funds did help to "achieve one of the
most important American objectives in Europe: centrist, pro-
American forces in both countries used the counterpart funds as
a tool to consolidate their positions."[37] The magnitude of U.S. aid
might have been small in relation to total European investment,
but most scholars now concur that it was large enough to limit
"the distributional consequences of stabilization by financing imports of consumption goods in quantities sufficient to reconcile
an acceptable standard of living with the costs of reconstruction."
The Marshall Plan, concludes Barry Eichengreen, "facilitated an
accommodation between European capital and labor over the distribution of income which permitted stabilization and liberalization and encouraged saving and investment. It ensured a role
for the price system in the allocation of resources in postwar Europe's social market economy." It also fostered the integration of
European economies and supported the European Payments
Union without obliterating the ultimate goals of free convertibility and multilateral trade symbolized by the Bretton Woods institutions.[38]

Marshall planners wanted to rebuild the German economy and
link it to Western Europe. In so doing, they sought to defeat Soviet
efforts to lure all of Germany into an eastern orbit. American officials worried that by offering markets, or territorial rectifications
in the east, or hopes of unification, the Kremlin might tempt West

Germans to look eastward for their salvation. Secretary of State George C. Marshall feared that should German reconstruction be thwarted, the worst of all scenarios might ensue: "a Germany controlled by the Soviet Union with German military potential utilized in alliance with the Soviet."[39] Marshall, Forrestal, and Secretary of War Robert P. Patterson argued over budgetary matters and unification issues. But as they formulated plans for the European Recovery Program, they had no difficulty agreeing "that Germany must cooperate fully in any effective European plan, and that the economic revival of Europe depends in considerable part on recovery in German production—in coal, in food, steel, fertilizer, etc., and on efficient use of such European resources as the Rhine River."[40]

The logic of America's grand strategy led in directions few officials anticipated in 1945. The decisions to rebuild the German and Japanese economies triggered new demands that required radical policy alterations. The French, for example, bitterly protested Anglo-American actions to raise the level of industrial production in the western zones of Germany, to merge the zones, and to establish German self-government. A revived Germany, the French warned, might act independently or in concert with Moscow. Washington's most influential diplomat in Europe, Lewis Douglas, informed Marshall that "if the French were assured of long-term United States defensive cooperation against German aggression, in other words, that we would fight on the Rhine in such an eventuality, the French would relax in their attitude regarding German industry and reconstruction."[41]

Policymakers in Washington were exasperated by French opposition to their initiatives in Germany. But Marshall understood the risks and burdens that centrist French governments were being asked to bear. Beleaguered by the Gaullists on the right and the communists on the left, Georges Bidault, Robert Schuman, Paul Ramadier, and other moderates desperately needed reassurance. Marshall promised to support the creation of a Military Security Board, to retain U.S. troops in Germany, and to allow France to participate in the distribution of Ruhr coal. He also agreed to coordinate emergency war plans, provide military assistance, and enter into talks for an Atlantic security treaty. When the foreign ministers Ernest Bevin of Britain and Robert Schuman of France came to Washington in April 1949 to sign the North Atlantic Treaty, Dean Acheson, the new secretary of state, took them aside to discuss German matters, including the occupation statute, trizonal fusion, the Basic Law, and reparations. Without the North Atlantic Treaty, Acheson confided to President Truman, "I doubt that we could have come to a successful conclusion of these agreements at this time."[42]

In order to ensure the success of their efforts to promote the recovery of Western Europe and to coopt German power, American officials entered into treaty commitments they had not previously contemplated. They also began revising their war plans, for the first time outlining strategies and requirements that would permit the United States and its allies to retain a foothold on the European continent should war erupt. General Albert Wedemeyer, the director of the Army's Plans and Operations Division, insisted "that the United States cannot permit the Soviet engulfment of Western Europe except as it may be willing ultimately itself to become the final victim." The Joint Strategic Plans Committee agreed that it was foolish to proceed with a "strategic concept which abandons Western Europe and the Mediterranean nations without a struggle and hands over to the USSR their resources, manpower, and industrial capacity for exploitation against us." For the immediate future, an emergency war plan had to be based on existing U.S. capabilities and it still envisioned the evacuation of U.S. troops from the continent. But this plan, it was now conceded, had to be "replaced rapidly and successively by plans, the strategic concepts for which hold forth an increasing measure of hope that Western Europe can be saved from Soviet conquest and occupation."[43]

American officials still did not expect a premeditated Soviet attack, but they realized that their own initiatives escalated tensions and made war more likely, albeit still improbable. Observing the demonstrations and riots in France and Italy, the growing repression in Hungary, and the coup in Czechoslovakia, Kennan and Charles Bohlen, America's ablest Kremlinologists, were not the least bit surprised. These were "logical developments . . . in the face of increasing American determination to assist the free nations of the world both economically and politically." "Subject to a squeeze play," wrote Kennan, the communists were making a desperate effort to undermine the European Recovery Program before it became a reality.[44]

Kennan and Bohlen were pretty certain the Russians would not go to war.[45] But not all U.S. officials were quite so confident. Intelligence agencies examined prospective Soviet responses to universal military training, selective service, and supplementary military appropriations.[46] Secretary of the Army Kenneth Royall asked General Lucius Clay whether the Soviets would attack if the United States signed an Atlantic alliance or embarked on a comprehensive military assistance program to the Western Union.[47] Undersecretary of State Lovett worried about how the Kremlin would respond to the London agreements on Germany.[48] When the Soviets did react with the Berlin blockade, Army Chief of Staff Omar Bradley confided to his predecessor, Dwight Eisenhower, "the whole Berlin crisis has arisen as a result of two actions on the part of the Western Powers. These actions are (1) implementation of the decisions agreed in the London Talks on Germany and (2) institution of currency reform."[49]

As tensions rose in 1948 a heated debate erupted over the magnitude of military appropriations. Secretary of Defense Forrestal and the Joint Chiefs of Staff warned that capabilities were not sufficient to meet commitments. The president, however, insisted on containing military costs as strongly as he insisted on containing Soviet expansion. Assuming that the Soviets would not go to war, that economic aid was more important than military assistance, and that prudent fiscal measures were critical to the health of the U.S. economy, Truman and his advisers sought to fulfill America's grand strategy without preparing to wage global war.[50]

Of course, they now realized that they were locked in a prolonged conflict with an inveterate enemy. The Kremlin consolidated its grip over Eastern Europe and East Germany. Europe was split in two. The outcome was regrettable but acceptable to U.S. officials. Their initiatives stymied the possibility of an adversary taking control of the resources of Europe and Asia. Their efforts also established the framework for the eventual reduction of barriers to the movement of goods and capital, thereby fulfilling their overriding strategic objectives.

American policymakers responded effectively to the transformed strategic landscape of the postwar years. They designed new policies, assigned priority to critical areas, and integrated economic, political, and military initiatives. They worked intelligently with indigenous elites of a moderate political disposition. Correctly gauging the adversary's aversion for war, observing its repressive actions in Eastern Europe, and grasping the minimal prospects for collaboration in an environment that was volatile, U.S. officials jettisoned their previous hopes for collaboration with the Soviets. Deciding to build positions of strength, they resolved to live with a pattern of Cold War tensions rather than permit the possible aggrandizement of Soviet communist power over critical areas of Europe and Asia. The Cold War became the acceptable tradeoff for achieving the larger strategic objectives of the United States.

During the late 1940s U.S. officials dealt effectively with many, albeit not all, of the key challenges of the postwar world. What made it possible to do so? The critical variables were a wise understanding of the lessons of the past, a shrewd sense of threat, a vast superiority in wealth and power, a democratic culture that placed a premium on compromise and accommodation, a consumer capitalism that had a vast appeal to people everywhere, and a keen sense of strategic priorities that was linked to tactical flexibility and improvisation.

Although much has been written about the lessons of the past and the application and misapplication of the Munich analogy, this is not what I have in mind. In four critical ways, the lessons of the recent past exerted a salutary influence on the course of

U.S. policy. First, Roosevelt's and Truman's key advisers grasped that the economic nationalism of the interwar years had been counterproductive. They knew the United States had to play a more enlightened role as a great creditor nation and as a potential hegemon of the world economy. Second, they believed that vengeful treatment of a defeated adversary had proven counter-effective. Memories of the flawed Versailles Treaty and the fate of the Weimar Republic were in the minds of Acheson, Dulles, Forrestal, Lovett, and Harriman when they set policy for the post-war treatment of Germany and Japan. Third, based on their recognition of how the Nazis had used Germany's latent economic power for military aggrandizement, they resolved that the revived strength of former enemies had to be coopted for the good of the larger world community through new sorts of supranational institutions or corporatist mechanisms. Fourth, they understood that the presence of U.S. power was essential for the infusion of confidence and the pursuit of moderation. Although they did not want to keep U.S. troops in Europe or Japan, American policymakers knew from the experiences of the interwar years that the French would not be persuaded to make necessary concessions without having their security guaranteed; they knew that the presence of U.S. troops in Germany (and Japan) bolstered the parties of moderation in neighboring nations and buoyed the confidence of moderate democratic forces in the former enemies themselves.

These lessons, in fact, were much more important than the lessons of Munich because in the middle 1940s U.S. officials believed that Soviet Russia was not Nazi Germany, that Stalin was not Hitler, and that military force was not the Kremlin's preferred means for advancing Soviet interests. Notwithstanding Stalin's record of brutality, top U.S. officials initially were predisposed to deal with him so long as they thought he would be responsive to their needs. What was important about the Munich analogy was that once U.S. officials decided to pursue their goals unilaterally, they could mobilize a widespread and bipartisan consensus by referring to the lessons of the 1930s. Such rhetoric resonated widely and catalyzed support from divergent domestic constituencies that never would have supported government aid programs like the Marshall Plan and entangling alliances like NATO without the recent memory of Munich and the failure to appease totalitarian adversaries.

But with regard to official policy, American leaders had made a much shrewder assessment of threat than their public rhetoric suggested. They knew they had to overcome the dollar gap, deal with the sources of socioeconomic discontent, and fill the power vacuums in Germany and Japan. They knew that in launching such initiatives they would exacerbate Soviet-American tensions. They were willing to accept the tradeoffs. And when the Soviets responded with anticipated repression and belligerency, officials used the evidence to catalyze support for yet additional initiatives.

These initiatives could not have been successful if the United States had not possessed infinitely greater power and wealth than the Soviet Union. This is not the place to analyze the extent of Soviet ambitions or the nature of Soviet intentions at the end of World War II. But whatever their ambitions and intentions, the Soviets had incomparably less power than the United States, and American officials were fully aware of this and willing to take advantage of it. Marshall, Lovett, Clay, and their colleagues had great confidence that their strategic air power and atomic monopoly would force the Kremlin to back down and avoid conflict. During the Berlin crisis in 1948 they might have felt some doubts, but when the Soviets did not challenge the airlift they became convinced they were correct in their judgments. The Russians, said Secretary of State Marshall, understood the power of the bomb, knew the Americans would use it in a showdown, and modulated their behavior accordingly.[51] The State Department intuited that Moscow would "probably offer limited political concessions in order to prevent a seemingly certain war."[52]

If superior power permitted the Americans to take risks that they might otherwise not have taken, superior wealth made them an attractive ally. In recent years, there has been much talk about an empire by invitation.[53] However persuasive is this argument, a critical ingredient was the magnitude of assistance that the United States could proffer. In comparison, the Soviets had nothing to offer but a messianic ideology. Wherever they went, they did not give, but they took; in fact, they plundered and raped with abandon. They did so in part because of the nature of their own system, and in part because of their own desperate economic conditions.[54]

The Americans handled their superior wealth adroitly. Even while they dictated the course of overall strategy, they did not impose solutions. American diplomats worked with middle-of-the-road politicians and responded to their needs and demands even while they remonstrated against them. They were often agitated by the French, scared by the Germans, dismayed by the Italians, surprised by the British, and worried about the Japanese. Fearful that rightist or leftist forces might displace moderates, American policymakers were willing to accommodate their partners. They understood the electoral concerns of their democratic allies abroad, indeed so much so that they were often willing to engage in covert actions to support them. But there is no gainsaying the fact that coming from a democratic culture, U.S. officials understood that policy and politics involved compromise.[55]

The United States could afford to compromise because its margin of security was much greater than that of any adversary or ally. As difficult as were the choices made by Truman and his advisers, they were never of the same consequence as those taken by the Russians or the French or the British. Whether the Kremlin did or did not seek to spread communism wherever it could, there is no question that its most vital security interests were engaged in Eastern Europe, Germany, and northeast Asia. After the devastation and travail of World War II, no Russian leader could have relinquished domination over the periphery or looked with equanimity on the revival of German or Japanese power. Certainly the French would not acquiesce in Germany's revival without multifaceted and extensive guarantees of their own security. The Americans, still relatively safe across the oceans, could demand the resurrection of German power without worrying quite so much about the results. Indeed they could demand that the Russians and the French face the consequences just as they required the Australians and Filipinos and Chinese to grapple with the most immediate ramifications of revived Japanese power. Although the United States did offer guarantees to help allay the anxieties of its allies, the geographic position of the United States afforded it the luxury of asking others to bear the principal security risks that inhered in the reconstruction of former enemies.

Although U.S. adaptations to a changing strategic landscape were largely successful in the years immediately after World War II, there were some ominous signs in the winds. To dissuade Soviet adventurism and countermeasures, U.S. policymakers relied heavily on the shadows cast by their atomic monopoly and strategic air power. But once the Soviets exploded their own atomic device and supported limited war in Korea, the confidence of U.S. officials withered. They now thought that in order to support their diplomacy they had to spend vast sums to bolster conventional warfighting capabilities as well as to maintain a superior strategic arsenal. Such thinking fueled an arms race that was out of all proportion to the benefits derived from increased military expenditures. This did not happen during the 1940s, but the mentality already was present.

So was the inclination to place disproportionate emphasis on thwarting the advance of revolutionary nationalism and communism in the Third World. Because they accorded priority to bolstering democratic friends in Europe, Roosevelt and Truman modulated their support for national self-determination in Indochina and Southeast Asia. Subsequently, U.S. officials opposed revolutionary nationalist movements because of the emphasis they placed on integrating Japan with markets and raw materials in Southeast Asia and because of the importance they attached to fueling the industrial economies of Western Europe and northeast Asia with the petroleum of the Middle East and Persian Gulf. Policymakers assumed that radical governments would deny their resources and bases to the Western world and/ or collude with the Eastern bloc. In their reactions to revolutionary nationalist movements, American officials vastly overrated the appeal and reach of Soviet communism and grossly underestimated the the self-interest that underdeveloped nations possessed in maintaining economic ties with Western Europe, Japan, and the United States.

This observation leads to a concluding irony. We now tend to assign great importance to the resonance of democratic capitalism as critical to the victory over Soviet communism in the 1980s. Yet in the 1940s U.S. officials often lacked confidence in the appeal of their own system. They cherished American core values and desperately wanted to configure a world in which these values could survive and prosper. But they doubted the extent to which others might seek to emulate the American experiment. Europeans, said Acheson, had "suffered so much," they had come to believe deeply "that governments can take some action which will alleviate their sufferings." They were ready to "demand that the whole business of state control and state interference shall be pushed further and further."[56] Acheson and his colleagues also doubted the ability of the United States to compete for the allegiance of Third World peoples who sought liberation and rapid modernization. Marxism-Leninism explained away their backwardness and the Soviet model of development through a command economy appeared to hold out the prospect of rapid industrial growth.

The doubts and apprehensions of U.S. officials interacted in peculiar ways with their own sense of wealth and power. Together, these qualities inspired both dazzling initiatives and overweening ambitions. The grand strategy of the United States worked, but not without the costs of an exaggerated arms race and not without failures that mired this nation in protracted wars in Korea and Vietnam. These conflicts eroded confidence at home in the grand strategy itself. They also caused immense woe abroad among people who wondered, at least for a while, whether America's grand strategy could be reconciled with their own well-being.

4

Reversal of Fortune: Britain, France, and the Making of Europe, 1945–1956

William I. Hitchcock

In 1945, few doubted Britain's claim to great-power status. Britain counted itself among the Big Three, victorious in World War II, an imperial nation capable of projecting power across the globe. The British economy, though strained to its limits by the cost of war, was thought to possess the resilience required to recover its once dominating position in Europe and beyond. Moreover, the triumphant election of the Labour Party signaled the arrival of a new set of governing ideals that reflected the popular desire for a renewed and reformed Britain. The challenge of recovering from the cruel blows of war would, it seemed, be met.[1]

By contrast, France in 1945 staggered under the weight of its defeat five years earlier and the ignominy of collaboration during the war. Its strategic position in Europe and beyond was seriously hindered by the enfeeblement of its armed forces; the economy had ground to a standstill; and the body politic lay divided and adrift, engaged in purges, recriminations, and a general settling of scores. The future looked grim indeed, with more than a few observers predicting civil war between the right and the resurgent communists.[2]

By 1956, however, a rather extraordinary and quite unexpected reversal had occurred between these two states. The Suez crisis of that year, like an x-ray during a long-postponed trip to the dentist, revealed the frailty and structural weaknesses of Britain's world position. Not only had Britain been humiliated by Gamal Abdel Nasser's cleverly conceived nationalization of the Suez Canal, but the crisis laid bare the degree of Britain's financial dependence upon the United States. Following Prime Minister Anthony Eden's resignation in the wake of the fiasco, a contrite Harold Macmillan concluded that Britain must reinforce its strained relationship with America, even if this meant overtly recognizing junior-partner status.[3]

France, of course, fared no better at Suez; yet the lessons drawn by the Quai d'Orsay were rather different from those registered in Whitehall. Suez reinforced a long-nourished view in Paris that Britain would in future be unlikely to stray beyond the limits of action imposed by the United States. France could not look to Britain for support of policies that might run contrary to the wishes of the United States. Instead, France chose to pursue the path of strategic independence by stepping up its own atomic weapons program, and pressed forward its policy of close economic integration with the other continental European states. With the Treaty of Rome in 1957, the explosion of France's first atomic weapon in 1960, and the Franco-German Treaty of Friendship in 1963, the foundations of an independent foreign and security policy were in place. As the historian Maurice Vaisse has noted, "Gaullist France was already on the horizon in 1956."[4]

France's decision to move ahead with the creation of the Common Market marked the culmination of a process, begun right at the conclusion of the war, to build new economic ties with the states of Western Europe. Pro-European policymakers had seen that an export-led economic recovery could only be achieved in cooperation with Germany and the Benelux states, rather than in open rivalry with them. This readjustment from a stance of hostility to one of qualified integration with Germany took some time to effect, but by the late 1950s, France was ready to embrace a high degree of transnational economic coordination. By contrast, Britain, not content with limiting itself to European concerns but too weak to project global power, found it difficult to adjust to postwar realities. In attempting to craft a multilayered grand strategy with a European, Atlantic, and imperial dimension, Britain overextended itself at a moment when it could least afford to do so. By the time Macmillan opted for a policy of retrenchment and European integration, France was reluctant to share the continent with its old Anglo-Saxon rival. The new Europe would continue to keep Britain at arm's length.

The postwar development of these two countries can be explained in part by their very different fates during the war: Britain's expectations had been raised by its triumph in a global struggle, while France's pretensions to grandeur had been badly damaged in 1940. Yet postwar planning and strategy also played an important part in how these two countries positioned themselves to deal with the radically changed international circumstances of 1945. It was here, in the process of recalibrating national strategy to the postwar terrain, that the French proved more flexible, innovative, and successful than their British counterparts. Against all odds, it was France—weak, divided, and beset by colonial warfare—that charted a more direct path to recovery than Britain.

Britain in the Postwar World

In July 1945, Sir Orme Sargent, then deputy undersecretary of state in the British Foreign Office, was asked by Foreign Minister Anthony Eden to prepare an examination of Britain's postwar position and future prospects. Sargent submitted a paper called "Stocktaking After V-E Day," in which he displayed a clear understanding of the swift rise to superpower status of Britain's two great wartime allies, the United States and the Soviet Union. It seemed likely, he wrote, that they would dominate Europe "unless we assert ourselves." Britain could best do this, Sargent thought, by promoting the "principle of cooperation between the Three Great Powers." A cooperative framework "will give us a position in the world which we might otherwise find it increasingly difficult to assert and maintain." Yet Britain could not simply rely upon the good will of the other powers. "We should increase our strength," he continued, "in not only the diplomatic but also the economic and military spheres. This can best be done by enrolling the Dominions, and especially France . . . as collaborators with us in this tripartite system. Only then shall we be able, in the long run, to compel our two big partners to treat us as an equal." Once this was accomplished, Sargent thought, Britain stood a good chance of being able to check the Soviets in Eastern Europe and the Mediterranean while also winning long-term American support for British interests.[5]

Three interrelated objectives had emerged as Britain's chief priorities: to restore great-power status and independence vis-à-vis the two superpowers; to renew influence in the imperial sphere; and to capture the leadership of Western Europe, principally as a means to enable the pursuit of the previous two goals. Yet Britain fell well short of all of these goals. Why?

The breakdown of the wartime alliance shattered the assumptions on which Sargent's paper had been based. Rather than three cooperative great powers working to restore a balance of power in Europe, two rival superpowers had emerged from the war, each determined to defend its interests and even expand its sphere of influence. Such an order worked against the kind of middle position that Sargent's memo had laid out. Still more important, however, the economic impact of the war severely hampered Britain's efforts to restore great-power status and to renew imperial influence. The gravity of the financial situation was spelled out by Treasury adviser John Maynard Keynes in an August 1945 memorandum for the incoming Labour Government. Keynes pointed to Britain's burden of overseas indebtedness, the increase in the costs of imports, and the trebling of the national debt. Britain had lost about one-quarter of its national wealth during the war. These desperate conditions called for American aid, which was offered only after months of wrangling. The $3.75 billion loan was to be repaid at 2 percent interest, and Britain would be obliged to join the General Agreement on Tariffs and Trade and agree to the free convertibility of sterling by mid-1947.[6]

The American loan did not remedy Britain's financial and economic problems; the crises of 1947, 1949, and 1951 were still to come. Indeed, structural weaknesses in Britain's economic position would continue to hamper the realization of the country's postwar objectives. The Labour government was also, of course, committed to radical new initiatives in health, housing, employment, and nationalization of industry—each of which had to be paid for. In these circumstances, the ambitions laid out in Sargent's memo appeared impossible to attain. During the occupation of Germany, for example, British policy was shaped by financial considerations. One of the principal reasons for the British decision to merge its zone of occupation with the American zone in January 1947 was that maintaining an elaborate bureaucratic and military structure in Germany simply cost too much. Bevin had to concede this, even though he knew that zonal fusion would tend to diminish British influence in the Anglo-American debates on German policy.[7]

Economic weakness also undermined Britain's efforts to achieve a renewal of the British Empire, though the connection between economic weakness and imperial collapse is not as clear-cut as one might expect. True, economic frailty certainly influenced the withdrawal from India, Burma, and Palestine, and had of course been central to the surrender of influence in Greece and Turkey. Similarly, Britain's vast financial debts to the empire, especially India, seemed to have altered the balance of power within the imperial structure. Yet it was precisely the economic crisis at home that placed the role of the empire in a new perspective. The colonies and dominions, as sources of foodstuffs and raw materials that did not have to be paid for in scarce dollars, were expected to be crucial in aiding Britain during the period of economic recovery. As John Darwin has shown, the result of this reasoning was an intensified program of colonial exploitation in Africa, Asia, and the Middle East throughout the 1950s, albeit one based on the principles of cooperation, development, and reform rather than colonialism.[8]

Despite the new language, the British failed to renew the empire. Not only did the United States criticize the persistence of British colonial designs; this so-called second colonial occupation led to the intensification of hostility to colonial rule among colonized peoples, as well as the improvement in bargaining position of colonial elites vis-à-vis their newly ambitious rulers. Finally, the retooled, multiracial Commonwealth that emerged in the 1950s did not prove an effective vehicle for maintaining Britain's global influence. Instead, it may have served only to prolong the illusion that Great Britain remained an imperial nation—an illusion so swiftly dispelled at Suez.

If the economic crisis had made unattainable the dual objectives of great-power status and renewed overseas influence, then perhaps Britain could find opportunities for leadership on the continent of Europe. The Sargent memo had spoken of the need to enroll France and the smaller Western European powers into a bloc that could enhance mutual security while providing Britain with increased status as the natural leader of such an organization. Ernest Bevin, from quite early on in his tenure as foreign secretary of the Labour Government, approved of the scheme. In August 1945, Bevin spoke of the need for some kind of European "grouping" based on mutual security and economic interests. However, Bevin delayed taking any action in this direction, primarily because he feared the negative impact such an association might have on Anglo-American efforts to encourage cooperation with the Soviet Union, and secondarily because France appeared woefully inadequate as an ally in 1945 and 1946. When Bevin did finally judge the time right to move toward closer cooperation with Europe, his objective was chiefly to lay the foundation for a European security alliance to which the United States would lend its support. His call in January 1948 for a "Western Union" of European powers was clearly this—"a sprat to catch the mackerel," by Bevin's own admission. Bevin caught his fish; the Brussels Treaty that emerged from his Western Union speech was the first step toward the formation of NATO in the following year.[9]

His contribution to the formation of NATO remains Bevin's greatest legacy as foreign minister, though it is not clear that the new security pact did anything to bolster Britain's claim to great-power status, that ambition laid out in 1945. In fact, it tended to reinforce the perception that Britain was but one of a team of weak European players in an alliance dominated by the United States. NATO, for all its value as a security alliance, worked against British exceptionalism. Furthermore, Bevin's focus on the security aspect of the emerging Atlantic alliance revealed a tendency in the cabinet to neglect, even disparage, the movement for European economic integration so avidly pursued by France and the Low Countries. Bevin and the Foreign Office looked with great skepticism upon the Hague Congress of May 1948, at which various schemes for European political unity were launched. It was natural to assume that such schemes would in any case fail without British participation. Britain remained very cool toward the newly formed Council of Europe, and also opposed French efforts to widen the powers of the Organization for European Economic Cooperation (OEEC)—the body called into being by the Marshall Plan to coordinate European recovery.[10]

The proposal made by French foreign minister Robert Schuman in May 1950 for a European Coal and Steel Community (ECSC) considerably raised the stakes of Britain's policy of abstaining from European integration. Economic officials recognized that the coal-steel pool might shift the balance of power in Europe away from Britain and toward a Franco-German condominium. Still, on economic and political grounds, the cabinet found alarming the proposal for a supranational High Authority, able to dictate British industrial policy. The Foreign Office saw the Schuman Plan as an ultimatum to Britain: join Europe or remain committed to Atlantic and Commonwealth ties. The choice, apparently, was an easy one to make.

Britain also chose not to seize another excellent opportunity to influence the direction of European integration, this one in 1955. In June of that year, the six states that constituted the ECSC met in Messina, Italy, to discuss proposals for the formation of a customs union among them. Though the Six were eager to have Britain join the scheme, the Eden government declined to do so. The Treasury took the same line as it had done toward the Schuman Plan. A common market would weaken Britain's economic ties to its colonies, would hurt the effort toward global reductions of tariffs through the GATT, and would remove the protections that British industry still enjoyed from continental competitors.[11] Perhaps most significant in explaining this persistent aloofness from Europe is that in the years from 1950 to 1955, as George Peden has pointed out, "Britain's economic position relative to that of her European neighbors still seemed sufficiently strong to make it possible for her to stand apart from European integration. The Commonwealth still took a higher proportion of British exports than the future EEC countries did"—twice as much, in fact. Yet British complacency was ill-founded. The patterns of British trade were changing in the 1950s, with a shrinking percentage going to the Commonwealth. Worse, Britain seemed to be left behind in the early stages of the European boom. Britain's total growth in output between 1952 and 1956 was just 15 percent, while Germany had reached 38 percent and France 20 percent. British industrial production simply wasn't keeping up with the continent.[12] In the wake of Suez, Harold Macmillan began to see that Britain could hardly remain at arm's length from the new European trading bloc. But by the time he had gathered the bureaucratic and political support to launch a bid for membership, it was too late: Charles de Gaulle had come to power, and he—using the EEC as a platform for French political objectives—proceeded to block Britain's effort to join the community for the next ten years.

In examining Britain's postwar record of recovery, one must avoid the temptation to be too critical. The postwar economic crisis was far greater than anyone could have imagined in 1945. The problem was not simply a temporary balance of payments crisis but structural weaknesses in the British economy, especially industry, the consequences of which were felt all the way into the 1970s and beyond.[13] This state of affairs conditioned British foreign policy, ultimately forcing Britain to walk in close step with the United States or else risk the kind of humiliation served up at Suez.

Yet it must be admitted that while Britain, especially the Labour government of 1945–51, skillfully handled an almost uninterrupted series of crises in the immediate postwar era, Labour and Tory governments alike failed to develop an overall national strategy that reflected the diminished capacities of the nation. British leaders overestimated the ability of the country to meet the challenges abroad. Great-power status, imperial renewal, leadership in Europe—Britain pursued all these policies at once in a somewhat haphazard, random way, assuming that they would be rather easy to achieve. Further, Britain consistently underestimated the importance of the European integration movement, and it did so for a number of reasons: hostility toward supranationalism, belief in the economic and political importance of the Commonwealth, confidence that Britain simply didn't need Europe as much as Europe needed it, and a conviction that to join Europe was somehow to be demoted to the status of France—a horrible thought indeed.

This failure reflects a weakness in the British government machinery, especially a lack of strategic planning in the Foreign Office. As Anthony Adamthwaite has pointed out, "the most significant feature of Foreign Office thinking was the absence, until 1949, of any machinery to monitor and coordinate views over the whole field of British policy." But even in the 1950s, British strategy-making came up short. Policy toward Europe, as Alan Milward has noted, suffered from amateurism, social prejudice, and a surprising lack of understanding of both the political pressures working behind the integration movement and the economic dimensions of it.[14] The failures of the professional strategists were equally glaring during the Suez crisis itself, when Eden sharply curtailed their role, coming indeed to view them with hostility and mistrust.[15] Without the support of a competent, dispassionate policy planning staff, and the political leadership to profit from good advice, the British government was ill equipped to adjust to a radically new strategic landscape after 1945—a terrain that demanded strategic flexibility and innovation.

France Faces the Challenge of Recovery

Next to the mixed record of Great Britain, let us place that of France. France's postwar leaders, like their British counterparts, had high hopes at the war's end for the recovery of their country's great-power status, a flourishing revival of the empire, and a new role as the leader of Europe. But unlike Britain, France was early on disabused of the notion that the first two objectives were realistic. What French statesmen did see was that the third goal—a new role for France in Europe— might well provide the means for a renewal of French economic and political influence, both on the continent and perhaps farther afield. It would be wrong to portray this transition as easy. France's colonial wars demonstrate the tenacious hold of the imperial idea upon certain sectors of the elite, especially the army and the colonial service. But France's colonial conflicts should not be allowed to obscure our view of the evolution within key sectors of the French administration of new ideas about how France could exercise power in the postwar world.

France at the conclusion of the war had little reason to be optimistic about ever again being considered a factor in world politics. Charles de Gaulle's brief presidency of 1944–46 did little to address the long-term problem of French recovery. His vision of France as a great and imperial power, equal to Britain and able to play a mediating role between the superpowers, was based on a wholly fantastical assessment of France's real weight in the world. Far more realistic were de Gaulle's successors, notably Georges Bidault, the architect of French foreign policy until 1948. "I am well aware," Bidault confessed to the American ambassador in early 1947, "that France is a defeated country, and that our dream of restoring her power and glory at this juncture seems far from reality."[16] France, like Britain, suffered through a terrible balance of payments crisis in 1947, to which was added spiraling inflation. Worse, French industry was badly in need of modernization, not just because of the damage of the war but due to the lingering effects of the economic crisis of the 1930s, which had halted new investment.[17] Nor did France's German policy before 1947 give comfort to those concerned with France's future. Great Britain and the United States, after vainly pursuing a policy of four-power cooperation, began to lay the groundwork for the economic rehabilitation of Germany—a policy that greatly alarmed the French policy establishment.

Still, despite these inauspicious beginnings, a broad plan for recovery—a recovery conceived both in domestic and international terms—did emerge within the French government in the three years following the end of the war. It was crafted by a rather small coterie of technocrats, mostly economic and foreign-policy officials who had learned vital lessons from the war: that power depended on economic productivity, not reputation, and that in order for the society to reach its productive potential, the state had to lay out a plan and mobilize the resources of the country around that plan. These were concepts totally new in France, which had since the nineteenth century been in the grip of orthodox economic gurus who sought at all times to diminish the role of the state in the workings of the country. The French planning commissioner, Jean Monnet, is only the best known of this new coterie of officials who were part of a crucial "mental conversion" in favor of productivity and expansion, and who kept French recovery on the rails despite the political turbulence that surrounded them. These men were the engineers of what Charles Maier has called "the politics of productivity"—a conscious effort to shift the terms of public debate in France away from divisive partisanship and toward the more universal themes of productivity, growth, and an increase in economic well-being.[18]

That said, the Monnet Plan, the investment strategy designed by Jean Monnet to restart key sectors of the economy, was not so benign as its authors claimed. The aim of the plan, after all, was to reinvigorate French industry and stimulate exports; but the stoking up of French exports according to Monnet's ambitious design required French access to German coal and iron ore supplies. Here, in the emerging battle for coal, the implications of the Monnet Plan for foreign policy become clear. French industrial recovery was predicated on access to German mineral resources, and that access presumed an international political settlement to ensure it. From an early stage in the thinking about their own recovery, then, the French had identified their chief economic and security requirements. And unlike their British colleagues, who sought to reestablish British power on numerous fronts, the French crafted a strategy for recovery that converged on one point: Germany. In order for France to prosper, a solution to the German problem would have to be achieved.[19]

The process did not prove easy. For most French citizens, whether in or out of government, the notion of a "good" Germany emerging from the ashes of the Second World War seemed an improbable idea. French diplomacy between 1945 and 1949 reflected this cautious attitude, as the Foreign Ministry remained reluctant to concede elements of sovereignty to Germany, and instead focused on building mechanisms for control and oversight in order to gain assurances that Germany would never again menace France. French planners sought guarantees of control over German industrial production, especially in the coal-rich Ruhr valley; insisted on maintaining elements of the dismantling program initiated by the occupying powers; and demanded a strongly federal and decentralized system of government for the postwar German state. Of course, French policy tended to conflict with the Anglo-American emphasis on a prompt restoration of Germany to economic health and political stability. The French continued to view Germany as the chief long-term security threat, but in the minds of planners in Washington and London, that role was by 1947 (and for some much earlier) accorded to the Soviet Union. Once the division of Germany was confirmed at the London Conference of 1948—a long series of meetings that effectively set the West German state on its feet—the French knew that they would have to alter their tactics for securing lasting controls and restrictions on German freedom of action. Rather than coercion, France would have to emphasize such features as economic integration, regional planning, and political cooperation—concepts that appealed to the palate of the American power brokers that were guiding the process of German recovery.

What is striking in this process of adaptation is the way the French managed to pursue their interests despite their weak international position and their dependence on American aid. The Marshall Plan, announced in 1947 by Secretary of State George Marshall but instituted only in mid-1948, actually provided France with a useful tool to achieve these objectives. Not only did the European Recovery Program (ERP) promise to deliver France from its own domestic economic woes, it called into existence a number of Europe-wide institutions designed to coordinate economic recovery across national lines. And since the British were skeptical about such international planning mechanisms, the French were by default left in a leadership role. Suddenly, the entire project of European cooperation depended on an active and supportive France. French planners knew this all too well. As Jean Monnet put it, "without us, 'European cooperation' is impossible. . . . And for we French, 'European cooperation' means that before any other problem is discussed, the position of Germany is defined."[20] France could use the ERP as leverage in its search for a favorable settlement of the German question. American postwar priorities appeared to be serving France quite nicely indeed.

The institutions created to promote a coordinated European recovery proved disappointing to most French (and American) officials, however. The OEEC, established in April 1948 to divide and allocate Marshall Plan aid, fell well short of French expectations. Paris gave prompt support to the idea, supported by the Americans, that the OEEC be granted far-reaching powers. By developing regional plans for economic recovery, the OEEC could help reestablish the European market for French exports, and it could promote trade liberalization on the continent, which would grease the wheels of the continental commerce on which the French economy largely depended. Furthermore, because the OEEC was supranational, and hence nonpolitical, it could provide political legitimacy for France's efforts to ensure that German recovery was deliberate and carefully supervised.[21]

The OEEC, however, was hampered from the start by the fact that its members were chiefly concerned with dividing up and then spending Marshall credits; the larger political objectives were quickly forgotten. Above all, British objections weakened the OEEC. By the start of 1949, the British cabinet resolved to limit its participation in schemes for economic cooperation with the continent. While Britain was ready to support the OEEC in its efforts to reduce intra-European trade barriers and to share technical information, British Treasury officials agreed that "on merits, there is no attraction for us in long-term economic cooperation with Europe. At best, it will be a drain on our resources. At worst, it can seriously damage our economy."[22] In the British view, real economic cooperation, built around a customs union, specialization of production, and coordination of investment, could only be achieved through political federation, and this Britain was dead-set against.

The failure of the OEEC to emerge as a strong mechanism for controlling German recovery—and the equally limp character of the Council of Europe, established in 1948—obliged French planners to return to the drawing board. The much-vaunted European institutions had not met expectations; nor had the narrower agencies like the International Authority for the Ruhr and the Military Security Board succeeded in holding back German recovery, for theirs was only an advisory role. Worse, from the French perspective, time seemed to be working against France's German policy, for faced with a deterioration of East-West relations in 1948–49—from the Prague coup of February 1948 to the Berlin blockade—military planners in Washington and London began to speak privately about rearming Germany. Before Germany could be rearmed, and thus granted a great role in the Western security and political community, French planners had to devise a lasting framework to contain German influence in Europe.

The solution was devised by the irrepressible Jean Monnet, and sprung on the world by Foreign Minister Robert Schuman in May 1950. Monnet and his advisers were particularly keen to construct some kind of framework that would contain German industrial power, or at least harness that power to France's own ends. In providing a mechanism for controlling and channeling Germany's coal and steel industries by pooling them with other European producers under the guidance of an impartial, binding High Authority, the French could realize what they had striven toward for five years: lasting controls on Germany's economic power and by extension Germany's influence in Europe. The Schuman Plan, which emerged in 1951 as the European Coal and Steel Community, locked France and Germany into an economic partnership, but it also marked an important political milestone on the road to a lasting Franco-German settlement. For now, whatever the outcome of the rearmament debate, the French could rest assured that Germany's powerful heavy industries would be linked to France's own.[23]

Despite the unqualified political success of the Schuman Plan, the quest for a lasting postwar settlement had not been entirely completed. The rearmament debate, launched in early 1950 at American insistence, once again compelled French leaders to fall back on the principle of using binding international mechanisms to contain Germany's freedom of maneuver. Following the outbreak of the Korean War in June 1950, a divisive and unproductive debate over Germany's contribution to European defense nearly destroyed the still-fragile Western alliance. France stood at the center of this struggle, deeply torn about finding an appropriate response to the problem of German rearmament. The French public, and many French leaders, maintained a strong aversion to the creation of a German army so soon after the end of the war, before Germany had proven its loyalty to the West. Worse, German rearmament, it was thought, was sure to provoke a reaction, perhaps even an invasion, from the Soviet Union. Yet the French government was under immense pressure from its Anglo-American allies to acknowledge that a credible defense of Europe would be impossible without a German contribution. The French sought to take the initiative on the issue by resorting to the principle of European integration as a solution. In an effort to obstruct the creation of a German national army, France in October 1950 proposed a European alternative: a supranational army in which member states pooled their resources, thus blocking the establishment of a powerful military force under German control. This plan seemed to complement Schuman's strategy of using binding integrative mechanisms to link France and Germany together; the European Defense Community (EDC) was a military analogue to the ECSC.[24]

The EDC scheme deeply divided the French political elite. Some felt that it offered the only chance to block the formation of a national German army, and was therefore a vital French interest. For these proponents, it was either the EDC or the Wehrmacht. Opponents felt the price was too high, for the EDC would require France to pool its own army with its European neighbors, and thus to lose control over one of the country's most hallowed institutions. From this point of view, French prestige, power, and independence would be gravely compromised by the EDC. Thus, though the French government in May 1952 signed the treaties of Bonn and Paris agreeing to a European army, a majority in the French parliament was already forming to make sure that the treaties did not receive parliamentary ratification. The bitter debate on this issue, however, often obscures the fact that there was a high degree of consensus on the overall stance toward German rearmament: France must win guarantees restricting German military sovereignty. It was the means, not the end, that provoked controversy.

Even before the French parliament rejected the EDC in August 1954, those in the French administration who opposed it had started to plan for an easier, more direct way to control Germany's future military power.[25] In a grand bargain struck at the end of 1954, France agreed to support German entry into the NATO alliance—something inconceivable four years earlier—in return for specific treaty restrictions on Germany's military independence. Germany's army would be limited to twelve divisions; the German General Staff would not be able to act independently of NATO; and Germany would be strictly prohibited from producing atomic, bacteriological, and chemical weapons—although France would retain this privilege. Further, Germany would enter NATO via the Western European Union (WEU), to form a smaller "core" of NATO. The purpose of this was to provide a monitoring system for arms production and procurement, so that Germany could not develop such capabilities on its own. France also gained a commitment from Britain, which had never agreed to join the EDC, to keep at least four divisions on the continent and never to withdraw them without approval from the WEU. France, through the deft use of integrative mechanisms, had achieved a stunning success: Germany would become an ally but remain militarily subject to allied control; Britain had committed itself to continental security; and French military (and atomic) sovereignty was in no way infringed.[26]

The London agreements assured that France and Germany would become allies within the Western alliance, a prospect that had seemed remote amid the recriminations over the EDC. Yet this victory had been won at a heavy price. The rejection of the EDC idea badly damaged the principle of European integration— the bedrock of the French bid for influence in Europe—and the French could blame only themselves. Indeed, the enthusiasm for integration visible in the wake of the Schuman Plan announcement of 1950 cooled in the French administration by 1952. To some extent, this was due to the economic troubles France faced following the outbreak of the Korean War, which caused a sharp rise in the prices of raw materials and a parallel increase in consumer prices in France. The Korean War also thoroughly alarmed the European military establishments, and France undertook a massive increase in arms expenditures, tripling the defense budget between 1950 and 1952. France's trade deficit, which had so laboriously been brought under control by

1950, once again grew, so much that even the modest steps France had made within the OEEC toward trade liberalization had to be abandoned in February 1952. Lacking confidence in the economy's ability to withstand the impact of foreign competition, the French government retreated to the ramparts of protectionism.[27] This policy not only failed to help the French economy recover its balance, it also worked against the European strategy that France had pursued since 1948: to use integration as a means to assert French leadership in Europe. By withdrawing from the OEEC-sponsored programs of trade liberalization, the French presented a picture to their European partners of economic weakness and political drift. When the EDC collapsed in August 1954, it appeared as if France had completely abandoned the principle of integration.

Yet just three years after the EDC fiasco, France entered into a far-reaching agreement—the Treaty of Rome—that created a customs union among the six states of the ECSC, and formed a European atomic energy agency called Euratom. It was a remarkable reversal for the "European" idea, which had been so badly tainted during the lengthy EDC debate. Once again, French planners perceived that their national interests would best be served by embracing a policy of economic integration and political cooperation within the European framework.

This turnaround was partly the work of the pro-European foreign minister of Belgium, Paul-Henri Spaak, who in the spring of 1955 began a campaign to "re-launch" the European integration effort.[28] Spaak knew that it would be unwise to push for anything too ambitious, given the state of public opinion in France, but thought that progress could be made in integrating certain sectors of the Western European economies, notably in the areas of transportation, electricity, and atomic energy. He also pointed out to the French that given the current international climate—the Austrian state treaty on unification and neutralization of that once occupied country had just been completed and the Soviets were making noise about a four-power meeting to do the same for Germany—the time was propitious to link Germany more securely to the West.[29] The French government was receptive to these overtures but knew that the still-strong hostility to supranationality that had killed off the EDC treaty would severely curtail any major new effort on European integration. Initiatives would have to be limited to specific sectors of the economy.[30] But Spaak pressed forward, and on May 18, 1955, in conjunction with his Dutch and Luxemburger counterparts, proposed that the six Schuman Plan countries meet to discuss both further sector-specific cooperation in energy and transportation, and the institution of a customs union among the six ECSC countries.[31]

The French government quickly warmed to the idea of a European agency for atomic energy. This scheme seemed to have many of the same advantages the Schuman Plan had offered in 1950. A European atomic program would restrict the development of an independent German one; it would put an end to the bilateral scramble to establish a special "atomic" relationship with the United States, as the Belgians, for example, had already undertaken; and it promised to spread the costs of research and development among a broad base of states. Provided that the European effort would not prohibit the development of a French atomic weapon, planning for which was already under way, Euratom offered France significant advantages.[32] It was no surprise, then, that the Germans should be considerably hostile to the scheme. Enjoying their newfound freedom in the international system, the Germans were reluctant to place this emerging new technology, which appeared to hold vast implications for German economic expansion, under a restrictive, French-controlled regime.[33]

The attitudes of the two countries were, however, precisely the reverse when considering the second topic raised by Benelux: a common market of the six ECSC countries. Aside from the political problem—there remained a high degree of residual hostility to integration in the French parliament—the French bureaucracy raised numerous objections on economic grounds. The Common Market required a common external tariff, but would this be set at the low level favored by Benelux or the high rate imposed by France? Also, the costs of production were higher in France due to its generous social benefits for the labor force (paid holidays, shorter working week, better pay for women); this social legislation would have to be adopted by France's neighbors to level the playing field. The problem of opening the heavily protected agricultural sector to competition raised serious objections, as did the possibility that a common market in Europe could weaken France's ties to its overseas territories. Finally, the French saw in the scheme a creeping supranationalism: once instituted, it would require a common political authority and perhaps a central bank, a prospect that would be thoroughly reviled by the National Assembly.[34] By contrast, the Germans embraced the Common Market proposal: reduced barriers to trade promised great things for the export-driven German economy.[35] Despite the public stance of Europhilia evident at the six-nation Messina conference, convened in early June 1955 to examine the Benelux proposals, the battle lines were drawn, and they remained more or less fixed for the next eighteen months.

Still, the French documents show that the government did not want to reject the Common Market scheme out of hand. During the long-running talks on Euratom and the Common Market (from July 1955 to April 1956) the French searched for ways to accept the Benelux proposals but within a treaty that offered certain safeguards and protections to French interests.[36] Why this effort to be conciliatory?

First, the French grew increasingly attached to the Euratom project. They saw in this plan a way of reinvigorating European integration, reclaiming some prestige for France following the EDC crisis, and above all they saw it as a useful and constructive way to contain German independence—and possibly the evolution of a special German-American relationship—in a field that was considered to have huge future importance in the European balance of economic power.[37] But in order to get Euratom, the French were going to have give the Germans and Benelux the Common Market. The linkage between the two treaties had become explicit by the winter of 1955–56, and the French were well aware of this.[38]

Second, the French were very concerned about the failure of the four-power talks held in Geneva during the second half of 1955 on German unification. High hopes had been raised in July when Khrushchev appeared conciliatory toward the issue of unification; by November, however, he had soured on the idea. French policymakers feared that the disappointment among the West German public would create pressure on the government to search for an all-German settlement, at the expense of the Western alliance. Without speedy and concrete results to give the Germans a sense that they belonged in the Western community and that they stood to gain from deeper association with it, the Germans might drift toward neutralism and appeasement toward the East.[39] As one French official noted, "In Germany, time is working on the side of nationalism."[40]

Third, the British reaction to both Euratom and the Common Market project was totally hostile, as Prime Minister Eden made clear in his talks with President Eisenhower in January 1956. The British and French had long tussled over the best means to secure European cooperation: the British favored the intergovernmental approach of the OEEC, while the French preferred integrative mechanisms that clearly bound Germany, such as the Schuman Plan. The British expressed little interest in Euratom, quietly pooh-poohing the meager accomplishments of their continental neighbors in the area of atomic energy; but the prospect of a common external tariff clearly scared them, especially because they believed that France would use its influence to insure that this tariff was set at a high level.[41] The persistent British effort to deny the validity of integration as a means to underpin a Franco-German settlement caused irritation in Paris. The French always wished to have Britain join the new institutions of "Europe," the better to balance out Germany's preponderant role. But by keeping Europe at arm's length, the British only made the French conclude that binding, supranational mechanisms to control Germany were all the more imperative.[42]

These pressures, deriving from the international arena, helped mobilize opinion within the French government in favor of the Common Market scheme, despite the considerable opposition to it evident among the technical services. And when the negotiators had become bogged down over details in the treaty, once again international events served to break the deadlock. The Suez crisis, which unfolded during the summer and fall of 1956, proved to be the catalyst for the compromise. Even before the actual Franco-British-Israeli invasion of the canal zone in November 1956, German chancellor Konrad Adenauer had begun to fulminate against American policy. Adenauer was already riled up against the United States for what he saw as its neglect of a European role in world affairs. He thought the Americans were too willing to accept, in tacit agreement with Moscow, a divided and nuclearized world. While the Europeans earned the wrath of the Third World and sought to contain it, the Americans stood aloof, expressing disinterest in the fate of Europe. The Suez crisis in Adenauer's mind only underscored the need for Europe to join together in a tight political union, so as to chart more effectively a European foreign policy that was not subject to judgment from Washington.[43]

As the dual crises of Suez and Hungary exploded in the early days of November 1956, French premier Guy Mollet—a "European" himself, who had supported the EDC—joined with Adenauer to intervene in the stalled Common Market/Euratom talks. Mollet, in a letter to Adenauer of October 31, bemoaned the failure of their respective negotiating teams to strike a compromise in meetings that had taken place on October 20–21. It was time, he believed, for intervention from the highest level to break the deadlock. Evidently Adenauer welcomed this gesture, and he traveled to Paris for a meeting with Mollet on November 6—the very day the Soviet invasion of Hungary and the Anglo-French invasion of Egypt reached a fever pitch.[44]

The minutes of this meeting are extraordinary. Adenauer and Mollet, who had come together to examine European issues, were sidetracked in their talks by the international crises. And the French-German meeting provided another opportunity for Adenauer to vent his anger at the United States. Suez, he claimed, was the fault of the Americans to start with, because of their mishandling of the Aswan Dam affair; but now the Europeans were the ones losing face. It was time, he said, to unite "against America." The Americans, he continued, had lost hope in a united Europe and were seeking a "pax atomica" with the Russians. The freedom given to the Soviets to crush Hungary was evidence of that. In the midst of Adenauer's rantings, Mollet was called out of the room to take a telephone call from British prime minister Anthony Eden. As recounted by French foreign minister Christian Pineau, this call deflated Mollet completely, for Eden told him that Britain—at the insistence of the United States—had unilaterally decided to call off the invasion. It was, as Pineau said, "un coup dur" for Mollet, and for any hope of independent European action in world affairs. Returning to the room, Mollet told Adenauer what had happened, and after an awkward silence, Adenauer gently encouraged his French counterpart with the telling phrase: "Now, it is time to create Europe! [Et maintenant, il faut faire l'Europe.]"[45]

In Pineau's judgment, this was a turning point. "Starting from this moment, when Western Europe felt, rightly or wrongly, that it could no longer count on the United States when its security was threatened, the only solution was the union of the Six, and the creation of institutions capable, if not of assuring their own defense, at least of bringing these countries closer and more tightly together on the economic plane." The actions of Nasser, Khrushchev, Eisenhower, and Eden had combined to push the French and Germans together. Almost immediately, on orders from Mollet and Adenauer, the negotiators resolved their differences—largely in favor of the French position. Within two days of the Mollet-Adenauer meeting in Paris, Pineau could report that the Germans had softened their attitude on Euratom, on harmonization of social policy, and on the safeguard clauses associated with the lowering of tariffs. When German foreign minister Walter Hallstein continued to object to bringing the French overseas territories into the Common Market because of the likely increase in costs for German imports of tropical products, Adenauer quickly stifled him. "Hallstein," he is reported to have said during the final negotiations, "stop boring us with your bananas, your coffee, your cocoa. The work we are engaged in is too important to be compromised by such minor economic considerations." Never had the political nature of the compromise wrought at the end of 1956 been more apparent.[46]

The formation of the European Economic Community had a profound impact on the subsequent development of Europe. France and Germany underwent a sustained economic boom that lasted until the mid-1970s, while Britain, outside the Common Market, struggled to keep up with these new economic dynamos. During the 1960s, Britain's average annual growth of GDP was 2.9 percent, which appeared sluggish next to Germany's 4.9 percent and France's 5.8 percent.[47] The economic ties on the continent were bolstered in 1963 when de Gaulle and Adenauer, two men of similar age and faith who shared a common social outlook and a distrust of American foreign policy, signed the historic Friendship Treaty, a culmination of almost two decades of Franco-German rapprochement. Britain remained on the sidelines, watching with concern and perhaps some envy these impressive continental achievements.

France had, of course, profited from the support of its allies in crafting this national strategy. The economic recovery depended on cooperation from France's European neighbors; the Franco-German settlement came to fruition because of Adenauer's willingness to concede the leadership of Europe to France and by his embrace of the "European" solution to the German problem; and, of course, the United States had played a vital role in offering France economic aid and security at a time of great vulnerability. It might be said that France had a "good Cold War." But French planners and strategists had been able to make the most of these advantages, while overcoming such significant obstacles as two ill-conceived colonial wars and a weak political system that failed to provide the country with strong executive leadership. The French officials responsible for foreign policy in the Fourth Republic had showed tenacity, vision, and effectiveness, traits usually associated with the phlegmatic Anglo-Saxons across the Channel. Here was a reversal of fortune indeed.

5

The Making of a Political System: The German Question in International Politics, 1945–1963

Marc Trachtenberg

In October 1963, Soviet foreign minister Andrei Gromyko had a long conversation with his American counterpart, Secretary of State Dean Rusk. The German problem was the focus of the discussion. "From the standpoint of the security of Europe and of the Soviet Union," Gromyko said, this "was problem number one." And Rusk agreed: the German question, including the complex of problems relating to Berlin, was obviously the most fundamental issue in East-West relations. "There was certainly no question about that," he said. Germany was "the point of the confrontation," and the German problem (including Berlin) was thus obviously the "number one" problem in "relations between the NATO and the Warsaw Pact countries."[1] The two men knew what they were talking about. The German question—and that meant, above all, the question of how much power Germany would have—did indeed lie at the center of great-power politics during the entire Cold War period.

Why was the German question of such fundamental importance? The division of Europe—the fact that the continent was divided by mid-1945 into two great blocs—by and large solved the basic problem of how the two sides, the Soviet Union and the Western powers, could get along with each other in the postwar period: the Soviets would do as they pleased in Eastern Europe, and the Western powers would have a free hand on their side of the line of demarcation. On that basis, the two sides could get along indefinitely; if that had been all there was to the story, there would not have been a Cold War—at least, not the sort of conflict that could conceivably have led to a third world war. The problem was that there was one great exception to that general rule, and this had to do with Germany. The Soviet Union could not allow the Western powers a totally free hand in western Germany; given their experience with Germany, given the fact that Germany is inherently a very strong country, given that they were in effective occupation of a very large part of prewar German territory, they had to be worried about a resurgence of German power. But the Western countries, for their part, given their sense of Soviet policy, had a certain interest in building up western Germany, creating a state there, and making that state a partner, with the same rights, more or less, as the other Western powers. This was a very real conflict; the most central interests of each side were engaged; and it was this clash of interests that lay at the heart of the Cold War.

But there is more to the issue than that. There was a fundamental theoretical issue involved. In dealing with the German question, people were in fact grappling with perhaps the most basic issue in international politics: the problem of how, at its core, international political life is to be organized. The great question is whether the international system should be based on the free play of political forces, or whether those forces need to be constrained in major ways. Should those basic forces be allowed to reach their own equilibrium, or should a system be constructed that permanently limits the power of major nations? In the Cold War context, whether such a system could be built turned essentially on what Germany's status would be. Could Germany—either a unified Germany or the rump West German state—be permanently kept from reemerging as an independent great power, strong enough to defend itself and to chart its own course in international affairs? Should the other powers even try to construct a system that would keep Germany from ever being able to challenge the status quo?

In the postwar period, it was by no means obvious that Germany could be kept down forever. Many people took it for granted that sooner or later Germany would once again become a truly independent great power. A system based on keeping German power limited would not be self-enforcing; would foreign countries be able, year after year, to mobilize the resources needed to keep Germany from becoming too strong? After the First World War, the Western allies had tried to impose a system of that sort, but the Versailles settlement—in essence, a set of constraints on German power—had collapsed very quickly. What the Germans called the "shackles of Versailles" had been thrown off during the Weimar period—that is, even before Hitler had come to power. After 1933, and even after 1945, the Versailles experiment was commonly seen as a disaster. The assumption was that a great nation like Germany could not be treated that way, and that a system based on constraint was simply not viable.

And if this was true of the interwar period, wasn't it doubly true after the Cold War began to set in? Now there was the additional argument, for some compelling in itself, that the West needed Germany as an ally and that Germany therefore had to be treated as a real partner—that is, as an equal. How could one say that German military power would have to be kept limited without at the same time implicitly saying that the Germans were not to be trusted? And yet an effective alliance in the long run could only be built on the basis of trust. If the Germans rejected discriminatory arrangements and insisted, as they had during the Weimar period, on equality of rights—on "Gleichberechtigung," the term used in both periods—then wouldn't the Western allies have to give way in the end? It was almost inconceivable that the West would employ really tough tactics to keep the Germans in line. But knowing that, wasn't it best to accept the inevitable, and to think in terms of a political system in which a strong German state was an integral part? A strong Germany might not be entirely to the liking of the Western countries, but such a state would be an effective counterweight to Russian power in Europe. Perhaps the West would like to keep the Soviet Union at bay and at the same time keep Germany down, but, the argument ran, it simply did not have the strength to do both things at the same time. The best course of action was therefore to permit a strong German state to come into being, and to allow that state to balance the USSR on its own.

By 1949, for example, George Kennan, then head of the U.S. State Department's Policy Planning Staff, was thinking explicitly along these lines. The idea, he argued, that the Western countries could keep the West Germans "properly in their place and at the same time contain the Russians" struck him as "unsound." The West was "trying to contain both the Germans and the Russians" but was just not "strong enough to do it." The answer, he thought, was to "look for a balance in Europe and Asia by permitting a situation to arise in which the Germans will have a stake in their own strength, where they will do things for their own sake and not for our sake." It was "not a bit pleasant," he admitted, and he had "little confidence" that the Germans would be what "we would call a westernized force." They would instead be "something between ourselves and the Russians," and might in that capacity be able to gather around themselves "the sort of in-between countries of Europe." They could then establish "a relationship which we could not establish," something that was "antagonistic" to both the "Russians and ourselves," but which would be "vigorous enough to back against the Russians."[2]

Kennan's advice was of course not accepted: the Western governments did not take this approach at all. And in fact even in 1949 Kennan's views were considered a little bizarre. Kennan did not think that a system based on the division of Europe between the Soviets and the Western powers would be viable; his assumption was that the arrangement would not work because both sides would be overextended, and that the only solution was to allow an independent power to emerge in central Europe that was neither "ours nor theirs."[3] But most officials—not just in the United States but in Britain and France as well—felt there was a good chance the Western countries could organize a viable system that would provide for the defense of Western Europe as a whole, including West Germany. And they also assumed that a defense system in which Germany took part would not necessarily lead to the reemergence of a strong and fully independent German state.

Western policy in the early 1950s was in fact rooted in assumptions of this sort. The Western powers at this time constructed a system—the NATO system—that provided an effective counterweight to Soviet power in Europe while at the same time limiting German power. Kennan, it seemed, had simply been wrong: one *could* contain both Germany and Russia at the same time. One could do it because the Soviet threat made West Germany dependent on the Western powers, and above all on the United States, for protection; unlike the Weimar governments in the 1920s, the West German government had a very strong incentive to reach an accommodation with the Western allies. But precisely because the Federal Republic was so dependent on America and its friends for protection, the Western powers did not have to rely primarily on formal controls to keep Germany in line and could afford to ease up on the occupation regime and allow West Germany to become a nearly sovereign country again. With the Red Army "just across the Elbe," the Germans, it was understood early on, would very much want to cooperate with the West.[4]

In other words, the assumption that the Soviet threat made the problem of dealing with Germany *more* difficult, because it forced the West to choose enemies and was thus bound to lead to the removal of the controls and to a distasteful resurgence of Germany as a fully independent power, turned out to be mistaken. The Soviet threat made it *easier* to deal with the German problem: the Germans were so vulnerable that they more or less had to accept the terms their Western protectors were willing to offer, even if those terms were in some absolute sense less than fully satisfactory.

By late 1954, the elements of a system had been worked out. In October of that year, Germany and the Western countries signed the Paris accords. This series of treaties, conventions, protocols, and unilateral declarations provided the legal basis for relations between the Federal Republic and the Western powers for the rest of the Cold War period. In this system, West Germany was not fully sovereign, and German freedom of action was limited in major ways. The Western allies had the right to station troops on German territory and to do whatever was necessary to provide for the security of those troops. The Germans could not force the allies to withdraw those troops, nor could they negotiate a reunification deal with the Soviet Union on their own. The level of German armament was limited and subject to foreign control. The German army was placed within the integrated NATO defense system and rendered incapable of conducting major military operations independently. Above all, the Germans were not allowed to build nuclear weapons on their own territory—or implicitly to have a nuclear force under their own control.

The system created in 1954 provided the basis for an effective defense of Western Europe. The NATO forces, now to include a German army, would provide a counterweight to Soviet military power on the continent. But because it limited German power and freedom of action in important ways—because it made Germany dependent on the Western powers, whose only real interest was the defense of the status quo in Europe—it also met the Soviet Union's number one security requirement, the control of German power. This was a system the USSR could live with; and because it provided security for Germany, and a bit more besides, the Federal Republic could also accept it. The 1954 arrangements therefore provided a viable basis for a stable international order.

Who in 1945 would have predicted that a system of this sort would be worked out? The normal assumption, perhaps, would have been that this kind of system—one in which German power and independence were fundamentally limited, indeed one based on the division of Germany—was something the Germans themselves would never accept, and that they would in fact revolt against it the same way they had revolted against the Versailles system in the 1920s. Kennan, for example, had assumed in 1949 that a West German government was bound to become "the spokesman of a resentful and defiant nationalism," and that "much of the edge of this resentment" would "inevitably be turned against the Western governments themselves."[5] But this, of course, was not to be.

Something very basic was at issue here in this argument about Germany. The core question had to do with how international politics works and what statecraft, at the most fundamental level, can hope to achieve. Should the Western governments try to build what are in a sense artificial structures to maintain stability? Or was the system-building approach perhaps bound to fail? What Kennan's view boiled down to was the idea that international political life was not all that malleable. His assumption was that it was natural, almost inevitable, that in the long run a great nation like Germany would not accept a system that kept it weak and dependent on foreign powers for protection. The constraints on German power were artificial: a viable system could not be built on arrangements of that sort. One could not indulge in what Kennan, in another context, called the "colossal conceit" of thinking that one could fundamentally change the basic nature of international politics.[6] One had to accept certain basic realities for what they were, and deal with them in their own terms.

But the opposite view, and what turned out to be the dominant view, was that stability depended on the construction of a system—that is, on the working out of arrangements that constrained the free play of political forces in important ways. It might be admitted, in this case, that Germany's eventual reemergence as an independent great power was in some sense "natural," but this did not mean it was inevitable, or that there was no point in trying to construct a system that would limit Germany's freedom of action in fundamental ways.

This very basic problem—whether political forces should be allowed to find their own level, or whether structures that could limit the free play of such forces need to be worked out—was a fundamental concern not just for statesmen after World War II. It is an issue that political leaders have always had to deal with, and indeed still need to concern themselves with today. Thinking about major issues of current policy—the question, for example, of the eastward expansion of the NATO system—is inevitably rooted in assumptions about the viability, or the necessity, of the system-building approach. The story of the making of the Cold War political system is thus of interest not only in its own right but also because of the extraordinary bearing it has on this very basic political problem.

In this context, there are three fundamental points that need to be made. The first—obvious to us now, but by no means obvious at the time—is that a system based on the constraint of German power could actually work. This system in fact turned out to be so stable that people lost sight of how remarkable it was and came to think of it as more or less natural—so much so that the whole idea that the German government in the 1950s and early 1960s sought an independent nuclear capability, and thus full political independence, came to be dismissed as almost unthinkable, at any rate until absolutely compelling evidence to the contrary was presented by Hans-Peter Schwarz in 1991.[7] The system-building approach is in no sense absurd, and cannot be dismissed as inherently unworkable.

The second point is that if it did end up working, this was by no means inevitable. A system was constructed, but this was the result of a rather bumpy and complex political process, and things could easily have gone in other directions. The implication here is that we perhaps tend to take things too much for granted: the system today is not quite as solid as it seems on the surface. Systems may perhaps be built, but putting one together is not quite as easy as it might seem in retrospect.

Third, this system worked because it was viable in power-political terms. System builders in the past—British premier Wil-

liam Gladstone in the 1880s, for example, and U.S. president
Woodrow Wilson in the period of the First World War—disliked
the very concept of power politics. Policy, in their view, had to
be rooted mainly in moral considerations; the power-political approach was supposedly in itself a source of tension and instability. But a purely moral policy was never successful. Power is too
fundamental a part of the international system to be swept aside
in that way.

But if fundamental power realities are taken into account, a
workable system can be constructed. And this helps explain why
the Cold War political system, the system built on the constraint
of German power, worked as well as it did. Germany was threatened by Soviet power, and this gave the Germans a very strong
incentive to reach an accommodation with the West. And the
Soviets, worried about a possible resurgence of German power,
for their part also had a strong incentive to accept the system the
Western countries had created, as long as it effectively kept the
Germans under control. In particular, the implicit threat of allowing Germany to go nuclear was an effective lever for restraining
Soviet policy. But for that element in the system to carry any
weight, Germany had to remain non-nuclear: if Germany ever did
develop a nuclear force, the threat value of its going nuclear
would obviously vanish.[8] The West was in a sense balancing between Russia and Germany, capitalizing on the fears each felt
about the other to hold each of them back and lock both of them
into a status quo–oriented policy. But this was a balance-of-
power policy of a peculiar sort, more structured, and indeed more
institutionalized, than the balance-of-power policies of the past.

How did this system come into being? It did not take shape
automatically as a by-product of the division of Europe after
World War II. It was not as though Western Europe immediately
and permanently became an American sphere of influence; nor
was it clear from the start that Germany would be contained
within a system dominated by American power. And it was not
even brought into being by the Paris accords: even in the late
1950s and early 1960s, the issue of German power—and that

meant essentially the issue of a German nuclear capability—was still very much an open question.

The reason the question remained open for so long had to do mainly with the attitude of the United States. The only way there could be an adequate counterweight to Russia in Europe without allowing Germany to reemerge as an independent great power was for the United States to remain committed to the defense of Western Europe. How could the Germans be expected to remain weak if the Americans were not there to protect them? The limits on German power—and above all, ultimately, the Federal Republic's non-nuclear status—and the continuing American military presence in Europe were thus two sides to a coin: these were the twin pillars on which the NATO system would rest.

But in the late 1940s a permanent American presence was by no means taken for granted. The U.S. government wanted the Europeans to pull together and form themselves into a "third force" strong enough "to say 'no' both to the Soviet Union and to the United States."[9] West Germany would be part of that Western European bloc; indeed the idea was that West Germany "should be regarded not as part of Germany but as part of Western Europe."[10]

West Germany should not be regarded as part of Germany? What an extraordinary thing to say! What could be more at variance with long-standing assumptions about what was natural in international politics? This sort of policy, the hallmark of which was the U.S. government's obsession with European unification, was thus system-building with a vengeance. The assumption was that deep-seated historical traditions could be essentially swept aside, that national feeling was highly malleable, that the state system was like putty to be reshaped at will.

This goal of a strong and independent Western Europe remained at the heart of U.S. policy even during the early Korean War period—that is, even after the American government had decided, in December 1950, to send a sizable U.S. combat force to Europe. Originally, the presence of that force was supposed to be temporary: after the Europeans had built up not just adequate military power of their own but an integrated European military system, which would prevent the Germans from being able to operate independently, the U.S. force could be withdrawn. It was only in mid-1951 that the American government shifted course on this fundamental issue.

As late as July 6, 1951, Secretary of State Dean Acheson, the real maker of American policy during this period, still felt that American forces should not remain in Europe permanently. But by July 16, just ten days later, he had reversed his position 180 degrees. It was a mistake, he now argued, to think that American participation in NATO would end "at some indefinite time in the future"; European integration was not a solution to "all problems including that of security against Germany"; the Western Europeans were not strong enough by themselves to "outweigh German influence" in any purely European defense organization that might be created; America therefore had to remain in Europe on a permanent basis.[11]

This new policy, however, lasted only as long as Acheson remained in office. A year and a half later, a new administration came to power committed to a very different kind of policy. The new president, Dwight Eisenhower, thought that sooner or later the Europeans would have to defend themselves—that Western Europe should become, as he put it, a "third great power bloc" capable of balancing the Soviets on its own. When that happened, he said, America could then "sit back and relax somewhat."[12] The enormous burden of defending Europe would be lifted from American shoulders. The United States could then reduce its military presence in Europe down to token levels, or perhaps even withdraw its forces entirely. From the start, Eisenhower, and Secretary of State John Foster Dulles as well, felt that a system based so heavily on American power was not natural: it was not "healthy" for the allies to be so dependent on America. They should take over primary responsibility for their own defense, so that the Americans should not have to stay in Europe forever.[13] The United States, the president thought, could not be "a modern Rome guarding the far frontiers with our legions if for no other reason than that these are *not,* politically, *our* frontiers. What we must do is to assist these people [to] regain their confidence and get on their own military feet.''[14]

Western Europe would have to be strong enough to stand up to the Soviet Union on its own. Ideally, the Europeans should unite politically, but if this could not be done overnight, then Eisenhower was perfectly prepared to see the Europeans, including the Germans, build up their strength on a national basis. The European forces, to be sure, would be coordinated within the NATO framework. Indeed, his hope was that with the withering away of the American military presence, NATO—and that meant a NATO with a strong nuclear force of its own, not subject to American control—would devolve into a purely European organization, with a European general as NATO commander. And he wanted this process of devolution to take place fairly rapidly—in fact, a good deal more rapidly than even the most self-reliant Europeans were prepared to accept.[15] But the Western defense structure, whether the NATO system or the European system he hoped would grow out of it, would be based on consent. The goal was no longer to keep Germany down—to lock it into the Western system and keep it dependent on the Western powers for protection.

Indeed, from the start Eisenhower was relatively unconcerned about the risk of Germany becoming too strong. It was not just that he felt the West needed Germany as an ally against Russia, and that the Federal Republic therefore had to be treated as a real partner—that one could not maintain discriminatory arrangements that reflected a deep-seated distrust of that country. At a more basic level, his attitude was rooted in a fundamental power-political calculation. To be sure, he admitted, a strong Germany had been a great problem in the past, but that was only because Russia had been weak. But now, with Russia so strong, he would ''take a strong Germany.''[16]

And that, of course, meant a Germany with a substantial nuclear capability under its own control. From Eisenhower's point of view, it was more or less inevitable that the major European countries would seek nuclear forces of their own, and he was not at all alarmed by the prospect of a German nuclear capability. If the Europeans were to stand up to the Soviet Union by themselves, they obviously would need to be fully armed with nuclear weapons; if there was to be no European federal union, those European nuclear forces would, in the final analysis, be under national control. For Eisenhower, this was normal and natural. And in keeping with his general philosophy, he wanted to help the Europeans, including the Germans, develop nuclear forces of their own—forces that would be under the ultimate control of the various major European governments. The State Department, and by 1959 even the secretary of defense, were opposed to this policy: they still felt that Germany could not be trusted with too much power. But Eisenhower disagreed: Germany, he said, "had been his enemy in the past, but on the principle of having only one main enemy at a time, only the U.S.S.R. was now his enemy."[17]

And the Eisenhower policy was in line with what the German government itself wanted. The Federal Republic sought, sooner or later, to acquire a nuclear force under its own control. The German chancellor, Konrad Adenauer, made his intentions quite clear in 1956 and 1957.[18] Germany, he thought, needed to produce nuclear weapons itself, perhaps in cooperation with France. What he was aiming at was real political independence: Germany could not forever remain an American "atomic protectorate"; it was "intolerable" that Europe was so dependent on the United States; a state incapable of defending itself was in his view no real state at all.[19]

It was perfectly natural that a leader of a major country whose security was directly threatened should be thinking along these lines. And it was perfectly understandable that the Germans in the late 1950s, like the other Europeans, should question whether the defense of Europe should depend so heavily on American resolve. Would the Americans really be willing to go to war for the sake of Europe if, given the growth of Soviet nuclear capabilities, such a war would inevitably result in the destruction of

American society? As Dulles himself admitted, this European concern was basically "rational."[20] The corollary was that the European countries, including Germany, could not really be expected to rely so heavily on America for protection, but instead needed nuclear forces of their own.

In the late Eisenhower period, it might therefore have seemed that the "system builders" had ultimately been proven wrong. The constraints on German power, and especially the most fundamental constraint, the one relating to the Federal Republic's non-nuclear status, were being thrown off; "natural" forces, and not human artifice, was evidently shaping the basic structure of international politics. And if things had continued along that track after 1960, there would have been no shortage of people to argue that once again the story shows that a great nation like Germany cannot be kept down indefinitely and that there was therefore no way that a system based on restraining German power could have served as the basis of a stable international order.

The subsequent course of events was to show precisely the opposite. In 1961, the American government changed course dramatically, and by 1963 a relatively stable system based on the constraint of German power had come into being. In time, people became so used to it that they assumed this kind of arrangement was natural, and indeed found it hard to believe that something fundamentally different had ever been possible. The Germans, it was said, had naturally never wanted to go nuclear in first place, and it was inconceivable that the U.S. government could ever have wanted the NATO allies to develop nuclear forces under their own control.

The reality was that a system based on a non-nuclear Germany did not come into being more or less automatically, and even in 1961 it was by no means taken for granted that such a system could successfully be constructed. The Kennedy administration certainly sought to keep nuclear weapons, and especially strategic nuclear weapons, out of German hands, and that fundamental goal lay at the heart of a whole series of policies it adopted soon after taking office—new policies on the control of NATO nuclear forces, on land-based strategic missiles, on a sea-based NATO missile force, and on nuclear forces under ultimate national control. The British were to be encouraged to get out of the "nuclear business," and the French were to be discouraged from developing a nuclear capability of their own.

But this was not because the Kennedy administration was really worried about British or even French nuclear forces in themselves. The real problem had to do with Germany. How could you say yes to the British, but no to the French? But if you said yes to the French, how could you then say no to the Germans? The best course of action was to say no to everyone, to tell the Europeans that they should just trust America to defend them and should accept "a single U.S.-dominated force."[21]

The assumption throughout the Kennedy period was that Germany would have to be kept non-nuclear, and that implied also that the United States would have to remain in Europe. But if America was unable to withdraw—if the burden of defense remained on American shoulders—then in exchange, the U.S. government felt, it had the right to call the tune politically. And that meant, in particular, it had the right to press for a political settlement that would stabilize the status quo in Europe. A key part of that settlement, it became clear beginning in late 1961, related to the Federal Republic's nuclear status. West Germany, as part of a general settlement that would, among other things, guarantee the freedom of West Berlin, was to remain non-nuclear.

The new thrust of American policy led to a great crisis within the Western alliance. Adenauer was deeply opposed to a policy that would keep Germany a second-class power forever. By the beginning of 1963, he was ready openly to join forces with the French in opposing American policy. The French president, Charles de Gaulle, had been deeply alienated by the policy the American government had been following since early 1961. Europe, more than ever, needed to develop a strategic personality of its own. France, he told Adenauer in January 1963, "understood" Germany's nuclear aspirations; it seemed at the time that the two countries might sooner or later build nuclear weapons on a joint basis.[22] De Gaulle was in revolt against the American-dominated system; Adenauer seemed to be aligning himself with de Gaulle; and if a Franco-German bloc emerged, with France helping Germany develop a nuclear force, the situation, from the U.S. point of view, might well become unmanageable. The Americans therefore forced the Federal Republic to choose: if the Germans wanted continued American protection, they would have to abandon their nuclear aspirations. And by mid-1963, it had become clear that they were going to accept these American terms. Adenauer's policy of alignment with France was repudiated by the Bundestag; Adenauer himself was forced out of office; and the Federal Republic agreed to sign the Limited Test Ban Treaty of 1963.

This treaty was not just a simple arms control measure. It was of fundamental political importance. It was directed essentially at Germany. The Germans could not test, therefore they could not build: the Federal Republic was being kept non-nuclear. This was something the Soviets very much wanted. But the United States was not making a simple present to the USSR. The Soviets, for their part, would have to accept the status quo in Europe, and in particular around Berlin. The connection was not formal; instead, the link was tacit and structural; the sense of connectedness was a product of the historical process that had given rise to the test ban treaty in the first place. On the Western side, the need to protect Berlin was a source of restraint; German freedom of action, especially in the nuclear area, was severely limited by the need to avoid provoking the Soviets. Conversely, the threat of Germany going nuclear if the Soviets moved on Berlin was an effective means of constraining Soviet behavior. The Soviets, for their part, had an interest in preserving West Berlin as a Western enclave; its hostage value was of considerable importance in the context of the German nuclear question. These linkages had become quite apparent by 1963; they all tended to tie everyone into the status quo.

Thus by late 1963 a system had more or less taken shape, and it was not a system that had resulted from the free play of natural forces. Germany would remain non-nuclear, and thus dependent on America for security; and American troops would remain on German soil indefinitely. German power was effectively limited, and limited by a system created by Germany's own allies. Even though the Cold War has now ended, this system remains largely intact. Germany remains non-nuclear, and American troops are still in Central Europe. Whether it will remain intact in the twenty-first century is certainly one of the great political questions of the post–Cold War period.

6

The Trials of Multilateralism: America, Britain, and the New Economic Order, 1941–1947

Randall B. Woods

The great conflict that began in 1939 and ended in 1945 destroyed the European balance of power in both a strategic and economic sense. Cataclysmic in its destructive power, World War II left the international community, and especially its European members, battered, gasping for breath, and searching desperately for a new order that would usher in an era of physical, economic, and social security. As policymakers in Washington and London grappled with the task of recasting the international economic system, however, they found that they were constrained by domestic politics as well as by competing national visions over what kind of system would best serve the recovering nations of Europe. The United States sought to maintain the economic advantage that the war had given it; the British were reluctant to relinquish their position as the world's greatest economic and financial power. Through a process of tough negotiation, compromise, and some coercion, these two states hammered out an international economic order that, despite its many faults, served to underpin the most rapid global economic expansion in history, and contributed to the ultimate success of Western capitalism in the Cold War conflict with communism. The story presented here reveals that even in times of grave international crisis and disruption, national economic rivalries among allies are to be expected; yet they can be overcome through judicious leadership and compromise.

Britain's vision for the postwar economic order rested on the foundations of "new liberalism." The concept, consisting of a pragmatic blend of state socialism, private enterprise, planning, and countercyclical deficit spending, transcended party lines in Britain, with its conservative adherents calling themselves reform Tories and its Labor advocates, liberal socialists. The approach seemed tailor-made for the war-damaged postindustrial societies of Western Europe because it promised social security without undermining democracy or diminishing individual liberty. But alas for Britain, which hoped to ride the crest of the new liberalism to a position of leadership in the European community, only America could provide the resources necessary to make this healing nostrum available to the continent.

As Paul Kennedy demonstrates in *The Rise and Fall of the Great Powers,* the United States emerged from World War II as the only true superpower. While the conflict ravaged much of Europe and Asia, America grew stronger. Its productive capacity actually increased by 50 percent during the war, its GNP rising from $88.6 billion to $135 billion.[1] Such economic power, especially when placed alongside the rest of the world's war-damaged and underdeveloped economies, made America's relative might analogous to that of Britain in 1815. According to Kennedy, and more recently Melvyn Leffler, the economic and strategic expansion of the United States following World War II was inevitable simply because of its preponderance of power.[2] The key question was how America would define its leadership role. In the United States during World War II, a battle still raged between the new liberalism and the old. With the coming of World War II the New Deal had gone into remission in America. Even those who advocated merely countercyclical deficit spending of a temporary nature to smooth out the bumps in the business cycle, were driven underground by the champions of laissez-faire and free enterprise. Not until 1947, when Europe appeared on the verge of economic disintegration and the forces of international communism seemed ready to spread westward and engulf the entire continent, did America decide to abandon its commitment to free trade and help foster European recovery. Moreover, the United States did so not by funding a global multilateral trading system but by encouraging the Europeans to form themselves into an integrated system that could effectively compete not only with the Soviet bloc but with the colossus of the New World as well.

Intimidated by the rising conservative tide in the Congress and among the American people, Franklin Roosevelt, Harry Truman, and their advisers searched for foreign policy strategies that would placate conservatives and at the same time ensure social justice, economic security, and physical safety both at home and abroad. The answer to their dreams appeared out of the past: multilateralism, that British-bred and British-led system of payments and trade that had prevailed in the Western world during the last quarter of the nineteenth century. Those members of the Roosevelt-Truman foreign policy establishment responsible for economic matters embraced multilateralism as a technique that would raise living standards at home and abroad without accelerating collectivist trends, while those concerned with armies and boundaries viewed multilateralism as the economic phase of balance-of-power realpolitik. But so strong was the conservative impulse in the United States that nationalists, bureaucratic imperialists, and special interests modified multilateralism into a machine to enrich America. As such it proved counterproductive to Anglo-American efforts to restrain Soviet imperialism and prevent the spread of communism into Western and Central Europe.

No matter how compelling the drama of World War II, Anglo-American leaders from 1941 to 1946 could not escape elections, nor could they avoid the socioeconomic issues that usually dominate domestic politics. Ever sensitive to the mood of the American people, which grew increasingly conservative during the course of the war, the administration of Franklin D. Roosevelt searched for a mechanism that would prevent unemployment in the United States and abroad after the war, rehabilitate strife-torn Europe, and simultaneously deflect charges from Republicans and southern Democrats that it was taking America and the world further down the road toward state socialism. The formula that the president and his advisers turned to as a panacea for the nation and the world's socioeconomic ills was multilateralism, a concept that called for a mutual, simultaneous reduction of trade barriers and elimination of currency controls by the United States and its trading partners. Goods and currencies, their value pegged to each other at a fixed rate, would flow freely across international boundaries, creating an interdependent world economy with each region specializing in the production of the goods and services it produced best. Multilateralism, Washington believed, would prevent unemployment in postwar America, rehabilitate war-torn areas in Europe and Asia, and raise living standards in the developing world.[3] In Roosevelt's view the concept was non-ideological and as such would allow him to avoid a divisive debate over how to distribute scarce resources. To his mind and those of other multilateralists there was no conflict between international cooperation and domestic growth.

Because Great Britain was the second largest non-communist trading nation in the world, and operated a relatively closed imperial trading bloc, it was the key to realization of the Roosevelt administration's multilateral dreams. At the Ottawa Conference in 1932 the United Kingdom and other members of the Commonwealth and empire had formed a trading conglomerate within which member nations awarded one another's exports preferential treatment. The drain on Britain's financial and material resources caused by World War II compelled the Exchequer and the Board of Trade to strengthen this bloc and generally to accelerate the trend toward governmental control of international finance and foreign commerce. The war cabinet authorized long-term bulk purchasing agreements with exporters of primary products, strictly limited imports from nations outside the sterling bloc, and refused to make sterling freely convertible into gold and dollars, thus limiting the ability of its merchants and those of the empire to buy from third parties, such as the United States. American policymakers perceived that if Britain used the leverage of blocked sterling balances to maintain and strengthen its trading and monetary union into the postwar period, multilateralism would never come to pass.[4]

As the war progressed, it seemed that the United Kingdom would do just that. During the two years from 1939 through 1941, when it stood virtually alone against the forces of international fascism, Great Britain exhausted its gold and dollar resources as it acquired the material and munitions with which to fight. Passage of the Lend-Lease Act in 1941 eased the strain on British finances, but the Exchequer was never able to recover. By July 1945 British gold and dollar resources had dwindled to $1.8 billion, while its external liabilities mounted to $13 billion. (At this point the United States had accumulated more than $21 billion in gold bullion at Fort Knox.) If the United Kingdom lowered its trade barriers without rebuilding and modernizing its industries and if it made sterling freely convertible, as multilateralism required, it would be drained of gold and dollars in the blink of an eye. Such an eventuality would mean not only the collapse of the internal economy but a British strategic withdrawal from Europe and the Middle East.[5]

With good reason, then, did Prime Minister Winston Churchill contemplate the future with a deep sense of foreboding as 1944 opened. Britain was in trouble, the Conservative Party was in trouble, and he was in trouble. World War II was destroying the traditional European balance of power, accelerating the United Kingdom's decline, and aggrandizing Britain's allies-cum-rivals, Russia and the United States. The United Kingdom faced the threat of financial and commercial domination by America and strategic eclipse by Russia, whose troops were then poised to occupy Eastern Europe. At home, the destruction inflicted by Nazi bombing, the collectivization spawned by the war effort, and memories of the depression had created an irresistible demand among Britons for measures designed to guarantee their economic and social security. The popular clamor for food, homes, and work alarmed the prime minister quite as much as Britain's declining international status because it pointed to a Labour Party triumph in the first general election after the war. The Conservatives, crippled by their historic inability to solve the unemployment problem, were in no better position to meet the political challenge from the left than the nation was to deal with the two rising superpowers.

One thing was clear to Churchill and his advisers, however: a simple continuation of imperial preference and protectionism was not going to solve the massive economic problems facing the country after the Axis powers had been defeated. Apprehensive though Churchill was at the specter of U.S. domination, he came to see Britain's salvation as well as his own and that of the Conservative Party in the establishment of a multilateral trading system buttressed by a massive program of American aid. A continuation of lend-lease or an interest-free credit during Phase II, the period between V-E Day and Japan's surrender, would allow Britain to reconvert part of its economy to civilian production and then to compete with the United States for foreign markets as the war wound to a close. In addition, such an arrangement would, he believed, enable Britain to retain its empire in the eastern Mediterranean and the Middle East, and make it possible for the Conservatives to provide the British electorate with an increased standard of living.[6]

The person charged with creating an international economic order in which Britain could safely do business was John Maynard Keynes. From 1941 until his death in 1946, Keynes served as chief adviser to the British Treasury on matters of wartime and postwar economic policy. Although 1941 saw him committed to protection and national policies to secure full employment, events late that year and early the next led Keynes to abandon his previous position and embrace multilateralism. Like Churchill and the Conservatives, he understood the overriding need for American aid to rehabilitate the British economy and to secure the nation's strategic interests on the continent and the eastern Mediterranean.[7] He also understood the dangers multilateralism posed to British markets and financial reserves. Keynes believed he could design institutions, indeed, fashion a new international economic order, that would simultaneously satisfy America's multilateral cravings and protect British interests. "For your private information," he wrote an American acquaintance in 1941, "I . . . am working [on] . . . a Utopian Plan which would solve all our problems on international lines. I call it Utopian because it is the sort of thing that never seems to happen. But it is entirely practical and requires nothing more for its success than a mental attitude on the part of the powers that be."[8] Keynes perceived correctly that in a multilateral world the United States would dominate every market, driving its competitors—especially Great Britain—into bankruptcy and draining its trading partners—again, especially Great Britain—of dollars and gold. What Keynes proposed was the creation of institutions that would provide debtor nations with the capital they needed to rehabilitate their economies and compete with the United States, and the gold and dollar resources they required to survive free convertibility.[9]

During 1943 and 1944 the British economist designed the International Clearing Union, an organization whose members would contribute to a huge central fund that would be used to finance international trade. Nations whose currencies were bought would have their accounts debited, and those that sold their currencies would be credited. Countries like the United States that ran huge trade surpluses with other members and thus accumulated massive reserves of dollars and gold would forfeit those reserves once they reached a certain level. The surplus funds would then be made available to debtor nations to support their currencies and to make their industries and agricultural systems competitive.[10]

The United States would have none of Keynes's Clearing Union plan. During World War II a battle raged within the Roosevelt administration over foreign economic policy. True multilateralists like Harry Hopkins and commercial experts in the Department of State wanted to provide Britain and the other creditor nations with the liquidity—gold, dollars, or credit—necessary for them to compete. Economic nationalists like Senator Robert Taft of Ohio and Treasury Secretary Henry Morgenthau, Jr., opposed a generous aid program either because they were genuine isolationists or because they looked forward to a world economy that would allow the United States a competitive advantage.[11]

Hopkins, special adviser to the president, was well aware of the political and economic possibilities of an active foreign loan policy. William L. Batt, a senior official on the War Production Board, Lauchlin Currie, deputy administrator of the Foreign Economic Administration, and Charles Taft of the State Department all assumed that "the condition of the economy of the United Kingdom is a matter of direct concern to the United States, and that our overall policy will take the U.K. welfare into consideration, in our own best interest," as Batt wrote Hopkins.[12] In the spring and summer of 1944 this informal network of advisers scattered throughout the bureaucracy began to articulate a variety of justifications for massive aid to Great Britain during Phase II and into the transitional period after Japan's surrender. Unlike most Americans, they understood that Britain was not economically self-sufficient. Foreign trade was its lifeblood. In order to pay for the $4 billion worth of goods it imported each year, Britain would have to export; in order to do that, it would need help rebuilding and redirecting its industrial plant. Without a healthy economy, Britain would find it impossible to carry out its occupation duties in postwar Europe. In addition, the Hopkins group argued, failure to aid the United Kingdom in a substantial way would prolong and even stimulate British imperialism, both economic and political. And, of course, they saw an economically healthy Britain as the key to a properly functioning multilateral world.[13] These economic internationalists were swimming against the tide, however.

In the aftermath of Pearl Harbor, isolationism—defined both as non-intervention in European affairs and as preservation of congressional prerogatives in foreign policy making—was forced into temporary eclipse. But the isolationists had no intention of allowing the Roosevelt administration full rein in foreign policy. They equated internationalism with surrender of American national sovereignty, executive control of foreign policy, and distribution of the nation's wealth among the less fortunate nations of the world. Republican congressional leaders like Arthur Vandenberg, Robert Taft, and Gerald Nye had opposed lend-lease in 1941 because they believed it would lead directly to United States involvement in war. They could hardly take that position after Pearl Harbor, but when the aid program came up for renewal in 1943, Republicans called for a comprehensive investigation. Senator Hugh A. Butler of Nebraska compared lend-lease to "the dole" and denounced it as a global Works Progress Administration.[14] In the fall of 1943 five members of the Senate Military Affairs Committee journeyed to Europe to investigate the American aid program. They reported subsequently to Congress that charges of widespread waste and mismanagement in the delivery of aid to the Allies, particularly the British, were true. The Senators accused Britain of using lend-lease supplies to win friends and influence people at the expense of the United States in the oil-rich Middle East and other strategically crucial areas.[15] During the 1944 presidential campaign, former GOP standard-bearer Alf Landon accused Roosevelt and his minions of indulging themselves in "mystical dreams" of raising the living standards of all the "heterogeneous" peoples of the world, at the expense of the American taxpayer.[16]

The parsimony so apparent among the nation's politicians was an accurate reflection of popular attitudes. A secret report prepared by Samuel Rosenman and his staff in late 1943 advised FDR that recent surveys showed that the American people were almost twice as interested in domestic as in international affairs. Two-thirds of those polled believed that the United States should not furnish aid to foreign countries if it would lower the standard of living in postwar America, and about half of those questioned believed that it would.[17]

In tacit alliance with the nationalist-isolationists in Congress were Henry Morgenthau, Jr., and his subordinates in the United States Treasury. The Treasury was determined to preserve America's monopoly of the world's supply of gold and dollars made possible by the war and to take advantage of the nation's superiority in money and material to establish an international financial system dominated by the United States. That Morgenthau wanted to transfer control of the national and international economy from private to public hands, from New York to Washington, made him no less a nationalist. (What made the alliance all the closer was that Morgenthau and midwestern Republicans were determined to end Wall Street's control of both the domestic and international financial structure.) As Keynes was designing his apparatus for international currency stabilization in the spring of 1942, the United States Treasury advanced its own plans for a stabilization fund and international bank for reconstruction and development. The principal difference between the Keynes plan and the American structures designed by Harry Dexter White was that the former aimed at securing British financial independence while the latter were intended to ensure United States domination of international finance.[18] That the Treasury's primary motive was the transfer of world financial leadership from London to Washington became clear as Morgenthau and White labored throughout 1943 and 1944 to hold British gold and dollar balances to a bare minimum.

By the time the Allied nations met at Bretton Woods, New Hampshire, in the summer of 1944 to design an economic order for the postwar world, economic nationalists from the Treasury Department were in control of the American delegation.[19] As a result, the institutions coming out of the Bretton Woods Conference—the International Monetary Fund (IMF) and the International Bank for Reconstruction and Development (IBRD)—were constituted so as to entrench and protect American domination of the new economic order. The IMF was a clearing union that established a central fund from which members could borrow to finance trade, but only on current account. Moreover, all debts had to be repaid. There was to be no international income redistribution, no global "Share Our Wealth" program, as Morgenthau put it.[20] The IBRD, funded at a paltry $9.1 billion (the Allies and the Axis were then spending $8 billion dollars a month destroying the world), would do no more than guarantee loans made by creditor nations like the United States to debtor nations like Britain and Peru. Finally, countries that maintained artificial controls on their currencies or that retained quotas, tariffs, and preferences would be disqualified from participating.[21]

Washington's commitment to commercial multilateralism was no less a fiction than its commitment to authentic financial multilateralism. In the midst of its campaign to persuade its allies to agree to a simultaneous, across-the-board reduction in trade barriers monitored by an international trade organization, the White House submitted to Congress a strengthened version of the Reciprocal Trade Agreements Act (RTAA). This legislation, the alleged centerpiece of the administration's trade liberalization program, passed both houses in the summer of 1945 by record margins, with the vote cutting across partisan, geographic, and ideological lines. Robert Taft voted for it. So did a number of other conservative Republicans even though the State Department represented it as part of a broad program of action on the international economic front.[22] That vote was made possible not by the conversion of economic nationalists and the guardians of special interests to the principle of free trade, but by their realization that RTAA as amended was a servant rather than an enemy of U.S. economic interests, narrowly defined. In the first place, the measure guaranteed national as opposed to international control of the tariff-making process. The RTAA provided for selective, item-by-item reductions, not across-the-board percentage cuts dictated by a multilateral convention or authority.[23] Moreover, the legislation contained a mechanism for the protection of domestic interests in every case—public hearings coupled with the "peril point" provision.[24] According to this mechanism, the Tariff Commission would recommend higher rates to the president if lowered schedules negotiated under RTAA in any case endangered the well-being of an American industry.

Keynes was troubled by the course of Anglo-American commercial and financial negotiations during 1944 and 1945. He understood the dangers inherent in the Bretton Woods structures: that they would strip war-weakened and developing nations like his of the protective devices necessary to preserve their markets and their currencies. Liquidity was the key to making any multilateral system work, and the Bretton Woods agreements did not provide that liquidity. Instead of protesting the IMF and IBRD, however, he acquiesced in their creation, even claimed them as his own and passionately recommended them to his government. He continued to believe that he could make the Americans see the light and that at the very least the United States would provide Great Britain, sure to be its principal ally in the dangerous postwar world, with the capital necessary to get back to its feet and compete.[25] He was wrong.

Less than a year after the close of the Bretton Woods Conference, the war in Europe was over. In July 1945 Britons elected a new government. Though they valued Churchill's services as wartime leader, British voters believed that his and the Conservative Party's laissez-faire, free enterprise philosophy rendered them unfit to preside over peacetime affairs.[26] They chose instead to give the Labour Party under Clement Attlee a clear majority. Not surprisingly, Labourites, particularly the left wing headed by doctrinaire socialists Aneurin Bevan and Emmanuel Shinwell, were deeply suspicious of multilateralism, seeing in it a plot by American capitalists not only to ensure U.S. dominance of the international economic system but to defeat socialism in Britain as well.[27] The moderate leaders of the party, Attlee and Foreign Secretary Ernest Bevin, were not particularly enamored of the concept either, but they were desperate that the United States not retreat into isolationism, once again leaving Britain alone to deal with economic chaos and potential military aggression on the continent.[28] Moreover, they, like Churchill, recognized that if the public's demand for food, work, and homes was to be met, Britain would have to secure a large postwar loan from the United States. Keynes, who remained in place as chief adviser to the Treasury, agreed and, in addition, saw a generous American loan as a means to make multilateralism palatable and save the IMF and IBRD.[29]

Throughout the fall and winter of 1945 a team of British financial and commercial experts under Keynes met in Washington with officials of the new Truman administration to work out details of a postwar credit. What Keynes and his colleagues wanted was a multibillion-dollar interest-free loan that could be used to jump-start the British economy. They promised to remove trade barriers and dismantle exchange controls but not for at least five years, and then only if Britain showed a favorable balance of trade. What they in fact received in the financial agreement of 1946 was a $3.75 billion loan at an interest rate of 1.62 percent. In return for the credit, the Attlee government agreed to recommend to Parliament passage of the Bretton Woods agreements and to accept the full obligations of the system within a year. Congress eventually approved the pact on July 15, 1946, and Britain was thus forced to accept full convertibility of sterling on current account in midsummer 1947.[30] Within six months of convertibility coming into force, British gold and dollar reserves were exhausted; with bankruptcy staring it in the face, the Attlee government made plans for a severe austerity program at home and a strategic withdrawal abroad.

It was not, then, that multilateralism did not work during the crucial period from 1944 to 1947. It was never really tried. The forces of xenophobia, isolationism, and nationalism that dominated American politics during and immediately after World War II succeeded in converting multilateralism into a blunt imperial instrument. The goal of relatively free trade, in which creditor nations provide liquid capital to debtor nations in order to maintain continual equilibrium in trade and payments, was in theory a worthy one. The architects of multilateralism in Washington and London erred not in designing their system but in continuing to press for its acceptance after it had been subverted by special interests, Congress, and the United States Treasury. In their determination to have half a loaf, Anglo-American multilateralists saddled Britain with a scheme that brought it to the verge of bankruptcy and that hampered Europe in its effort to fend off the forces of international communism. Fortunately for Great Britain and Western Europe, however, World War II, unlike World War I, was not followed by a twenty-year period of American isolationism.[31]

In the wake of the financial agreement of 1946 British officials found themselves stretched on a Procrustean bed. The nation had only three means available to pay for its imported food and raw materials: money earned from services such as shipping and insurance, from foreign investments, and from manufactured exports. But the war had crippled the nation's merchant marine and forced the liquidation of over half of its foreign investments. At war's end many of Britain's industries, particularly those engaged in production for export, were outmoded and capital poor. By December 1946, despite the American loan and a severe austerity program that included the rationing of bread, Britain had reached only its prewar level of production. At this point, nature chose to demonstrate its indifference to human suffering. The winter of 1946–47 turned out to be one of the harshest in modern history. Temperatures dropped below zero, and snow fell in record amounts, paralyzing the transportation system. By February 1947 more than half the nation's factories lay idle as the mining of coal came to a virtual standstill. World War II and the elements were even less kind to the rest of Europe. The vagaries of the weather hit continental Europe with equal severity, just at a time when a yawning dollar gap was opening up: Europe, eager to import U.S. goods, as yet had no means to pay for them. The result was a deep economic crisis that threatened to deliver the coup de grâce to the still fragile social fabric of postwar Europe.

Despite neo-isolationism and congressional parsimony, widespread sympathy for Europe's plight developed in the United States in 1946–47. Accounts appeared in the *New York Times* and other nationally syndicated papers of ragged, starving children, teenaged prostitutes, and disintegrating families; such tales aroused the nation's humanitarian instincts. A number of Americans were aware, moreover, that Europe had been their nation's primary trading partner prior to the war and that an economically enfeebled Europe would retard America's growth. Finally, there were those in the United States, particularly congressmen and government officials, who believed America would have to come to Europe's rescue in order to fend off the twin threats of Soviet imperialism and communist subversion. The only reason that members of the conservative coalition voted for the financial agreement of 1946, ungenerous and short-sighted as it was, was that the State Department justified it as necessary to strengthen Britain for the forthcoming struggle against the Soviet Union and the forces of international communism. Quite simply, in 1946 American conservatives, who had concluded that communism posed a greater collectivist menace to free enterprise than socialism, joined with liberals, who had decided that the Soviet Union rather than Great Britain represented the forces of imperialism and autocracy, to support a program of foreign aid to save the social democracies of Western Europe.[32]

By the spring of 1947 Congress and the American people had come grudgingly to support those American policymakers who were arguing that modified multilateralism was not sufficient to achieve the reconstruction of Europe. Instead of continuing to press London and the other European capitals to participate in an international economic free-for-all with the United States, officials of the Truman administration set about helping the continent to develop an integrated economy modeled on the internal American market. The system would eliminate internal trade barriers and monetary controls and lead to the creation of a European economy that could stand up ideologically and physically to the threat posed by international communism and, not coincidentally, better compete with the United States.[33]

With the economic situation in Western Europe deteriorating daily and the popularity of the Italian and French Communist parties growing apace, Secretary of State George Marshall directed his staff to work out a program of aid. The fruits of their labor, subsequently known as the Marshall Plan, were made public in a commencement address the secretary delivered at Harvard University on June 5, 1947. In his speech Marshall reviewed the devastation, pestilence, and insecurity that plagued Europe. He called upon Britain and the nations of the continent to frame an integrated plan for Europe's recovery. When it had devised a scheme for economic rehabilitation, Europe could count on the United States to supply "friendly aid." There were stipulations: the United States would not fund a collection of national shopping lists from Europe—there would have to be an integrated plan—and the scheme must provide for the economic reconstruction of Germany.

On July 12, 1947, representatives of sixteen nations met in Paris to discuss European reconstruction.[34] At the urging of the British and the Italians, France shelved its objections to a rehabilitated Germany, accepting the argument that an economically stable Germany, contained by a non-communist European community, was safer than an impoverished and alienated state outside that community. The Paris conference prepared and submitted its plan for European reconstruction in the last week in September. It envisioned the continuation of a Committee on European Economic Cooperation (CEEC) to negotiate priorities, quotas, and aid levels with the U.S. implementing agency, and it promised to work toward all of the goals Marshall had outlined. The following spring, after a concerted propaganda campaign by the Truman administration on behalf of peacetime aid to Europe, Congress passed the Economic Cooperation Act of 1948. The bill authorized an appropriation of $5.3 billion for the first twelve-month period of the program. These funds were to be disbursed and administered by a new agency, the Economic Cooperation Administration (ECA).

The ultimate goal of the European Recovery Program (ERP) was the establishment in Western Europe of healthy national economies that would be independent of outside assistance. In its report the CEEC had committed itself to four major undertakings in pursuit of that goal. The participating nations were to make every effort to increase industrial and agricultural production; to establish and maintain internal financial stability; to expand foreign trade; and to fashion mechanisms of economic cooperation.[35]

Ironically, the European beneficiaries of Marshall Plan aid were skeptical of any scheme impinging on their national sovereignties. They were particularly resistant, therefore, to the last two objectives of the ERP, the creation of a customs union and a currency clearing scheme. Leading the way in opposing U.S.-led efforts to force integration through these mechanisms was the Labour government of Clement Attlee. During the latter half of 1947, a global shortage of dollars, the fuel and grain shortages that followed the winter crisis of 1946–47, and the rising costs of imports from the United States combined to slow the British recovery almost to a halt. Coming as they did on top of the Exchequer's July decision to honor the terms of the Anglo-American Financial Agreement, these developments created a catastrophic drain on the nation's dollar and gold reserves. Indeed, by August those reserves were dwindling at a rate of $176 million a week.[36] Participation in a customs union and a currency clearing agreement, Treasury and Board of Trade officials argued, would only make matters worse. Britain continued to conduct twice as much business with the Commonwealth as it did with Western Europe. By turning westward, the United Kingdom would sacrifice trade with the Commonwealth without offsetting gains on the continent, where British goods faced stiff competition from those produced by French, Italian, and, potentially, German industries. Incorporating the Commonwealth into a European union would not work because it would lead to the scrapping of empire preference and a trading system built on sterling rather than dollars.

American planners met the objections of the British and others jealous of their national sovereignties by agreeing to emphasize increased production and inflation control in the short run and to confine such matters as a customs union and monetary clearing agreement to the planning stage.[37] Washington would insist on a supranational planning authority, but it would be temporary, with the power only to allocate resources, set production targets, and theorize about further integration. American officials such as the newly appointed undersecretary of state Robert Lovett believed that getting bogged down in rigid schemes for currency stabilization and a customs union would only exacerbate tensions with the European governments and delay the economic recovery, which was the ultimate guard against communism.

The CEEC (renamed the Organization for European Economic Cooperation in 1948), sometimes cajoled and sometimes coerced by the ECA, made great strides forward in both industrial and agricultural productivity. The millions of dollars in machine tools, tractors, seed, and fertilizer distributed by the ECA had a pump-priming effect on Europe's economy. As a result, by 1951 Europe had actually surpassed the target of a 30 percent increase in aggregate industrial production. Gains in agricultural production were not as spectacular but still stood at 11 percent above the 1938 figure by 1951–52. During this period the ECA attempted to utilize its control over counterpart funds—local currencies put up by national governments to match U.S. aid—to force participating governments to balance their internal budgets and restrain the growth of wages. Altogether, the ECA approved the release of $7.56 billion in local counterpart funds, nearly all of which was used to finance deficits on current account or to pay off old debts. Inflation persisted, but given the ERP's emphasis on increased productivity and investment, ongoing price rises were perhaps inevitable. Resurrection of commerce within the European community was the third major objective of the Marshall Plan. In September 1950 European participants concluded the Agreement for the Establishment of the European Payments Union. During the eight and one-half years of its existence the union financed $46.6 billion worth of intra-European trade.

The European Payments Union was also part of the fourth objective of the Marshall Plan—the institutionalization of economic cooperation among members of the OEEC, leading, if possible, to the political unification of Europe. The Truman administration and Congress strongly favored such steps because they assumed that economic integration would lead to self-reliance, and that both economic and political unification would pave the way for the strongest possible defense against the forces of international communism. The OEEC itself did not prove an adequate forum to pursue economic integration, however. From its inception, the OEEC was hamstrung by a dispute among its members as to its proper function. Led by France, a group of Europeanists called for a truly autonomous body, in which members relinquished part of their national sovereignty, that would operate centralized institutions. Great Britain and several other states objected vigorously. The Attlee government conceived of the OEEC as an instrument for intergovernmental consultations and negotiations rather than as a supranational agency with the authority to tell member states what to do. In the end, Britain and its allies triumphed. In truth, during the life of the Marshall Plan the OEEC served merely as a coordinating agency for individual national aid requests submitted to ECA by the participating states.

What emerged from the European-American dialogue that began in 1947 was an economic order that focused first on the rehabilitation of the national economies of Europe with limited moves toward European integration. The IBRD and the IMF were left to deal primarily with the developing world. As Alan Milward and others have pointed out, the $13.3 billion (the final figure is still in dispute) distributed under the Marshall Plan was necessary because multilateralism as modified by the Bretton Woods and Anglo-American financial agreements did not work.[38] He does not dispute the argument made by historians Michael Hogan and Charles Maier that American policymakers opted for the "politics of productivity" over outdated and potentially divisive free trade, laissez-faire mechanisms, but argues that Marshall Plan aid was only marginally important. The nations of Europe were already on their way to recovery when the United States intervened. What he implies, correctly, is that Washington had at long last embraced the new liberalism—a pragmatic blend of state socialism, free enterprise, planning, and countercyclical deficit spending—an approach that Britain and the other states of Europe had been espousing for years. Although he underestimates the importance of the ERP in priming the European pump, Milward points to an important fact: the success of the Marshall Plan was due to its origins in a nation with a mixed economy and political institutions rooted in democracy and individual liberty, which was willing to extend aid to nations with roughly similar institutions and economies. Whether authentic multilateralism— that is, a global system characterized by minimal trade barriers and currency stabilization agreements, in which creditor nations supplied the liquidity to make the entire system run—could have served in lieu of the new liberalism remains a moot point. Given the history of political internationalism, however, it most probably could not.

Third World Nationalism and the Great Powers

7

Tony Smith

In surveying the international system at the end of World War II, leaders of the great powers spent comparatively little time thinking about the future political development of what has come to be known as the Third World. Yet in the course of the Cold War, the Third World became a major theater of ideological and sometimes military conflict. The war had wrought profound changes in the colonial empires that would contribute to a loosening of the bonds of control. In the postwar landscape, one of the least anticipated and least understood dimensions was how to control the process of decolonization and Third World nationalism that began to unfold in the late 1940s all across the globe. None of the powers most closely implicated—Britain, France, and the two superpowers—handled the challenge well at all.

Interest in the end of European empire gains in importance when we remember that it was but part of a global shift in power bringing greater sovereignty to the peoples of Asia, Africa, and Latin America. Because decolonization coincided with communist victories in revolutions in China in 1949 and Cuba in 1959

(and with communist bids for power in other countries as different as Greece, the Philippines, and Vietnam), as well as with
strong anti-Western expressions of nationalism in countries as
different as Iran and Guatemala, the retreat of Western European
powers from Asia and Africa came to seem to many in Washington and Moscow as a global development of epic proportion that
each capital soon set out to control. The correct way, then, to
study the great powers' perception of decolonization is to situate
their reaction within the greater story of the triumph of nationalism in Asia and Africa in the post-1945 period and to ask what
the emergence of this new force meant with respect to five hundred years of Western dominance of the international system.

I propose to review this extraordinary political transformation
by reflecting on two seemingly opposed but actually closely related kinds of misperception that decolonization and attendant
nationalism elsewhere in the Third World gave rise to—one that
overestimated its significance and the other that, as a result of
the overestimation, *underestimated its force.* A great power's
overestimation of the importance of this control reflected the extent to which these world capitals mistakenly saw their own vital
interests dependent on mastering these weaker peoples of Asia
and Africa. Whatever their other differences, such an evaluation
was true of London and Paris, of Washington and Moscow. By
contrast, underestimation of the force of decolonization resulted
from a great power's desire to control Third World nationalism,
presuming it could turn this force to its own ends, when in fact
it was far more difficult to control this tiger than leaders in these
northern capitals often realized.

The point, simply put, is that the great powers failed to understand that although Third World nationalism was powerful locally it was not so important globally (unless a great power came
so to define it, at which point it might become important indeed).
However significant the rise of Africa and Asia (and one might
add Latin America) seemed in the 1950s, from the perspective of
the 1990s it is tempting to conclude this was much ado about
nothing, that it did not in fact signal the long-awaited "decline

of the West." To be sure, seen in retrospect a century from now, when China may well be dominating world affairs, this rise of non-European nationalism may be seen as the precursor to great events. But such a development should not obscure the fact that the great concern aroused from the 1950s through the 1970s was rather thoroughly misplaced.

The discussion has two sections. The first compares the British and French reactions to colonial nationalism, asking why the spread of nationalist demands for self-determination after 1945 was not sensed earlier by the colonial powers, and why the British fared relatively better than the French in facing the challenge colonial nationalism presented. The second analyzes policy in the United States and the Soviet Union, with particular attention to the overestimation in both countries of the weight Third World nationalism would have on the global balance of power.

France and Britain

How often it happens that what appears in retrospect to have been an inevitable historical development, one every commonsensical observer should have anticipated at the time would take place, was to those who lived before the experience an improbable if not inconceivable occurrence, one nobody who understood how the world operated actually anticipated. So it was with the fall of the Soviet empire and then the Soviet Union between 1989 and 1991, and so it was with the decolonization of the European empires in the period running from the independence of India in 1947 to that of Algeria in 1962 and the simultaneous rise to power of outspoken nationalists in governments as different as China and Cuba (and, if I may stretch the time horizon a bit, Iran in 1979).

One might think that the European powers would have had a clear sense of the nationalist upheavals that would confront them with the defeat of Germany and Japan in 1945. Nationalism was hardly a new concept on the continent of Europe, and its ability to dissolve previously longstanding empires had been made abundantly clear with the disintegration of the Russian, Austro-Hungarian, and Ottoman empires in 1918. The Western European states were now in the unenviable position of themselves being badly beaten by war (even if not actually defeated), so why should they expect less to happen to them than had happened to their erstwhile enemies a generation earlier?

Here is part of the answer. Having seen the depths to which countries deprived of their imperial possessions could sink, London and Paris (as well as Brussels and The Hague) understandably recoiled at the notion that this could be their fate as well. Hence late in 1944 when Winston Churchill was informed of an American plan to get the Europeans to make "early, dramatic, and concerted announcements" of specific steps and dates by which their empires would become independent states, the British prime minister famously declared: "There must be no question of our being hustled or seduced into declarations affecting British sovereignty in any of the Dominions or Colonies. Pray remember my declaration against liquidating the British empire. If the Americans want to take Japanese islands which they have conquered, let them do so with our blessing and any form of words that may be agreeable to them. But hands off the British empire is our maxim and it must not be weakened or smirched to please sob-stuff merchants at home or foreigners of any hue."[1]

Similarly, a few months later at Yalta, Churchill again reacted strongly to an American proposal that the forthcoming United Nations be given a trusteeship over colonial empires reminiscent of the mandates earlier held by the League of Nations. As the American minutes on this session of Yalta report: "Churchill interrupted with great vigor to say that he did not agree with a single word of this report on trusteeships. He said that under no circumstances would he ever consent to 40 or 50 nations thrusting interfering fingers into the life's existence of the British Empire. As long as he was Minister he would never yield one scrap of their heritage. He continued in this vein for some minutes (asking) how Marshal Stalin would feel if the suggestion was made that the Crimea be internationalized as a summer resort." During this tirade, it is interesting to note, a pleased Uncle Joe "got up from his chair, beamed, and at intervals broke into applause."[2]

Charles de Gaulle, though not present at Yalta, felt precisely the same way. He once lectured Roosevelt on the dangers to stability in Europe should France develop "the psychology of the vanquished." De Gaulle attacked Roosevelt's suggestion of colonial independence as an American scheme to take over French possessions (provoked by Churchill and FDR's ruminations at Casablanca in 1943 and then by concern over French positions in sub-Saharan Africa, the Middle East, and Southeast Asia), declaring "as was only human, [FDR's] will to power cloaked itself in idealism." De Gaulle then went on to insist to the American president: "The West must be restored. If it regains its balance, the rest of the world, whether it wishes or not, will take it for an example. If it declines, barbarism will ultimately sweep everything away. . . . This is true of France above all, which of all the great nations of Europe is the only one which was, is and always will be your ally. But [France] must recover her vigor, her self-reliance, and consequently, her role. How can she do this if she is excluded from the organization of the great world powers and their decisions, if she loses her African and Asian territories—in short, if the settlement of the war definitively imposes upon her the psychology of the vanquished?"[3]

Accordingly, de Gaulle organized a conference of high colonial officials in Brazzaville, the French Congo, early in 1944, the purpose of which was to reform so as to preserve the French empire in its totality. Although the conference proposed to promote the economic development of the colonies, improve education, end forced labor, extend civil liberties, and provide for the political representation of the colonial peoples in the future National Assembly, the preamble to the document summing up the conference forcefully declared that any "idea of autonomy, any possibility of evolution outside the French bloc of the empire; the eventual establishment, even in the future, of self-government in the colonies is out of the question." Just so there would be no ambiguity on the matter, the words "self-government" were actually written in English.[4]

The most momentous consequence of the thinking coming from Brazzaville was to occur in September 1945, when with Japan's defeat and critical British help (over American objections) de Gaulle dispatched a French occupation force to Indochina. By late 1946, what Paris meant by colonial reform became painfully evident as the French launched an attack on Vietminh forces in Hanoi and Haiphong, designed to extinguish the communist government in the north. By then, de Gaulle was no longer in power, but his policy was now firmly adopted as that of the Fourth Republic.

To this point, I have made British and French reactions to the rise of colonial nationalism appear quite similar. But they were not. Although many British looked to reform the empire in order to preserve it, and few indeed were aware of the great changes that were afoot, nonetheless in their institutions and their values they were far more attuned to the possibility of decolonization than were the French. In the Labour Party, some welcomed the devolution of power to the colonies, whereas the Conservative Party—long attached to empire as an antidote to class conflict and for its economic potential—remained intransigent. Yet while party labels certainly mattered, the British left was nonetheless much more progressive with respect to decolonization than the left in France.[5]

Aside from the party differences and the party system, where the French multiparty framework was far more difficult to coordinate than the British, three other features of British imperialism allowed it to accommodate the demand for emancipation more easily than the French did. First, the British had a long tradition of informal great-power influence, whether in Asia, Latin America, or the Middle East, an "imperialism of free trade" in the phrase of John Gallagher and Ronald Robinson, that predisposed them ideologically to the notion that their interests could be preserved without direct political control. They knew, from the troubles of holding Ireland to the experience of Commonwealth association, that there could be positive alternatives to formal empire. The British may have taken inordinate pride in beholding a map of the world with large patches of color indicating their imperial possessions, but they seldom made the mistake of letting pride dictate policy, as the French often did.

Hence, even among peoples whom they did rule directly, the British liked to talk about eventual self-government, which they linked to imperial governing procedures that allowed locals some share of power. When, therefore, London was confronted with demands for self-rule on the part of imperial nationalists, they had in practice (though not so much in theory) a process of devolution that allowed them to handle the situation more readily than the French, who with their talk of assimilation had preferred to bring colonial representatives to sit in the National Assembly.

It is nonetheless worth noting that in the aftermath of formal empire, the French proved for more than a generation far more successful at establishing an informal neo-empire in much of Africa, while London's hope that it could exert substantial influence through Commonwealth ties was soon to be completely disappointed. The cooperation between authoritarian elites in Francophone Africa and Paris—exemplified most clearly in repeated French military interventions and the participation of these countries in a French Community Franc Zone controlled by Paris—is simply without parallel in British experience. Today, after the tragedy of Rwanda and the collapse of the Mobutu government in Zaire (renamed the Congo in 1997), French power is finally greatly diminished—but its imperial afterlife outlasted that of the British.[6]

A second way the British were favored relative to the French was by the character of the nationalist demands they encountered. In India and Ghana, London had the simple good fortune to deal with nationalists who, while determined, were also restricted in what they could do by local political concerns to avoid popular revolutionary mobilization that might be impossible for these elites to control. By contrast, in Indochina and Algeria, the French faced nationalist revolutionaries who suffered under no

such limitations. To some extent, of course, this second distinguishing feature of French from British rule reflected the first: the
British had been more willing to allow a colonial elite to form
with whom they could later negotiate independence than the
French—except in sub-Saharan Africa, where elites like Félix
Houphouët-Boigny in the Ivory Coast were quite eager to be free
of control from Paris but extremely reluctant to enter into protracted warfare to bring it about.

Finally, the British were favored by their closer position to the
United States. For some time, London had viewed its "special
relationship" with Washington as one that would make it the
privileged junior partner of the colossus of the West. By contrast,
the French had come to distrust what Charles de Gaulle often
referred to as Anglo-Saxon ambitions to reduce France permanently in great-power status. In contrast to the ease with which
the British transferred power to the United States in the eastern
Mediterranean (occasioning the announcement of the so-called
Truman Doctrine in March 1947), the French had no such trust-
ing relationship with Washington. Indeed, mistrust in Paris continues even today. Among the reasons for France's support of the
Hutu government in Rwanda in 1994, for example, was that the
Tutsi exiles in Uganda had become Anglophones, depriving
themselves of any sympathy among the French.

As these considerations suggest, the British were far better prepared to deal with the rise of colonial nationalism than were the
French. By the same token, they were not unduly alarmed by the
Chinese Revolution either, advising Washington repeatedly in
1949 to extend immediate recognition to the PRC for the sake of
economic interests and to avoid driving Mao into Stalin's hands.

Yet lest I should be accused of being unduly Anglophile, I
should close this discussion of a general European underestimation of the power of Third World nationalism by referring to
events in Iran and Egypt between 1953 and 1956, where the British were far from progressive in their policy. Whether it was the
tirades against Mohammad Mossadegh in Tehran on behalf of
British petroleum or the ill-fated attempt to reverse Gamal Abdel

Nasser's seizure of the Suez Canal in cooperation with Israel and France, the British, in the person of Anthony Eden, were every bit as pig-headed, arrogant, and self-defeating as the French were to prove themselves in Vietnam and Algeria. Here, in short, was the time and place—the Middle East in the mid-1950s—in which Britain showed how deeply it too could underestimate the power of Third World nationalism.

The United States and the Soviet Union

Just as the European colonial powers underestimated the strength of Third World nationalism, partly because of their over-estimation of the importance of holding on to their empires, so too did Moscow and Washington accord these developments an inflated importance in their superpower rivalry—and with deadly consequences to both (not to speak of the local peoples directly involved, from the Afghanis to the Vietnamese).

Consider first the Soviets. Since the founding of the Third International in 1919, the Bolsheviks had essentially argued, as the apocryphal line put it, that "the road to Paris passes by Peking." Here in the Third World was the "reserve army of labor," the cheap raw materials, the vulnerable markets that capitalism would be obliged to try to control in its efforts to avoid its internal contradictions. Building on Rudolf Hilferding and Rosa Luxemburg, Lenin had articulated a line in *Imperialism: The Highest Stage of Capitalism* in 1917 that was to be much improved upon by the theorists of the Third International in the 1920s before emerging as "dependency theory" in the West in the 1970s, where it did so much to give intellectual fuel to efforts to expand the Cuban Revolution, including the claims of liberation theology.[7]

In the interwar period, the Soviet Union had also explored the political utility of working not only with communists but also with "objectively progressive" Third World forces such as "national bourgeoisies" who were anti-Western. In countries as different as Afghanistan, Turkey, and China, for example, Moscow had found it could form something of an international "united front," fashioned from a common interest in opposing Western "imperialism."

This policy continued after World War II. The recently released papers in the Wilson Center's Cold War International History Project, worked on most authoritatively by John Lewis Gaddis, suggest that Stalin saw the Chinese Revolution (as did Mao) as an epochal event ushering in the next stage of socialist global expansion. As a result, Kim Il-sung's proposal to reunite the Koreas by war eventually met with the approval of both Stalin and Mao not only for the sake of what it might do to the Korean peninsula but also for the sake of the greater good of socialism internationally.[8]

Whatever the excesses of the talk about "monolithic international communism" in the United States in the 1950s, there was, in fact, in communist circles a sense of the wholeness of their movement. Whether in Greece or the Philippines, Guatemala or Indochina, communism followed the current environmental slogan to "think globally, act locally." The result was a millennarian or chiliastic faith, whereby the force of change in the Third World would sweep all before it elsewhere. Even after the Sino-Soviet split opened in the late 1950s and early 1960s, China kept the flame alight although now arguing that Moscow was insufficiently revolutionary for the task, that Beijing instead was now the capital of the age of enlightenment. At the same time, again in the 1960s, much the same argument was to be heard from the little island of Cuba, where Fidel Castro was holding forth on the need for revolution throughout Latin America and Africa. "Two, three, many Vietnams," declared his associate Che Guevara: "The Andes will be the Sierra Maestra of all the Americas." With the end of the Portuguese empire in Africa in 1974, the Cubans were to be found aiding the establishment of communist governments there as well.[9]

In short, Moscow, Beijing, and Havana all overestimated the importance of Third World nationalism, seeing it as an important element of the struggle against the West when, in fact, it was no

such thing. Ultimately, involvement with Third World nationalism was to weaken each of the superpowers, not help them in
their titanic struggle. Indeed, in the unlikely event that either of
them had gained undisputed leadership of these regions, there is
little reason to think the course of the Cold War would have
thereby been noticeably affected, given that the major dynamic
of the American victory concerned its leadership of Western Europe, North America, and the leading economies of the Pacific.
In this struggle, Africa and most of Asia and Latin America were
simply not important stakes.

If the Soviets gave special importance to developments in the
Third World, the United States became inclined to do so as
well—partly because of the evident appeal of communism there,
partly because of a previous interest in these regions held for the
sake of American concepts of world order that go back to Woodrow Wilson's time.

Thus, from the lend-lease agreements and the Atlantic Charter
of 1941, through its wartime planning for a postwar order in
1944–45, Washington saw the independence of the colonial
world as a goal it hoped to foster. Just as the United States had
welcomed the end of Spanish rule in Latin America in 1823, and
in 1919 had participated in carving up empires in Eastern Europe
and the Middle East in what Wilson had explicitly called "the
globalizing of the Monroe Doctrine," so in the 1940s FDR and
Truman looked forward to a postwar order free of what the State
Department repeatedly called great-power spheres of influence.
For a time, to be sure, Roosevelt anticipated the Big Four acting
as world policemen, each with a part of the globe under its special control. But in short order he advanced the idea instead of a
United Nations that would function more effectively than the
League ever had and that would be the home of those countries
freed by the war against the Axis and by the eventual spread of
national self-determination worldwide.[10]

Part of the motive for this policy was undoubtedly economic.
The United States had always opposed mercantilism and the imperial orders to which it generally belonged. Getting the British

out of India, the Dutch out of Indonesia, the French out of Indo-china, and keeping the Soviets from annexing Eastern Europe made sense in terms of U.S. business and financial interests.

But American support for open international markets had a political provenance as well that went back to British arguments for free trade in the first half of the nineteenth century. The basic idea was that fair trade meant peaceful political relations. Poli-cymakers saw imperialism in substantial measure as the effort to gain through force what could not be had through open economic competition. Economics should be depoliticized by allowing the market, not governments, to determine trade and investment de-cisions.[11]

The political consequences of this thinking were that the West-ern Europeans should decolonize and the Soviets should stay within their 1939 borders (which might be rectified but only with the assent of the subject populations). In taking this stand, Wash-ington was aligning itself with Third World nationalism—that is, globalizing the Monroe Doctrine to the four corners of the earth, much further than Wilson had ever dared to think of ex-tending it.

The positive side of American policy was evident when the Philippines was given its independence on July 4, 1946, and when Washington welcomed new sovereign governments in In-dia and Israel in 1947 and 1948. Such easy identification in the-ory of the United States with nationalism abroad was short-lived in practice, however. For in many lands, nationalism had shown itself better at undermining the old authoritarian or multinational imperial order than at providing stable modern government in its place. So it had been in the aftermath of World War I in Eastern Europe and the Middle East, so it is again today in the aftermath of the Soviet collapse, and so it certainly was in the late 1940s and early '50s as decolonization proceeded apace. The biggest wrinkle for this new wave of nationalism at mid-century, how-ever, was how it would relate to communism.

Some did not care much whether these regions became com-munist or not. Why bother to intervene in Asia, Africa, or Latin

America in an effort to control these problems of Third World nationalism? George Kennan had early argued that so long as the position of the United States was strong in Western Europe and Japan, there was no reason to expend our resources and energy to assure the emergence of pro-American governments elsewhere in the world. The stakes were simply too negligible relative to the effort that would have to be expended to make the enterprise worthwhile. In sum, it was one thing to see that Third World nationalism was a force to be reckoned with, quite another to commit the United States to a forward policy dedicated to controlling political order in these regions.[12]

For a brief period, such thinking predominated in Washington, which initially refused to see Ho Chi Minh as this country's enemy. But as the Cold War unfolded, beginning in 1947, the seemingly insignificant players in the Third World began to appear as pawns with a meaning greater than themselves in a global struggle. As the name Cold War indicates, the central divide between the United States and the Soviet Union traced at Yalta remained stable. Elsewhere, however, the confrontation is better described as *hot*.

Such an appellation is particularly correct in Asia, of course, where the outbreak of the Korean War settled Washington's mind on how to view China. Although it was already apparent from the lessons of Tito's Yugoslavia that the United States could work with some communist governments, Chinese-Soviet collusion in Korea indicated that elsewhere the kind of grudging acceptance that emerged toward Yugoslavia would be risky to duplicate. Washington had already successfully countered communist bids for power in Greece and the Philippines, and now it would be prepared to do so wherever such challenges emerged—as was soon to happen, in Iran in 1953 and Guatemala and Vietnam in 1954, at a time when the British were dealing successfully with a communist insurgency in Malaysia.

Just as Moscow overestimated the importance of the direction Third World nationalism took in the thirty years following World War II, so also Washington read far more into these events than they deserved. But there was an insidious logic to the way these developments appeared in the United States. Greece could be argued to be a Western security concern. Iran had oil. Guatemala evoked concerns based on the Monroe Doctrine that even George Kennan invoked. Vietnam may have seemed a strange place for American intervention, but in the context of the Korean War, where it could well be argued that Western determination was being tested, it came to have new significance. And then there was the Cuban Revolution, with its announced goal of turning the Western hemisphere into a revolutionary cauldron, and its eventual success in Nicaragua, which in turn threatened traditional American paramountcy in all of Central America.

So like other great powers before it that sought to demonstrate their resolve by putting out brush fires for fear they might lead to wider confrontations, the United States overreacted to the emotional rhetoric of Third World nationalism wherever it appeared to be critical of its interests or policies. Meanwhile, the Soviet Union was having its own difficulties with its imperial possessions throughout the Third World and even within its sphere of interest in Eastern Europe.

In short, like Britain and France but on a more global scale, both the United States and the Soviet Union overestimated the significance of the Third World in their struggle with each other, and as a result both found themselves underestimating the difficulty of controlling foreign nationalism once they decided it was important. Ultimately, it was the Soviet Union that had the harder time of it.

Here the most critical factor seems to have been that the United States relied more on informal hegemonic controls that allowed important elements of client countries to be autonomous than did the Soviet Union, whose hand weighed far more heavily on their clients' decision making. The edge the United States enjoyed is explained by its preference for democratic or at least consultative frameworks that left a real dimension of initiative to local actors. The United States' own political apparatus was never as tied in to the control of foreign peoples as those in the Soviet Union but instead usually made clear distinctions about where the water's edge began. In addition, the United States presided over the international economic system in a way that offered substantial reward to those elites who agreed to play by rules set in Washington. As a result of these two factors, the American imperial-hegemonic system never proved as burdensome as that emanating from Moscow and so proved better able to ride the waves set up by the nationalism of the weak. America's empire was, then, informal while the Soviets' was formal, and it was the latter, not the former, on which history passed a death sentence.[13]

Indeed, the Cold War ended in good measure because of Moscow's inability to control nationalist forces, in Eastern Europe, in Central Asia, and certainly within the Soviet Union itself. Washington may have been damaged by its efforts to control similar forces in Asia or Latin America—and may have wrought terrible damage to the peoples there as well—but as current European hopes to see NATO enlarged or Mexican hopes to see NAFTA consolidated suggest, the competition between these two systems East and West always favored the West.

Let me then conclude by restating the lack of understanding that typified nearly all the great powers in this great historical drama: by overestimating the importance to themselves of controlling Third World nationalism, they thought in ways that led them to underestimate its real power and soon were swept away by its force. To estimate it properly was to see that while it was a force that brooked no local opposition, its weight on the outcome of the Cold War might well have been treated as negligible. The misperception in Paris and London, Washington and Moscow, was to suppose that somehow national greatness depended on hegemonic control in Africa and Asia (and by extension in other relatively weak parts of the globe as well).

Some students of the period are likely to contest this assessment, feeling that however brutal U.S. imperialism was in these regions, it was ultimately a necessary part of winning the Cold War. I disagree. Events of tremendous local significance may have little or no impact on a global balance of power—unless of course they come to have such a large role by virtue of the great power's definition of their importance, as the French and Americans demonstrated in Vietnam, the British at Suez, and the Soviets in Afghanistan. In sum, an analysis of how the great powers viewed Third World nationalism in the postwar period gives little hope that elites will think rationally about how to defend their interests but instead will overestimate or underestimate trends not only to their own detriment but especially in a way that damages the weaker peoples who find themselves manipulated by these powerful outside forces.

Security and Order After the Cold War

The United States, the Cold War, and the Post–Cold War Order

Philip Zelikow

It is impossible to analyze the settlement of the Cold War without comprehending what was being settled. In other words, a theory of settlement must be accompanied by a theory of what the Cold War was about. The Cold War can best be understood as the final phase, lasting nearly half a century, of a long global struggle between two fundamentally different conceptions for the organization and governance of modern society.

That struggle began as the international system of the nineteenth century was coming to its end in the bloody chaos of World War I.[1] Out of those ruins arose a new conception of government and society, one that had not held power anywhere before the war, and was offered as the ultimate response both to the industrial revolution and to the modern requirements for total war. This form of governance claimed unlimited power over its subjects in order to transcend the traditional divisions of society and unite them in pursuit of utopian ideals. These ideals differed, principally between a focus on a global conflict of nations and races or a global struggle of social classes. But all these varieties of totalitarianism were united in their hostility, even revulsion, toward the liberal democracies. Once the Bolshevik regime had survived the trials of civil war in Russia and the fascist dictatorships also began attaining power, first in Italy, the battle lines were drawn around the world. By early 1941 the totalitarian states held most of the world's military power. But then the two most powerful states in the world, Germany and the Soviet Union, went to war against each other.

The Cold War Becomes Evident, 1943–1946

The Cold War began as the outcome of World War II was coming into view. As the danger of the German, Japanese, and Italian dictatorships was being contained and pushed back, the kindred threat of Soviet communism returned to the foreground of Western attention. Between 1943 and 1946, Western political thinkers, in and out of government, were not sure whether or how they would cooperate with Soviet communism. The views of traditional, conservative anti-communists were clear enough, and were sharpened by the philosophical breadth and rigor offered by Friedrich von Hayek, whose warning in *The Road to Serfdom* received enormous attention on its publication in 1944.

More influential for postwar Western governments dominated by the center-left were the views of anti-communist leftists that were hardened by the crucible of world war. For this group Arthur Koestler's *Darkness at Noon* attracted great attention as the war was ending, and their great exemplar was (and is) George Orwell. Orwell's *Homage to Catalonia* had foreshadowed the opinions shaped by his experiences in the Spanish Civil War; his critique of Stalinism, *Animal Farm*, had been censored by British authorities in 1944 but appeared in 1946, to be followed three years later by *1984*.[2]

Soviet views toward the West reflected an unremitting hostility that had been muted and qualified by wartime needs but never forgotten. The global class struggle would resume once the war was over. This hostility could express itself either in the form of the more pragmatic geopolitical maneuvers advocated by some Foreign Ministry professionals in 1945–46 or in the expected return to old global battle lines, indicated by Stalin's speech of February 1946. But there was never any Soviet analogue to the kind of cooperative power sharing apparently envisioned by Franklin D. Roosevelt.[3]

Indeed what is striking about Roosevelt's vision, and the general tenor of American policy between 1943 and 1946, is not naïveté about the Soviet Union so much as a general complacency about the intensity and stakes of the postwar conflicts to come. Stepping back from the work of the few concerned specialists, the overarching theme until the summer of 1946—whether in policy toward occupied Germany, or on the fate of the atomic bomb program, or any other regional or security issue—is weak analysis, high-level inattention, or just plain neglect. The Cold War was therefore one-sided until American complacency was disturbed and the United States began reacting with growing urgency to dangers and moves that were initiated by others.

Shoring Up the Defenses, 1946–1952

Complacency was disturbed when the Truman administration had to contemplate seriously how it might respond to Soviet threats against Iran and Turkey, and then to the debilitation overtaking Western Europe. The initial responses were to put the American national security establishment back into some minimal order, reestablishing an atomic weapons program that was falling apart, developing significant plans for waging World War III against the Soviet Union, and building the organizational capacities that solidified into the postwar national security state. Aid programs were developed for Greece and Turkey, followed by a much more ambitious program of economic sustenance for the rest of Europe.

When the Americans shook off their passivity in 1946 and 1947, the Soviet government responded with energy, though not sophistication. Moscow consolidated its control over Eastern Europe, began bringing its conventional forces in Europe back to large-scale combat readiness, and determinedly sought to stop, or reverse, the economic Westernization of Germany by squeezing Berlin. The effort failed, and helped bring together the signatories to the North Atlantic Treaty, in 1949. This much is familiar. Historians have sought for decades to assign responsibility in the reciprocal spiral of growing hostility. A great virtue of John Lewis Gaddis's recent contribution to the debate is his attempt to distinguish the strategies of Moscow and Washington, honing in on the absolutely central issue of consent versus forcible coercion.[4]

The other great distinction between Soviet and American policy was between the desire on one hand to revise the existing political and social order, attacking it violently if needed, and the desire on the other to defend that order, preferably through democratic evolution. Moral judgment here depends on the judge's view of whether the existing order was evil or tolerable, and of the methods being employed to attack or defend it. While those methods often became all too equivalent, the ideals of the two sides were never identical.

Leaders in Moscow, or in Peking, always looked for and idealized the revolutionary champion who could take up the victorious struggle for socialism, by whatever means were necessary. Achievements were objective and did not acquire their status from popular consent. Washington, in contrast, always searched for the elusive progressive democrat who could reform the abuses that caused unrest while winning power with ballots, not bullets. That each side often settled for less than what it wanted should not obscure the differences in their aspirations.

What may be less obvious about this phase of the Cold War is the defensive pessimism in American policy and the optimistic opportunism evident on the other side. The Americans, to Mao Zedong's great surprise, chose not to mount a serious contest between 1946 and 1948 for the greatest prize of all—the fate of China. In 1949 Washington's plan for war in Europe was a replay of World War II, starting with a long retreat off the continent and a slow, problematical fight to win it back. The evanescent atomic advantage was some consolation, but not enough.

In 1949 Washington thought of Asia as a series of tough choices over what could be defended and what must be abandoned. Japan would be held, but perhaps at the expense of giving up on Taiwan, Korea, and Indochina. The only other consolation was in the hope, among some, that the contest might remain diffuse and waged with words rather than guns. Many of Truman's officials thought the hope was vain, but in early 1950 the president still planned further cuts in his defense budget.

The Korean War changed all that. As it had in 1940–41, the United States began to mobilize in earnest for war. But after China intervened, the American choices were constantly shadowed by a sense of weakness. An indefinite war of attrition in Korea seemed intolerable, but all the alternatives aimed directly at China risked war with the Soviet Union, and that was a war Washington felt it might well lose.[5]

A Precarious Preponderance, 1952–1957

During 1952 the initiative in the Cold War began passing from the Soviets and Chinese to the Americans. The United States was the first to test thermonuclear weapons. Though a Russian test soon followed, the United States was building up a far greater capacity to produce such weapons and deliver them against faraway targets. The North Atlantic Treaty had turned into a military organization with U.S. combat divisions deployed in its support and an aroused Europe engaged in rearmament, now including Germany. The dramatic increases in defense spending of 1950 and 1951 were now paying off in large numbers of aircraft, tanks, and every other kind of military hardware. The Truman administration, followed by Eisenhower, adopted a more assertive approach in Korea, plainly more willing to consider widening the war in order to bring it to an end.

Soviet attitudes became noticeably more defensive, especially in the confused aftermath of Stalin's death. After putting down a revolt in East Germany, the Soviet government concentrated on protecting the existing regime and abandoned any pretense of seeking unification in Germany. A more confident America, in contrast, was willing to push harder and gamble more on allowing German unity. Khrushchev's denunciation of Stalin in early 1956 led to more unrest as Poles and, especially, Hungarians tested the continuing Soviet commitment to forcible coercion. The Chinese also chose to make significant concessions to gain a Korean armistice, and Mao displayed more prudence in his relatively generous approach to the Geneva talks on Indochina and during the first Taiwan Straits crisis of 1954–55, never pushing beyond what the Americans seemed ready to allow.[6]

The American confidence led Washington to a series of policy initiatives, from the Baghdad Pact, and other projects for the Middle East, to covert actions in Iran and Guatemala. The initiatives included contemplation of ideas for unsettling Eastern Europe, especially with "psychological warfare," and the consolidation of a new strategic concept for defending Europe that would make a stand in Germany, resting this forward defense on a bristling arsenal of nuclear weapons.

Yet this confidence was shadowed by a constant sense that the moment would pass as the American thermonuclear advantage was canceled out by the inevitable Soviet nuclear buildup. Marc Trachtenberg has ably analyzed the dilemma American planners faced in thinking about whether or how to use their "wasting asset."[7] If Soviet and Chinese leaders noticed these debates, as they probably did, and thought about how they would have resolved Washington's dilemma had they been in Washington's place, it is not hard to see why they displayed such prudence and moderation.

The Crisis Years, 1957–1962

During November 1956 the Soviet bloc violently sealed the fissure that had opened in Hungary just as Western cohesion visibly cracked over the issue of Suez. To make matters worse,

Khrushchev apparently convinced himself that his threats to use nuclear missiles against Western Europe had really played a major part in crumpling the Anglo-French assault against Egypt.[8] In 1957 Khrushchev defeated the effort to unseat him led by his principal rivals and, heralded by the first tests of intercontinental-range missiles and the Sputnik satellite success, he began asserting the power of his new medium-range missiles to check any American resort to its nuclear defenses in Europe.

Once again it was the West's turn to feel defensive and react to initiatives from the other side, first with stopgap deployments of their own crude missiles to Europe. Fortunately one of the only Americans not infected by the gloomy mood of inferiority and danger was Eisenhower himself, who saw no need to offer loud reassurances.[9] Swelling with optimism about Soviet power, both real and feigned, Khrushchev and Mao contemplated new initiatives as they met in Moscow for the fortieth anniversary of the Bolshevik Revolution, in November 1957.[10]

Mao moved first, with little advance notice to his Soviet ally, by igniting another crisis in the Taiwan Straits. Little is known about his decision making during this period, but the crisis seems significantly more dangerous than the earlier Taiwan Straits confrontation of 1954–55, as Mao actively contemplated the prospect of war with the United States and successfully obtained at least some commitments of nuclear aid from an ambivalent and worried Khrushchev.[11] Just after Mao stepped back from the brink, blaming the quality of Soviet support, Khrushchev stepped up to it by demanding that Western forces leave Berlin.

American diplomacy remained reactive and defensive, if anything becoming even edgier, after Kennedy succeeded Eisenhower. The Berlin ultimatum that Khrushchev had suspended was renewed. The deadline was staved off at the end of 1961 with a promise of diplomatic action. But the two sides publicly admitted their talks were deadlocked by the end of April 1962, even as the Americans were bolstering the credibility of their nuclear commitment to Berlin by trying to assert their (quite real) superiority in strategic nuclear weapons. These factors were a critical backdrop to Khrushchev's effort to complete the secret deployment of scores of ballistic missiles into Cuba just before he planned to bring the Berlin crisis to a climax in November 1962, when—as Khrushchev put it—he would give Kennedy "a choice: go to war or sign a peace treaty." But the Cuban missile crisis intervened. Khrushchev's gambit failed; the promised final confrontation over Berlin was abandoned.[12]

Instead the Soviet government moved toward the modus vivendi solution on Berlin that Moscow had scorned when Kennedy had offered it (infuriating Adenauer) in the spring of 1962. The Soviet-Chinese relationship had fractured, especially after the Soviets refused to deliver an atomic bomb to China in 1959 and Khrushchev had a last, unpleasant set of talks with Mao. The split had become publicly evident during 1960, when the Soviets cut off economic aid to China even as Mao's Great Leap Forward was stumbling into economic ruin and mass starvation. By the end of 1962 neither the Soviet Union nor China could sustain its prior confidence about its power or place in the world.

War in Asia and U.S.-Soviet Détente, 1963–1974

The Soviet and Chinese governments chose very different paths in solving the problem of how to catch up to and surpass the West after the setbacks of the early 1960s. After a short period of retrenchment Mao chose the path of full-scale revolution. At home this took the form of the Great Proletarian Cultural Revolution. Abroad this was evident in a militant readiness to confront the United States, most immediately in Vietnam. There China apparently made the crucial strategic choice to accept a risk of general war with the United States by agreeing to defend North Vietnam even as North Vietnam, with Chinese as well as Soviet aid, poured arms and troops into the war against South Vietnam and its American ally.[13]

The Soviet Union, however, chose a more conservative path, avoiding any direct and violent challenges to the West's status quo while steadily devoting massive resources to a buildup of every category of armed strength. National liberation movements received steady but cautious, bureaucratized support. The relieved states of Western Europe were increasingly able to pursue local agendas while arranging their modus vivendi with Moscow. The Americans were distracted by the Vietnam War, yet the détente with Moscow frequently led both the Johnson and Nixon administrations to hope (vainly) that the Soviets might help put out the fires burning in Indochina. The era was marked by a remarkably blithe acquiescence to the Soviet-led invasion of Czechoslovakia, the Ostpolitik treaties, the Quadripartite Agreement on Berlin, the sluggish SALT/ABM negotiations and agreements, and the Helsinki Final Act (1975) that said the existing borders in Europe were "inviolable" (while leaving open the possibility, which seemed quite academic at the time, of peacefully negotiated adjustments).[14] Despite Kissinger's energy and pyrotechnics, the underlying U.S.-Soviet agenda did not change much when Nixon succeeded Johnson.

The Last Crisis Years, 1975–1985

The U.S.-Soviet détente did not break apart at once. Like the debris slowly exposed by a receding tide, three issues became apparent as détente aged. First was a contest in the Third World that seemed to be escalating, not abating, and turning decidedly against the governments or factions favored by the United States. The conquest of South Vietnam by North Vietnam, which had by then adopted the USSR—not China—as its principal patron, was a humiliating blow given an extra dramatic edge by the Khmer Rouge victory in Cambodia. Cuban intervention, with Soviet funding and supplies, tipped the scales in Angola, then Ethiopia, as the United States effectively abandoned the field. The Soviet invasion of Afghanistan in 1979, coming on the heels of the revolution that swept away America's principal ally in southwest Asia, Iran, accelerated the turn in government and public opinion that was already well advanced.

Second, as the Soviets gained parity (or superiority, as some perceived it) in strategic nuclear forces, apparent Soviet advantages in theater forces redoubled Western unease. This was the context for the belief that the Soviet introduction of a new generation of intermediate-range ballistic missiles, the SS-20s, challenged détente by upsetting an already precarious status quo.

Finally, and perhaps most interesting, is how the relaxation of overt international tension between East and West drew greater attention to the fundamental political and social differences between the two systems that had seemed so important in the 1940s. Seemingly narrow issues, like Jewish emigration from the Soviet Union or the treatment of famed dissidents like Andrei Sakharov or Alexander Solzhenitsyn, resonated because they spotlighted this earlier, larger, and enduring source of conflict. By 1979–80 unrest in Poland became, especially for the Soviets, a far more potent sign of internal decay within their empire. A Soviet invasion of Poland was narrowly averted, but the Polish government was forced to impose martial law by the end of 1981.

In Asia Mao's complacency about American retreat became evident after Washington, in 1968–69, chose withdrawal from Vietnam rather than further escalation. China secured an assurance that Washington and Moscow would not collude against Peking and granted a de facto armistice in the Cold War in Asia. The armistice turned into a genuine rapprochement between the United States and China, with growing security cooperation, founded on common hostility and fear toward the Soviet Union, after Deng Xiaoping triumphed over his rivals in the succession struggles of 1976–77.

In Europe and the Third World the United States and its allies began a major program of rearmament. The Soviet Union and its allies were confronted with overt and covert military moves around the world. The most dangerous year, in every sense, was 1983. The titanic political battle over deployment of NATO intermediate ballistic missiles reached its height; fears of nuclear war became acute (especially on the Soviet side, especially after an ailing Yuri Andropov gained supreme power); and Soviet combat forces deployed to Lebanon and Syria came perilously close to direct combat against Israeli and possibly even American forces. All of this occurred alongside bloody fighting in Afghanistan, Central America, and southern Africa.

The Second Détente, 1986–1988

Neither Gorbachev's accession to power in 1985 nor Reagan's reelection led to an immediate change in the confrontational policies of either superpower. But both were uneasy about the level of tension. Gorbachev accepted the basic American conceptions for new phases of nuclear arms control: deep cuts in strategic nuclear forces and some form of zero or near-zero option for intermediate-range missiles. After setbacks on the battlefield in Afghanistan in 1985–86, partly the result of enlarged U.S. aid to the rebels, Gorbachev also made the decision to withdraw from that war.

The United States moved too. In his memoirs, the longtime Soviet ambassador to the United States Anatoly Dobrynin argued: "It may sound like a historical paradox, in particular for Reagan's admirers, but if the president had not abandoned his hostile stance toward the Soviet Union for a more constructive one during his second term, Gorbachev would not have been able to launch his reforms and his 'new thinking.' Quite the contrary, Gorbachev would have been forced to continue the conservative foreign and domestic policies of his predecessors in defense of the nation against America."[15] Instead the Americans and Soviets signed a treaty on intermediate-range nuclear forces and were pushing hard on strategic arms reduction. Even the talks on conventional armed forces in Europe stirred to life. In the Third World, Soviets and Americans gradually disengaged from Afghanistan, made progress toward settlements of their disputes in southern Africa, and the U.S. policy in Central America foundered on the rocks of the Iran-contra scandal.

In Europe the new détente meant a renewal, even a consolidation, of the modus vivendi agreed upon during the Ostpolitik years. When West Germany's Christian Democratic party regained the chancellorship in 1982, Helmut Kohl felt grudgingly obliged to adopt the legacy of Ostpolitik as his own. The continuity was reinforced as Kohl also inherited the longtime foreign minister, Hans-Dietrich Genscher.

In relations with East Germany, for example, the East German head of state, Erich Honecker, received a red carpet welcome to the Federal Republic in 1987. The West Germans wanted to persuade the GDR to do good things (treat their citizens better, let them travel). This meant that the East German government needed to be reassured and stabilized. Such an approach shared the same goal as American policy, but the strategies differed. Timothy Garton Ash summarized: "The governing metaphor of [the American policy of] differentiation was that of 'carrots and sticks.' East European rulers were thus considered to be, at heart, donkeys. In the behavioral psychology of the German idea of détente, by contrast, East European rulers would appear to be, at heart, rabbits. The rabbit will freeze if you fix him in the headlights. If you frighten him too much, he may even bite. But speak to him gently, offer him carrots—above all, lots of carrots—and he will relax, loosen his grip."[16]

In truth, neither approach achieved very much inside East Germany (or Poland). West Germany helped to sustain a communist government that grew more hard-line in the late 1980s even as Soviet policy, at home and abroad, moved toward political reform. West German money helped the East German government avert unrest and maintain one of the most centralized and oppressive political systems in the Eastern bloc. West Germany's effort to reassure the East Germans produced no noticeable movement in the GDR leading toward eventual unity. Instead it tended to reinforce the conventional wisdom that territorial unification was out of the question.[17] This hard judgment on détente in Europe should be tempered, though, by three considerations. First there were the humanitarian benefits received by some East Germans and the opportunity to sustain small groups of peaceful dissenters. Second, there was the well-hidden but growing economic dependence of the Eastern European economies on Western cash, as well as the Soviet commodities provided at subsidized prices. Third, the strategies of reassurance, especially from West Germany, did pay dividends in Bonn's relations with the Soviet Union. Years of West German cooperation clearly softened Soviet attitudes about the FRG and built up at least a shallow reservoir of trust, at least among some Soviet officials, toward the West Germans as a new nation that had genuinely broken with its past. Asked in October 1988, after visiting Moscow, whether Gorbachev might someday offer unity to the Germans, Chancellor Kohl was scornful. "I do not write futuristic novels like [H. G.] Wells," he replied. "What you ask now, that is in the realm of fantasy."[18] Perhaps Kohl was musing just a bit about himself, too, when he wrote nearly a decade later that "the times had too powerful an effect, too much resignation, and also—one must say it—betrayal of the inherited path."[19]

Reagan did give a memorable speech in Berlin in 1987, standing at the Brandenburg Gate and challenging Gorbachev to "open this gate" and "tear down this wall!" It was a speechwriter who had come up with these words, not the foreign policy professionals. The secretary of state at the time, George Shultz, does not even mention the matter in his detailed memoirs. As Willy Brandt later wrote, Reagan may have "publicly called on Gorbachev to get rid of the Wall. But in negotiations with the Russians he set other priorities and certainly did not put in question the division of Germany."[20]

By the end of 1988 the Soviets had abandoned the old notion of the "socialist alternative."[21] They were ready to be integrated into the international system rather than isolated from it. They intended to join a transformed Europe on full and equal terms. What did all this mean for the Cold War? It obviously meant new chances for easing the U.S.-Soviet military rivalry. It meant that the Soviet Union no longer felt a special obligation to support fraternal socialist movements in the Third World or prop up regimes that would at least ally themselves with the socialist camp. In Europe it meant that Moscow would want friendlier political and economic relations and arms control talks to reduce concerns about the armed forces deployed by the opposing alliances, NATO and the Warsaw Pact.

By the end of 1988 the United States appeared to be defining an end to the Cold War as the achievement of three general goals: (1) to stabilize and reduce any danger from U.S.-Soviet rivalry in the development and deployment of nuclear forces, (2) to defuse and ameliorate any major areas of tension in the U.S.-Soviet competition for influence or advantage in the Third World, and (3) to persuade Moscow to move toward respect for the fundamental human rights of its citizens as a basis for full Soviet participation in the international community.

By the end of 1988 Margaret Thatcher, George Shultz, and Mikhail Gorbachev all thought that, by these standards, the Cold War was over. Thatcher, the most warlike of Cold Warriors, declared publicly in November 1988, "We're not in a Cold War now." Shultz also judged in retrospect that at the end of 1988 the Cold War "was all over but the shouting."[22]

But the Cold War was not over at the end of 1988. Europe and Germany were still divided, and hundreds of thousands of troops faced one another across the heart of the continent. The relaxation of tensions again exposed the ideological underpinnings of the conflict, as in the 1940s. The basic difference in the organization of society, one system relying on consent and the other relying on coercion, still lingered. Michael Mandelbaum caught the point, publicly, in early 1989; Bush and some, but not all, officials in his new administration had privately come to the same conclusion.[23] In their view the concluding era, and the basis for a settlement, would arise only from common agreement on the limits of coercion, the coercion that held the Soviet empire together.

The Revolutions in Central Europe, 1989–1990

The rapid pace of events in 1989 and 1990 has led less attentive observers to notice only the blurred rush to an end that, because it came so fast, seems to have been preordained by what came before. The inference is false. Many momentous choices were made in those turbulent months, and they were real choices between real alternatives, as revealed—for instance—by the quite different course of events in China.

As it had so often before, Poland was the first nation to test the limits of Russian coercion in 1989. The crisis arose from the unexpected outcome of parliamentary elections in June of that year, negotiated to provide a broader basis for Polish government actions to address the country's economic problems. When, to their surprise, Solidarity's leaders found they had swept these elections, the Soviets first faced the question of whether they would accept installation of a non-communist government in the Warsaw Pact. The Polish crisis reached its climax in August and September, resolved by a compromise in which a non-communist prime minister took office, while the defense and interior ministries remained under communist control and the government promised to remain in the Warsaw Pact. Hungary was able to follow the Polish example.

With the Polish crisis and national unrest inside the Soviet Union (Estonia, Armenia and Azerbaijan, Georgia, Ukraine and a special party plenum of its Central Committee) dominating the foreground, Moscow had little time to address the burgeoning crisis in East Germany, set off by the floods of refugees into Hungary and Czechoslovakia seeking an exit to the West. When East Germany's domestic crisis reached an acute stage, in October 1989, Gorbachev did engage but persuaded himself that the "Chinese solution" of using force was unnecessary, since a new, reformist communist government could recoup the situation.[24]

After the inadvertent opening of the Berlin Wall in November 1989, a crucial phase of diplomacy, led by West Germany and the United States, reestablished unification as the goal for German developments, then organized a diplomatic process to achieve this goal. I have detailed that intricate story elsewhere, and there is no need to recapitulate it here.[25]

The key point, however, was the ambition of the U.S.–West German agenda, to undo the status quo that had held for more than forty years. The Soviet, British, and French leaders were only the most important to react with alarm; their concerns were widely shared in other capitals and among outside commentators. The concerns were philosophical and pragmatic. Gorbachev put the philosophical point to Bush. Having already declared that two German states "was the decision of history," he attacked the U.S. view that, as Gorbachev summarized it, "the division of Europe should be overcome on the basis of Western values." The Soviet leader warned that if "policy is made on that assumption the situation could become quite messy. You used to make similar accusations against the USSR—the export of revolution."[26] Thatcher, too, felt the West "should respect Gorbachev's wish to keep the Warsaw Pact frontiers."[27]

French president François Mitterrand feared that the German crisis could bring Europe back to the brink of general war. He repeatedly evoked analogies to 1914, said "these people are tinkering with a world war," and, talking to Thatcher on one occasion, used an even more startling analogy to describe British-French-Soviet inaction in the face of German developments. "We find ourselves in the same situation as the leaders in France and Britain before the [second world] war, who didn't react to anything. We can't repeat Munich!"[28]

The Settlements of 1990

The German developments did move forward, however, as the Americans and West Germans outmaneuvered potential opponents during the first months of 1990. Having framed the unification issue starkly for the first, and last, elections in East Germany held in March, their diplomacy received a boost from the unexpectedly clear endorsement of Kohl's favored candidates. This momentum was then channeled into a plan, during the spring and summer of 1990, that would embed German unification into a larger framework for settlement of the most important political and military issues in European politics.

The United States wished to obtain Soviet acquiescence to an abrupt realignment of the European balance of power. American officials hoped to consolidate the democratic revolution in Eastern Europe, reduce Soviet military power on the continent generally, and eliminate the Soviet military presence in Germany. American forces, though fewer in number, would remain. These goals could be achieved only if the Soviet Union suffered a reversal of geopolitical fortunes not unlike a catastrophic defeat in a war.

But these same officials wanted the Soviets to accept this result and believe that they retained an appropriate, albeit diminished, role in European affairs. In the nineteenth-century international system, accommodating the interests of a defeated power was a familiar aspect of balance-of-power politics. Defeated powers were "compensated" for the loss of valued territory with other, perhaps less valued, land. In this way the victors sought to cushion the blow to the vanquished and protect the settlement. In the present, more enlightened, age, such compensation for political losses was not possible. The answers had to be sought in less tangible marks of power and influence. The resulting settlements, signed between September 1990 and the end of 1991, determined the contours of the post–Cold War strategic landscape.

The first group of settlements were the Final Settlement for Germany (September 1990), the Treaty on Conventional Armed Forces in Europe (CFE), and the Charter of Paris (both at the same gathering in November 1990). The German developments also propelled a transformation of the European Community. France and Germany accelerated European integration, not only the existing plans for monetary union but also new plans for an ambitious political union, propelled by a series of pivotal summit meetings between December 1989 and July 1990. So another element in the first group of settlements was the Maastricht Treaty establishing the European Union, finally signed in December 1991.

These agreements settled the German question in postwar European politics with a takeover of the East German state by the West, not a merger, with a united Germany as a full member of the Atlantic alliance and all its forces integrated under multinational military command while not subject to unique legal limits, with U.S. and other Western forces still on German soil and Soviet forces out, and with Germany tightly integrated into a strengthened European Union.

The settlements established that the dominant institutions for the organization of European politics would be the North Atlantic alliance and the European Union. The first offer to open NATO's doors to Eastern European envoys came in July 1990, to be followed a year later by the North Atlantic Cooperation Council, then the Partnership for Peace, and most recently a process for expanding the formal membership in the alliance. The Conference on Security and Cooperation in Europe would become an Organization (CSCE to OSCE), providing a normative framework for European dialogue along lines drafted in the West, codified in the Charter of Paris and its predecessor documents.[29]

The Revolutions in the Soviet Union

Poland, then above all Germany, had tested the limits of Soviet power in Central Europe. The diplomacy surrounding German unification, including the CFE Treaty, played a critical part in accelerating the crisis of authority within the Soviet Union itself. Obviously these developments emboldened rebellious nationalists throughout the USSR. Less obviously, receiving little public notice, were the ways in which Gorbachev's policies undermined his political base. The alienation of former hard-line allies like Yegor Ligachev was already well advanced, but these foreign policy issues were decisive in alienating the Soviet military and many party regulars in the Central Committee and the ranks of government and party officialdom. If there had been a coup against Gorbachev in August 1990, one of his chief advisers recalled, the German question "would have been in the forefront. . . . Look at the Central Committee, two-thirds of them were against Gorbachev and Shevardnadze."[30]

Gorbachev in turn, largely under the pressure of conducting this diplomacy, effectively abandoned the traditional institutions of Soviet collective rule, bypassing the Politburo almost entirely from the spring of 1990 onward. He weathered the storm at the July 1990 Party Congress, largely by letting Eduard Shevardnadze absorb hours of assaults and urging support for his promised program for economic reform and a promised all-Union treaty that would resolve the nationalities problems. Gorbachev's opponents had no organized alternative on the domestic issues.[31] But, as they returned to foreign affairs, Gorbachev and Shevardnadze proceeded to negotiate agreements that were almost disconnected from the rest of the government. In the CFE case, for instance, the Soviet military reacted by planning massive circumvention of the agreement even as it was being signed. Meanwhile Gorbachev backed away from his more radical economic reform plan and, in the fall of 1990, began trying to rebuild his support among the conservatives.[32] Top aide Alexander Yakovlev resigned in November. Shevardnadze's position became untenable after the first wave of settlements were concluded, and he resigned his post in December 1990 as the unrest at home began to boil over.

The decisive test of the limits of Soviet coercion arose in the Baltic republics, especially Lithuania. The Lithuanians had joined in the mass popular protests that marked the nationalist unrest of August–September 1989 but, having followed events in Central Europe, they then took the crucial step not only of electing nationalist rulers but of formally throwing down the gauntlet to Moscow by declaring independence in March 1990. The first acute period of tension came to a climax in May 1990, with violence narrowly headed off by the Lithuanians' agreement to suspend their declaration. During 1990 other republics followed the Lithuanian example but avoided a forceful confrontation. That confrontation was brewing, however, and in the fall of 1990 the country became more clearly polarized between those determined to sustain central Soviet power, led by KGB chief Vladimir

Kryuchkov, and the assorted factions rallying behind local autonomy and democratic rule. Each side feared, with reason, that the other was planning for revolution.

In January 1991 the violence flared in Lithuania as a government-led crackdown began but then stalled as Gorbachev, at the center, equivocated. Gorbachev was torn between the pressure from Kryuchkov and his allies and pressure from foreign countries, his few remaining reformist aides, and his conscience—oppressed by the spectacle of bloodshed and mass protest. His indecision allowed the Communist Party's apparatus of repression to decay further. Local potentates asserted de facto power; party officials began looking out for opportunities to convert the assets they controlled into ways to make hard cash; and Gorbachev was elaborating a deal to grant substantial autonomy to local republics. On the eve of the signature of the Union Treaty, which would replace the Soviet Union with a new "Union of Sovereign States," Kryuchkov and his allies in the security ministries attempted to strike first by implementing their own long-nurtured hopes for declaring a nationwide state of emergency. But the planning was poor and none of the plotters had a public profile or following comparable to Gorbachev or the newly elected Russian leader, Boris Yeltsin. The security forces largely refused to carry out the orders given to them and the coup collapsed in a few days. Gorbachev now stood atop a center that, as a governmental entity and as a place on the political spectrum, had ceased to exist.[33]

The Settlements of 1991

The American approach to these developments had two major dimensions. The first was to offer guidelines for political change and Western recognition of the new states. These principles, announced at the beginning of September 1991, called for (1) peaceful and democratic self-determination, (2) respect for existing borders with change only occurring peacefully, (3) respect for democracy and the rule of law, (4) regard for human

rights, particularly minority rights, and (5) respect for international law and obligations. The fifth point had a subtext—it
meant respect for the first group of settlements, and for recently
concluded agreements on the control of nuclear arms.[34]

The key settlements for this phase of revolutionary turmoil
were signed in December 1991, first in the Brest Declaration (December 8), in which the leaders of Russia, Ukraine, and Belarus
declared the dissolution of the Soviet Union (to be replaced by a
"Commonwealth of Independent States"), and then in an agreement at Alma-Ata (December 21) in which the Central Asian republics ratified the new arrangement. The American interests in
the character of the settlement may have simply reinforced the
prior inclinations of the leaders involved, but there is evidence
that, as Secretary of State James Baker discovered at the time, all
these leaders shared in their time of weakness and turmoil an
"intense desire to satisfy the United States."[35]

The second major aspect of the American approach focused on
the nuclear armaments of the superpowers. The long-discussed
and significant Strategic Arms Reduction Treaty (START I) had
been signed in Moscow in July 1991. The U.S. policy was aimed
at securing continued adherence to this accord and doing much
more to centralize control over the nuclear forces of the former
Soviet Union. To this end the Bush administration, in an extraordinary rush of action during September 1991, bypassed the idea
of seeking a formal treaty on shorter-range forces and announced
the unilateral redeployment or planned elimination of practically
all short-range nuclear missiles, as well as a series of new initiatives for another sharp reduction of strategic arms (including
MIRVed ICBMs). This September 1991 initiative created the conditions for consolidation of all nuclear arms under the control of
Russia and pledges of non-nuclear status from all the other republics, signed in Lisbon (May 1992), and conclusion of a START
II treaty (August 1992).[36]

One aspect largely missing from the American approach was
an equally dramatic engagement in the economic reconstruction
of Eastern Europe and the Soviet Union. The omission will seem

significant to any scholars who have studied the postwar settlements following the first or second world wars. Germany and France had advocated large-scale initiatives for assisting the Soviet Union as early as the spring of 1990, but their positions had little analytical work beneath them and the American stance was dominant.

There was a stance. Consultative mechanisms were put in place, attention was paid, and studies were launched. But Washington's basic strategic approach was to wait for the governments in the East to take the initiative of adopting massive and credible plans for market reform and then to seek Western aid in support of those reforms. Other than the aborted effort of August–September 1990 the Soviet government never took the needed initiative, settling for some significant stopgap aid wangled from the German government, especially in the first weeks of September 1990.[37] The Russian government only began undertaking the requisite commitments in negotiating for establishment of a currency stabilization fund and related large-scale aid in 1992, which did produce a meaningful Western response. The Eastern European governments did more, but the Western response remained modest, as neither the Americans nor the Western Europeans articulated or organized a strong policy, with one notable exception: the currency stabilization fund for Poland.[38]

Key Features of the New International System

The two and a half years between mid-1989 and the end of 1991 were the busiest period in American diplomacy since 1951 (though 1961–62 and 1983–84 are close runners-up). The activity involving Europe and the Soviet Union was accompanied by the Gulf crisis and war, establishment of a new Middle East peace process, negotiation of the North American Free Trade Agreement with Mexico, peace talks to end conflicts in El Salvador and Nicaragua, the invasion of Panama, settlements in southern Africa, major unrest in China, a new settlement in Cambodia, and the slide into civil war in Yugoslavia, with the United

States playing an unusually central role in every one of these separate sets of negotiations. As with other especially intense phases of American foreign policy, time is needed to sort out just what happened. But the system in place by the end of 1991 has remained intact for a decade, so perhaps we now have enough distance to gain a bit of perspective on it.

The system is founded on the largely latent, but evident, supreme power of the United States. The United States sits atop all three major hierarchies of world power—political, military, and economic. Its influence is accompanied not by ever vaster expenditures of money around the world but by wide adherence to its norms for the international order. Joseph Nye has discussed the concept of "soft power"; C. John Ikenberry and Charles Kupchan have also hypothesized (as early as 1990) that after periods of great turmoil the leaders in secondary states "seek alternatives to existing norms that have been discredited by events and in which new norms offer opportunities for political gains and coalitional realignment."[39] American aims have displayed great continuity. The United States is a status quo power, seeking change only if it enlarges the number of democratic states that accept the existing hierarchy of world power. "Rogue" states are isolated and targeted for possible military action.

The new system also has adequate institutions for organizing cooperative action. An informal concert of the great powers has taken shape, consisting of the United States, Britain, France, and Germany. Japan has some ex officio involvement. Chairs have been pulled out for Russia and China, but these countries prefer to loiter around the table, unsure about whether they really want to sit down and join in. Nor are the great powers sure about whether active participation by Russia and China is really either needed or useful.

The members of the concert agree that they like the current list of great powers and do not wish to see any additions or subtractions; that they wish to deter or avoid any serious international conflict; that domestic behavior is a proper subject for international discussion, though not much action; and that they need an open world economic system with relatively free flow of capital and goods. The only institutions needed for this tacit concert are those that give opportunities for effective consultation and provide some capacity to coordinate rapid, effective action by ad hoc political, military, or economic coalitions. NATO and the International Monetary Fund are especially useful for the latter role. Those and several other institutions provide opportunities— sometimes too many opportunities—for desired consultations.[40]

Much of the past seven years has been consumed with consolidating the new system. Its main strategic problem is how to deal with outsiders. Some outsiders want to come in. Debates over NATO enlargement have, unfortunately, diverted too much attention from deciding how to deal with larger and more troublesome outsiders.[41] The chief concerns are Russia, East Asia, and the Muslim world.

Russia has still not decided, fundamentally, whether it will accept an order and hierarchy in which it will not be "the new Rome." In talks with China, and even more recently with the temporarily annoyed French, Russia flirts with organizing some heterodox order with no evident principles beyond a desire for even more unrestrained commerce and resentment of the current government of the United States.

In East Asia, the Cold War never attained the kinds of settlements arrived at in Europe. The point is important. The Cold War clash with China ended with an uneasy rapprochement founded on little more than a common hostility toward the Soviet Union. Under Deng Xiaoping, and now the elite group headed by Jiang Zemin, China also sought, and still seeks, wide access to Western capital and Western markets. It seeks to join those parts of the Western-influenced international order, like the World Trade Organization, that will help achieve that goal (but with weak commitment to the actual norms underpinning that order). China never signed an Asian equivalent to the Charter of Paris, no documents to display a durable convergence in thinking about legitimate social and political orders either. That void has become more and more obvious since 1989. On the fundamental social and political issue—consent versus coercion—China and the West have little common ground beyond the uneasy truce in the Taiwan Strait.

The Muslim world is divided. Some parts are overtly hostile to the United States and what it represents; other states are aligned with America. Unfortunately American policy in this region has remained relatively inert for years, and fractures have opened up between Washington and its principal allies in Europe, and in the Middle East.

But there is one great continuity in the new international system that has emerged after the Cold War. The domino theory is alive and well. The dominoes are not countries falling before communists. Instead the dominoes are countries debating whether to stand by the less tangible, pervasive norms of the new system, in which the litmus word is "rogue" rather than the old word, "totalitarian."

In his thoughtful history of the domino theory, Frank Ninkovich explained why the notion of tests becomes so important. In a conception he traces back to Woodrow Wilson, the spectators are the mass of world opinion in a globe of fragile, often nondemocratic, developing or even developed countries. Certain issues become elevated, often by commitments of prestige or might, into enormous tests that will demonstrate, to the mass of spectators, whether or not the norms will be sustained. Only with this analysis can we begin to comprehend why a country as remote and unimportant as Laos could become so significant to Eisenhower and Kennedy in 1960–61, and why a genuinely important test, like Berlin, could summon a defensive threat of global thermonuclear war. "On the face of it," in Ninkovich's words, "third-world brushfire wars might be no more than the military equivalent of insect bites, but they could easily transmit the fatal contagion of doubt in a perceptual climate where American credibility was under fire and Western morale once again shaky."[42]

The new system is thus like the Cold War system, and unlike that of the eighteenth and nineteenth centuries, in the way "tests" can still acquire a disproportionate place in world politics, reverberating in a global echo chamber, amplified by the media networks now linking the world. Bosnia became such a test, and the belated vigor of international action in 1995 salvaged some respect, though not enough to preserve the so briefly ennobled status of the United Nations. Iraq may become another. But if this analysis is right, the essence of statecraft in the new system will be in how the great powers work together either to avoid a test or to choose one with deliberation, ready to then meet the challenge of performance on the global stage.

9

**Europe After
the Cold War:
Realism, Idealism,
and the Search
for Order
Without Empire**

Gregory Flynn

There is a striking convergence in each of the three post-war moments examined in this volume: in each period, the same basic debate has reemerged, a debate between realists and idealists over the basis for order and its possibilities. Following World War I and World War II, early thinking about a postwar system was dominated by idealists who sought both to establish a new basis for order, and to remove from Europe certain elements of order, both domestic and international, that were thought to have caused the wars to begin with. In both cases, institutions were created that were intended to embody new norms and a collective approach to security. And in both cases, idealism was sooner or later overwhelmed by geostrategic realities, in part because the institutions of idealism were not powerful enough to transform those realities.

Though framed by the same contest between realists and idealists, the period after 1989 has been different from its predecessors, at least until now. Geostrategic realities not only have not overwhelmed the search for a more normatively based, institutionally anchored European order; they have rather reinforced this search. At the same time, idealist constructions have not yet been able fully to mold the strategic landscape in a way that has either erased all geostrategic concerns or provided definitive answers to Europe's security problems. Idealist institutions and geostrategic realities have assumed a relation of constructive tension to each other, and this tension has defined much of the shape of the new Europe. It is also important that there now exists a wider consensus in Europe on the basic conditions of its order than at any other time in this century.

One of the crucial reasons for Europe's different experience after the Cold War lies in the geostrategic situation itself. As implausible as it might have seemed just a short time ago, the post–Cold War "settlement," which resolved the issues concerning Germany's status that had been at the origin of the Cold War in the first place, did not produce any fundamentally revisionist powers. Moreover, the unstable region between Germany and Russia, which had so long led to tension between them, no longer had the same geostrategic value for either power. This dramatically changed the way in which the states in the region confronted their problems, as well as the way the international community would have to deal with these problems.

The collapse of the Soviet Union has, however, left a more ambivalent geostrategic legacy. On one hand, Europe will no longer be the strategic battleground for two superpowers; on the other, Russia's unpredictable future has created deep strategic uncertainty for Europe. It is clear that the domestic outcome in Russia will determine whether Russia remains "outside" Europe and thus whether European security might still have to be organized against a hostile outside power. Nonetheless, although there exists a clear potential for Russian revisionism, the number of actual places where Russian revisionism and Western security interests would collide are few—the Baltic states may prove to be the only real case. And many, perhaps most, of the contentious issues between Russia and the West continue to appear susceptible to collective management within international institutions.

Moreover, even a Russian return to a nationalist, authoritarian regime would not undo the profound geostrategic change brought by the Soviet Union's collapse.

A second and no less essential part of the reason for the outcome of the post-1989 debate is the new level of consensus across Europe on the basic principles by which societies, economies, and political systems should be ordered. The collapse of communism and the embrace of political pluralism and market economics has left the continent functionally homogeneous in its political structures for the first time since the Congress of Vienna attempted to put Humpty Dumpty back together again after the French Revolution—and this in spite of the fact that the transformation of the states of east-central Europe and Russia remains incomplete. Without wanting to attribute a century and a half of European wars solely to the absence of consensus on principles of domestic order (as the continent moved away from monarchies and through the turmoil of the industrial revolution), there is much truth in the notion that states that share domestic principles of order tend to have an easier time arranging their relations with one another. And to the extent that one of those principles is the peaceful resolution of disputes through an apparatus provided by states, there are substantial implications for the strategies states pursue to create international order.

The third critical ingredient to the emerging European order, one for which neither realist nor idealist approaches has had an appropriate or effective answer, is the fact that most of the sources of conflict are internal to states rather than interstate in nature. The weakness of the states that have become independent or free again after the collapse of the last great European empire has left many of them incapable of managing the ethnic and national cross-pressures that were set loose within their borders. In the past, such issues in the region were dealt with through realist means: imperial (including communist) suppression, war, or both. Neither, however, is a tool currently sanctioned by the international community. Moreover, there is little appetite even among major powers for "realist" involvement in these matters because such involvement is simply no longer cost-effective. But the idealists do not have a comprehensive answer either: no matter how much consensus there is on the norms of social and political order, the absence of usable tools to enforce these norms clearly weakens their effectiveness.

The result is a hybrid situation, where multiple state strategies have been pursued because each seems to provide part of the answer. The residual geostrategic doubts about Russia require a continuing capacity to balance the country's strategic power, but the possibilities inherent in the Russian transformation have also led to ongoing attempts to engage Moscow and bind it into a durable cooperative security framework with the West. The instabilities in east-central Europe have required the international community to develop new tools to prevent or control conflicts. The complex mix of tasks has meant that no one institution has emerged to dominate the new European order. Instead what has taken shape is a somewhat awkward, multilayered institutional framework in which specific institutions absorb those responsibilities for which they are most appropriate.

As is always the case, the events of the post–Cold War transition appear to be part of a coherent narrative only after the event. The major powers reached their initial accord on geostrategic conditions only after intense negotiations and a frenetic attempt to stay on top of events as Germany moved toward unity. In the end, however, Germany was united within an institutional framework that altered the threat from German power, and thus resolved Europe's core strategic problem over the past century. If this issue had not been resolved, then Europe would definitely have been more dominated by realist considerations than it has been and residual uncertainties about Russia would have an entirely different meaning. While Germany's long-run position after unity still remained a preoccupation for some, including some Germans, the institutional framework has helped to attenuate concern over the past few years—in spite of some discord about how to adapt that framework to meet the security challenges of the new Europe.

Equally, it took time and considerable bloodshed in the former Yugoslavia before the countries of Europe began a concerted effort to deal with the legacies of the collapsed empires. While the local situation in Yugoslavia was very much dominated by realist/power considerations, the major powers had little taste for pursuing traditional realist solutions, something that their own domestic politics also precluded. The problems on the ground were probably not susceptible to such an approach in any case. The search for a collective approach to deal with the instabilities that arose within the states of east-central Europe—that is, for the functional equivalent of empire—was as uncertain and contentious as the struggle over German unity.

These two struggles are the most important stories of the search for order in the early years of post–Cold War Europe. Given the ongoing uncertainties about Russia, it is clear that they do not necessarily represent the end of the story. Moreover, there are still a considerable number of ways in which collective efforts to strengthen democracy and prevent conflicts could fail. Nonetheless, this postwar transition in Europe has been profoundly different from those earlier in this century, both in the breadth of its geostrategic stability and in the depth of collective commitment to the building of order on the cornerstone of democratic governance. It will be much more difficult for "geostrategic realities" to undermine the foundation that has been created, even if that foundation undoubtedly remains vulnerable to other factors, most notably to economic conditions in the states in transition. This chapter traces the evolution of the post–Cold War order in Europe between 1988 and 1992, and the bases of strength it created.

The Collapse of the Soviet Empire and German Unification

The earliest phases of transition out of bipolar Europe were a peculiar combination of excitement and caution, of disbelief and hope. Western policymakers concentrated much of their attention on two problems: how to encourage the Soviet Union to allow change to continue by assuring it that the West was not attempting to take advantage of the situation; and how to make sure that support for Western institutions was not eroded by attempts to create a framework to embrace change.[1] The moment the Berlin Wall fell, however, diplomacy in Europe changed dramatically.

This chapter will not rehearse those events that led to German unity.[2] The importance of the outcome—unity within NATO—had vast implications for the post–Cold War European strategic landscape. It was nothing less than a resolution of the problem that had been the root of European instability since the rise of a single German state in the nineteenth century.[3] The fact that German unity could occur at all, and in this form in particular, speaks volumes about how much international relations in Europe had been transformed by the forty-five years of the Cold War. It also left Europe in a condition unprecedented in the modern period: the basic geostrategic situation had been accepted by everyone, so there were no fundamentally revisionist powers and discussions focused on how a security architecture might be created to ensure that the new situation would not work against any country's strategic interest.

All studies of German unification have pointed to the almost uncontrollable cascade of events from November 1989 to October 1990, the complexity of the interactions and judgments, and how much the personalities of key players (along with some luck) helped determine the outcome. Of interest here is only the narrow, if key, question of why the geostrategic outcome of Germany reunited within the framework of NATO proved an acceptable, if not the most desirable, solution to all four powers. U.S. assumptions and policies differed substantially from those of the other three powers. From early on, the Bush administration did not ask whether German unity would occur but how it would occur.[4] It was the only one of the four powers to base its policies on this premise so early. Once the conclusion was drawn that unity was going to happen, no alternative arrangement to a united Germany in NATO could possibly produce security in Europe on terms that would satisfy U.S. needs. Much of this judgment was premised on the the central role that NATO was thought to have played in bringing about the collapse of the Soviet empire, and its continued role as a guarantor of security and stability on the continent. Part of the calculation was purely geostrategic: even if Soviet cooperation was needed to achieve German unity, Soviet power still required balancing, and balancing that power would be difficult with a united Germany outside NATO. Moreover, a new Europe with Germany outside NATO would be geostrategically unstable at best. Thus, the United States focused all its energies on creating the necessary outcome, as implausible as that outcome seemed. The precondition for success was seen to be reassurance of the Soviet Union that this outcome in no way represented the West taking advantage of Soviet weakness.[5] Concretely, this also meant adapting NATO in an effort to persuade Moscow that the NATO into which a united Germany would be integrated was fundamentally different from the NATO of the Cold War.[6]

From the Soviet perspective, many alternative outcomes would have been preferable: a united Germany in NATO presumably did not become acceptable until it proved unavoidable.[7] What enabled the Soviet Union to acquiesce to the outcome was an evolution in Soviet thinking that had many strands, but which assuredly did not come together until that moment in the Caucasus when the final deal was struck.[8] Almost certainly, the institutional framework of European integration, which had helped make the Federal Republic into a different kind of Germany, was central among these strands: it provided a context within which German national aspirations became embedded in larger collective endeavors, and which created unparalleled prosperity in Western Europe to which the Soviet Union needed access to deal with its own internal crises.[9] A new attitude toward Germany had begun to emerge in the late 1980s as a part of a general reevaluation of Soviet policy toward the West.

From what we know of the story inside the Soviet Union and of the negotiations over German unity during the crucial months from November 1989 to July 1990, the above considerations had produced nothing more than a general desire to refashion relations with the West in order to promote reform of the Soviet system.[10] There was certainly no plan to reshape the geostrategic structure of Europe. In the end, it may well have been Soviet weakness that was the crucial factor determining events. Moscow set loose forces it could not control, and the Kremlin could not prevent an outcome that was "one of the most hated developments in the history of Soviet foreign policy."[11] A strong Soviet Union almost certainly would never have permitted this result. But it is important to note that the Soviet Union did not emerge as a revisionist power from the phase of diplomacy that produced German unity, presumably because a united Germany within NATO was ultimately judged to be less of a threat than the alternatives available in 1990, and because NATO itself had begun to modify its posture and to reach out to the East.[12] None of the above is a causal argument; it is clear that the primary causes of Soviet policy can be located in the domestic conditions that produced *glasnost* and *perestroika*. But it does help explain why the outcome finally proved acceptable to the Soviet Union, as it would not have been at the outset of the process.

France and Britain, more clearly than the Soviet Union, wished German reunification to take place within the framework of Western institutions if it had to take place at all. Both, however, were early opponents of reunification, and would have been very happy to see the division of Germany continue as relations between East and West on the continent were restructured. Yet both countries lacked any significant power to inhibit the move toward unity.[13] In the end, their role was comparatively limited in the rush to German reunification and they were forced (especially the French) to concentrate their attentions on maintaining the viability of Western institutions in the face of this dramatic change.[14]

The Europe that emerged from the process of German unification was different from the Europe that emerged from either of the two previous searches for postwar settlements in this century. The absence of any revisionism among the major powers stems from the fact that the unity of Germany was seen not so much as a fundamental geostrategic loss or gain as a confirmation that the geostrategic landscape of Europe had changed profoundly over forty-five years. German unification in 1990 was a proclamation that the institutional framework that had reconciled West Germany's needs and interests with those of its neighbors could do the same for the whole of Germany. This was more a matter of hope than conviction for many, however, and thus it was important to ensure that both the framework and the behavior remained firmly anchored in the new situation.

From the spring of 1990 onward, the major actors focused on strengthening those dimensions of the institutional framework that each believed made German unity acceptable, and on adapting those institutions to make them adequate to the task of managing the new Europe. At the same time, the key actors differed as to what they felt was most important in making unity tolerable, and also in what they felt had been most important in bringing about the new situation. These differences produced some frictions and unease in the West, particularly in the transatlantic relationship.[15] During this period, which was to last for roughly a year and a half, the most significant and revealing agendas were those of Germany, France, and the United States.

Germany had in many ways been responsible for its own unity. Helmut Kohl and Hans-Dietrich Genscher had seized the moment and they and their colleagues had achieved something that none had thought he would experience in his lifetime. But the new Germany owed a great deal to others who had helped make unity possible. And there were still doubts about the new Germany in many parts of Europe, and even across the Atlantic. Germany's primary foreign policy objectives were to alleviate these doubts and to prove that the new Germany would not be different in any strategically problematic way from the old West Germany. Germany's two main concerns were relations with the Soviet Union and with France. Its two most important institutional strategies were centered on the CSCE and on the European Community, respectively. The objective of each was reassurance.

Since the Ostpolitik of Willy Brandt, most German political elites had believed that German unity would come as the result of Europe overcoming its division. For Genscher, and increasingly Kohl, the CSCE had been in large part responsible for creating the conditions that permitted German unity to take place.[16] It was not simply the success of Western security institutions in deterring aggression and bankrupting the Soviet system, but the success of efforts to bridge the divide in Europe and to dismantle fear-based images of the other, which had allowed the Soviet Union to accept German unity. The importance of the CSCE in German thinking during this period is found in the significance Genscher attached to having a formal benediction of German unity at the meeting of CSCE foreign ministers in New York on the eve of unification.[17]

Reassuring the Soviet Union, in the German government's view, necessitated the creation of a European institutional architecture that gave the Soviet Union a continuing role in security affairs—not a replacement for Soviet hegemony, but an equal role within the architecture for the new Europe. The CSCE was considered the appropriate institution for this role, because it had been "responsible" for the conditions that had permitted German unity, because security in the new Europe was to be based on instruments of cooperation, not confrontation, and because it was the only one of the three main institutions surviving the Cold War that had any role for the Soviet Union.[18] The Germans were instrumental in the diplomacy leading to the Paris summit in November 1990 at which the Charter of Paris was signed. The charter launched a new CSCE that was designed to develop mechanisms to prevent conflict and play a greater role in an all-European dialogue over European security. While the CSCE would remain a durable pillar of German policy, reassurance of Moscow also had a special importance until the Soviet Union ratified the 2 + 4 Treaty in March 1991.[19]

The European Community was the other institutional focal point for German policy. The objective was to reassure the French, but also to reassure Germany itself that the primary source of its postwar identity was not only intact, but capable of being adapted to meet the new circumstances. Already during the course of 1990, Germany and France had begun consultations about the future of the European Community, resulting in a serious mutual commitment to deepen the economic, political, and security integration of Europe. While there were considerable differences between the two countries' precise visions of the future shape of Community institutions, these consultations became the driving force behind the Intergovernmental Conferences on Economic and Political Union, initiated the Franco-German Corps, which gave further substance to the inextricability of French and German security, and ultimately led to the Maastricht Treaty signed in January 1992. Few sacrifices could have signaled Germany's powerful commitment as clearly as its agreement to give up new layers of sovereignty in the name of European integration, and specifically the deutsche mark, at precisely the moment the country had regained full sovereignty.[20]

France during this same period was preoccupied by its relationship with the strengthened Germany and concentrated its energies on the future of the European integration process. As long as Germany remained anchored in an integrated Western Europe, France would have a powerful influence over it (in spite of the devaluing of France's nuclear role that came with the end of the European stalemate). Thus, François Mitterrand's answer to German unity was more European integration, and a deepening of Western European institutions. The result was the Maastricht Treaty. A European Union would harness German power in a way that France, while it would formally sacrifice some sovereignty in the economic domain, would actually gain more say over the future direction of Europe, even in economic terms, than it currently possessed. An enhanced European Union would also provide the means by which European states could play a stronger role in world affairs, and Mitterrand, like his predecessors, saw this as a means of projecting French influence in the new context. Indeed, given the changes under way, the only way for France to retain any claim to some measure of independence would be through Europe. There was also an undercurrent of belief that the end of the Cold War would bring the long-awaited drawdown, if not complete withdrawal, of the U.S. presence in Europe, and that the European Union provided the only possible framework for maintaining a geostrategic balance over time with the Soviet Union.[21]

To the extent that France worried about the changes going on in Eastern Europe or the Soviet Union during this period, it was motivated by the fear that German concern with instability in the East could get in the way of strengthening Western European integration. Mitterrand had launched his idea for a European Confederation already at the end of December 1989 at least in part to prevent the European Community from becoming weakened by pressures for its enlargement eastward. He saw the need for a framework to reach out to Eastern Europe, but believed that there was no plausible way for the countries of Eastern Europe to become members of the European Community in the foreseeable future.[22] The confederation was meant to provide some form of reassurance to the former members of the Soviet empire, while buffering the core framework within which France had to manage its relationship with the more powerful Germany.

The United States saw its allies' desires to strengthen the CSCE and European integration as a threat to NATO and to the U.S. role in Europe, precisely those factors that it considered to have been most responsible for bringing about the changes in Europe. The Bush administration also believed that its European partners might ignore the continuing geostrategic requirements for European security and stability in the euphoria of the moment. Europe was vulnerable in the absence of a counterbalance to Soviet power, and NATO was the only institution capable of providing the necessary counterbalance. For key members of the National Security Council staff, NATO was also the only institutional framework capable of sustaining a continued American role in the new Europe, because only NATO would have the popular resonance necessary to maintain support in the American public for involvement in Europe after collapse of the Soviet threat.[23] American efforts were concentrated principally on the political and military adaptation of NATO to the challenges of the new Europe.

During this period, considerable controversy arose between the United States and its NATO allies. The most acute frictions came in connection with European efforts to create the institutional basis for a common foreign and security policy.[24] On February 22, 1991, Reginald Bartholomew, undersecretary of state for security assistance, circulated a memorandum to the European allies in which he warned against doing anything that would weaken NATO or exclude the United States from key European security deliberations.[25] Throughout that same spring, there were considerable tensions over the creation of a rapid reaction force that might be used in connection with conflicts on NATO's periphery, with the French in particular seeing this very much as a test of Europe's capacity to organize itself and the United States wanting all such forces to be under full NATO control.[26] The Europeans showed consternation at what they considered inappropriate American heavy-handedness, which some saw as proof that the United States wanted to continue its dominant role in Europe through its position in NATO despite the profound changes that had taken place in the European strategic landscape.[27] The dispute seemed to reach a peak with the Franco-German announcement on October 16, 1991, of the creation of a Franco-German Corps, which was to form the nucleus of a future European army.[28] Undersecretary of State Robert Zoellick, who had played a key role in shaping American policy toward German unification, wrote a lengthy letter to his German counterpart reminding the German government how important the United States had been in achieving German unity and asking for caution in German policy on the pursuit of a Western European identity in the security area.[29] Finally, at the NATO summit in Rome on November 7–8, President Bush asked NATO allies for a formal reaffirmation of support for the U.S. role in NATO.[30]

What is most interesting about the various actors' institutional preoccupations is precisely how little each represented new thinking for new circumstances. Each in fact represented a continuity of thinking about the role of institutions in the European strategic landscape. Although that landscape had just been transformed fundamentally by the unification of Germany, the means by which a united Germany was to be integrated into the new Europe was a reaffirmation of the institutional framework that had managed the last phase of the Cold War and helped bring about its end. It is not surprising under these circumstances that national objectives for institutional adaptation were an inextricable blend of steps designed to accommodate new circumstances, combined with the reinforcement or correction of what each had always seen as the strengths or flaws of prevailing institutional arrangements. Thus, new fears were very much updated versions of old fears: would Germany's anchoring in the West be loosened, and would the embrace of a vision of a whole Europe undermine the system that provided core security and made the vision possible in the first place?[31] As a consequence, new strategies were very much old strategies in new circumstances, and new debates were very much old debates in a new context. In the past, stalemate had produced a dialectic about how the status quo might be improved without undermining it. Now the absence of formally revisionist powers was doing the same. The year and a half after German unity was basically spent trying to formalize the architecture of the new Europe in a way that would not fundamentally alter relations among the key actors.

The Challenge to Idealism

In the search for a postwar settlement in the late 1940s, geostrategic considerations ultimately overwhelmed idealism and an East-West stalemate enforced a division of Europe that was to endure for over four decades. The same idealistic mix of universal values and collective security emerged once again in the late 1980s as the barriers between East and West finally crumbled. The rhetoric of the "common European home" was more than just rhetoric for many, especially for the Germans who saw the transcending of Europe's division as a means to a more secure order. Until July 1990, they also saw this as the necessary precondition for German unity; and afterward it remained a way to confirm its conditions. The new Europe was to be whole and security was to be achieved cooperatively, through shared norms and values at least as much as power balances.

The basic premise of this new security was that of Kant and the liberals who espoused democratic theories of peace. The same premise had been the basis for early U.S. policy for reconstructing war-torn Europe after the Second World War, but its application had been cut short by the emergence of the Cold War. Having been successfully applied to the western half of Europe since that time, the opportunity now existed to extend that success eastward. This time, however, the roles of the United States and the states of Western Europe were largely reversed. Although by no means insensitive to the transformations taking place in Eastern Europe, the United States was more concerned with consolidating the geostrategic situation. The states of Western Europe were more concerned with the nature of the states that were emerging to the east and less inclined to acknowledge potential geostrategic threats. The transformation of the Soviet empire convinced Western European states that security and stability on the continent could be based primarily on the conversion of communist states into societies sharing Western values.[32]

Eastern Europe's emergence from communism and rapid embrace of the principles of Western democracy and liberal market economics gave considerable grounds for optimism. Moreover, this time around the geostrategic "sorting out" of Europe did not overwhelm the idealistic agenda. On the contrary, the confirmation of a unified Germany within Western institutions was a declaration of support for a Europe organized according to basic Western economic and political norms. The catalog of principles that had formed Basket 1 in Helsinki were no longer simply a way to codify international order while agreeing to disagree on legitimate sources of domestic order. The new consensus on approaches to governance meant the Helsinki norms that had helped bring about the new Europe could also guide it.

The breakdown of bipolarity, however, set loose forces that were far more difficult to manage within this framework than the unification of Germany had been. The implosion of the Soviet Union altered the geostrategic situation in fundamental if not clear-cut ways, and the breakup of Yugoslavia demonstrated that the norms that were to guide the new Europe had little force in the struggle for power in Eastern Europe. At least part of the region between Germany and Russia was more volatile than had been hoped, and the international community had no means to deal with what had become the most important problem for the new European order: the basic weakness of the states that emerged from the collapsed empires in east-central Europe. None of Europe's institutions had been designed to deal with this kind of situation and none had the tools to cope with the challenge. The institutions that had been capable of absorbing Europe's most difficult strategic problem of the past century and a half—the weight of a united Germany—were virtually powerless in the face of individuals who were ultimately willing to slaughter masses of people in order to consolidate domestic political gain.

As Yugoslavia crumbled throughout the second half of 1991, the international community found that its efforts to help only aggravated the crisis. Despite the Western belief that international order stemmed from the quality of the internal order of states, and despite the fact that the basic norms of Western domestic order were increasingly shared throughout Europe, international relations were still structured by the basic norm of sovereignty. States are basically constituted to deal with other states and are proscribed from legitimately intervening in the internal affairs of one another. The challenge to international order this time around, however, was coming from within states rather than between them. During the early period of change in Eastern Europe, much Western diplomacy was focused on the need to protect the integrity of states, including Yugoslavia. The Bush administration's diplomacy was committed to the preservation of a single Yugoslavia long after most of its allies had concluded that this was a lost cause, reportedly because Washington feared the example of a Yugoslav breakup for the increasingly volatile Soviet Union.[33] Once jawboning had failed to halt the breakup of Yugoslavia into its constituent parts, however, the only real means available to the international community to bring events under control was to recognize the newly constituting states, thereby internationalizing the problem. At this point, at least in theory, more weight could be brought to bear in the name of the principles of territorial integrity, non-use of force, and peaceful change.

The effect of the recognition of Slovenia and Croatia in the winter of 1991–92, however, was to accelerate the Yugoslav crisis rather than bring it under greater international control.[34] Using the principle of self-determination as justification for the right of secession (external self-determination), in the absence of carefully negotiated agreements to guarantee the rights of minorities (to provide internal self-determination), was utterly inappropriate in a region of the world that was so ethnically heterogeneous.[35] The international recognition of Slovenia and above all Croatia, in the absence of guarantees to the Serbian minority in the Krajina, only helped assure a violation of the basic Helsinki norms, as it gave neighboring Serbia the perfect excuse for forcibly pursuing its own nationalist agenda of a Greater Serbia.

The good news, given that this all occurred as the Soviet Union was itself decomposing, was that none of the major powers tried to use the Yugoslav situation to posture for geostrategic gain. This surely testifies to the basic geostrategic stability of the continent during the period: history provides ample illustration of precisely how such volatile regions can draw major powers into the quagmire with disastrous results for peace. Indeed, this is all the more remarkable precisely because, just over a year after German unity, the collapse of the Soviet Union did alter the geostrategic situation in Europe once again. That the Soviet Union and then Russia was so little tempted to use the situation to compensate for its own loss of stature points to how much had in fact changed in Europe.

The primary international "strategy" for the former Yugoslavia thus became collective containment of the conflict.[36] This confirmed the basic geostrategic stability that Europe had found with German unity in NATO. The collapse of the Soviet Union, however, did reopen the geostrategic calculus in Europe, and precisely for the region that was most likely to experience instability. Had the Soviet Union continued to exist, the situation in Eastern Europe would have been strategically different than at any time in the previous century. Sandwiched between Moscow and Berlin, the problems of the peoples of this region had always been resolved as part of the geostrategic contest between the two great powers. After the Cold War, neither the Soviet Union nor Germany had any need to dominate the region in order to achieve security, as long as the region remained relatively stable and was not dominated by anyone else. For the first time, the difficulties of nationhood and statehood in Eastern Europe could have been approached in a way that was determined primarily by local conditions.

With the collapse of the Soviet Union, however, the situation became more unstable and less predictable. If the Soviet Union was not a revisionist power in the wake of German unity, it was not at all certain that Russia would not become one again. And from Eastern Europe's perspective, if Russia became revisionist, it was not at all certain that this revisionism would naturally stop at the boundaries of the former Soviet Union. As a consequence, the collapse of the Soviet Union produced a crescendo of claims for rapid membership in Western institutions, particularly NATO, taking advantage of a potentially narrow window of opportunity.

This is not the place to rehearse the debate over the enlargement of NATO, or of the European Union for that matter. These debates were in any case almost entirely part of a subsequent chapter in the development of the new Europe, one that did not begin in earnest until 1993. The point being made here, however, is that the collapse of the Soviet Union put the security of east-central Europe onto the agenda in a different way, for it would have been almost impossible to conceive of any push for incorporation of much of the region into NATO had the Soviet Union continued to exist. The new strategic circumstances also made it all the more imperative for the international community to arrive at an approach for dealing with the instabilities set loose by the collapse of the Soviet and then Russian empires. For if these could not be controlled in an acceptable way, they would almost certainly unleash pressures for strategic posturing or revisionism.

In the winter of 1991–92, the main concern was to find a collective way to prevent any more Yugoslavias. In theory, the new Europe could be one with a divided peace, with some states having more security than others. But a multiplication of situations like that in the former Yugoslavia could resuscitate geostrategic competition, and would pose a fundamental threat to the basic values upon which the new order in Europe was to be built. A continent seeking to base its security on shared norms would have great difficulty turning a blind eye to fundamental violations of those norms. If nothing else, domestic political pressures could force at least some countries to become involved in the name of humanitarian principles. And if some countries would have to become involved, it was imperative that collective mechanisms existed for orchestrating exactly how the international community could become involved. It was simply implausible that the major powers, no matter how much they did not want to be drawn in, could simply cordon off every little brush fire, creating the fire breaks necessary to let them burn themselves out. And given that the area in which instability might occur had become both larger and geostrategically more problematic, it was not guaranteed that collective containment would work forever without more formal mechanisms to channel it and give it form.

Conflict resolution had already been a focus for policymakers' attention since the summer of 1990, primarily in the context of the CSCE, as its participating states sought ways to enhance its role in the new European architecture.[37] Participating states had made a series of tentative steps, as they wrestled with the difficult normative issues involved in legitimating international involvement in domestic conflicts. In January 1991, in Valletta, Malta, member states created a new mechanism by which parties to conflicts could invite third parties to join in the search for solutions.[38] In June of the same year, an emergency mechanism was created with which the CSCE could take up a crisis politically without unanimous consent, a mechanism that was used repeatedly to discuss the Yugoslav situation during that summer and fall.[39] And in November 1991, in the Moscow meeting on the CSCE's Human Dimension, yet another mechanism was created whereby groups of member states could send a mission to investigate a conflict situation within a member state, even against the will of that state.[40] Finally, in January 1992 at a meeting of foreign ministers, the CSCE gave itself the power to take political action against a member state against its will if it was considered in violation of its human rights commitments, a power that was subsequently used to suspend Yugoslavia's membership in the organization. As innovative as these efforts may have been, however, they proved two things very clearly: that states do not like to codify ways to infringe upon the sovereignty of another state, no matter how egregious the behavior of that state; and that legalistic approaches to conflict resolution were bankrupt. The kinds of conflicts that cause the breakup of states highlight the basic contradictions in the norms that states embrace, and these conflicts are not susceptible to formalistic arbitration.

During the spring of 1992, the participating states of the CSCE began to shift their focus and set about creating the means to intervene in potential conflict situations, in what would later be called preventive diplomacy. Although there was substantial disagreement within the CSCE about both principles and mechanisms, it would be wrong to study what happened during the spring and summer of 1992 as primarily a matter of competing state strategies. Differences within the policy communities of member states frequently ran as deep as the differences between member states. The process reached a culmination in the summer of 1992 in the Helsinki II document, which gave birth to a range of creative mechanisms by which the international community could become involved in managing the conflicts born of weak states throughout east-central Europe.[41]

Along with the unification of Germany in NATO and the collapse of the Soviet Union, the decisions taken in Helsinki are almost certainly the most important part of Europe's new order to come out of this period.[42] The mechanisms created there, particularly the High Commissioner on National Minorities, as well as the impulses given for the wider usage of Fact Finding Missions and Mission of Long Duration, were an inventive way for the international community to become involved in conflict situations internal to member states without having to resort to formal decision-making procedures. Helsinki II, without formally proclaiming so on high, represented a fundamental reinterpretation of the norms by which states would interact in Europe. The catalog of principles from Helsinki I was not touched, but the principles were given new content and a new hierarchy, and means were created to promote actively these norms, if not to enforce them. To use the most recent addition to the international relations theory lexicon, the content of the European order was newly constructed at Helsinki. Most important, self-determination in the new Europe would once again primarily mean internal self-determination. The problems in east-central Europe were judged to stem from inadequate civil societies and weak states; these could not be resolved through the creation of more weak states. And even if the means were modest, nonintervention as a principle was clearly relegated to a position inferior to the rights of the international community to be concerned with unstable domestic situations in member states that could spill over and affect international security. At the same time, although member states gave themselves the power to intervene in the affairs of other member states, they by no means undertook a fundamental abrogation of the principle of sovereignty. The interventions in question, while they violate, at least in theory, the external sovereignty of states, are aimed at strengthening the internal sovereignty of these same states, thus strengthening the international system of states and thereby European order.[43]

The story of post–Cold War order formation in Europe obviously does not end with Helsinki II. Indeed, in an important sense, that order is still taking shape in debates over NATO and EU enlargement and the future of Russia's relationship with the rest of Europe, as well as in the continuing transitions to democracy throughout Central and Eastern Europe. Nonetheless, 1992 does mark the end of an important phase in the formation of Europe's order after the Cold War. By this time, the states of Europe had reaffirmed their commitment both to the institutions that provided the framework for German unity and to a European order based on democracy. But they had also discovered that they were willing to go only so far in developing formal mechanisms to help consolidate democracy in the transition states of Central and Eastern Europe. Despite these limits, what transpired during the period between 1988 and 1992 adds up to more of an order than is generally acknowledged, and has left Europe less vulnerable to the principal difficulties that plagued order formation on the continent after World Wars I and II.

Six years further into the process, Europe has still not succumbed to the reflex of geostrategic posturing in search of order, despite the fact that events easily could have called forth this instinct. This attests to the strength of the institutional framework that embraced German unity in removing fundamental revisionist tendencies in Europe. To be sure, Russia could once again become a revisionist power. There is good reason to believe, however, that such revisionism, although it would affect how Europe would have to organize its security toward the outside world, would have little effect on the way European order would be organized internally. It would mark Russia's self-exclusion from Europe, with the boundaries of Europe increasingly defined by the homogeneity of basic norms of political and economic organization. This in itself is a profound difference with the past, as, either way, Europe will no longer be organizing its security "against itself."

That one can now make such an assertion stems not only from the removal of Germany as a strategic issue at the heart of Europe but from the importance of the collective approach to conflict management in Central and Eastern Europe that developed in response to the collapse of Yugoslavia. Collective instruments may not have prevented tragedy in the Balkans, but they may well have prevented a worse tragedy by facilitating the involvement of the international community in preventing similar conflicts while providing a means for states to avoid posturing against one another in response to potential conflict situations. The situation in Central and Eastern Europe after the collapse of the Soviet Union could have looked very different if Germany had not been firmly anchored in Western institutions and if the problems of these states' transitions had not been declared a collective interest.

The biggest difference between post-1989 Europe and earlier periods of European order formation in this century lies in the fact that the most important challenges to order have been from conflicts within states rather than from conflicts between states. Indeed, it has been the uneven quality of states, where "quality" is defined in terms of a state's ability to provide order internally, that has caused the greatest difficulties for implementing the international order that all states of Europe subscribed to in the Charter of Paris, signed in November 1990. That order was to be based on democratic governance, substituting both for other forms of domestic regimes and for external domination. Democratic institutions have not been strong enough, however, to control the ethnic and social cross-pressures that have divided many countries east of the European community after the collapse of communism. This has left Europe in search of a functional equivalent of empire until such time as the basic sources of order that have come to dominate the western half of the continent during the Cold War can take root in the east.

Instead of idealism being overwhelmed by the new strategic realities, the states of the CSCE reconstructed the basic rules of the game of international relations in Europe in order to allow international involvement inside member states in conflict situations that potentially could cause international instability. This had the benefit of both helping to control these conflicts and inhibiting the impulses that some states might have had to become involved in the absence of international presence. At the same time, it also did not take long before the states of the CSCE discovered the limits of the new normative framework they had created. While the new mechanisms quickly proved effective in the Baltic republics and Moldova, they could not prevent further deterioration in the former Yugoslavia, nor halt the wars in Nagorno-Karabakh or, somewhat later, in Chechnya.

Perhaps most important, strengthening the internal sovereignty of states requires more than a rewriting of interstate norms. It requires long-term investment in the economies and civil societies of countries. In other words, a system based on norms actually requires the same type of durable engagement as one based on old-fashioned empires and geostrategic posturing. It is in theory safer, in that wars are assuredly more easily avoided, but it requires no less staying power, and perhaps even more. Whether the states that will determine the ultimate outcome in Europe have this kind of staying power is still an open question. Domestic populations in most Western countries, and even apparently in Russia, are not much more interested in spending money than they are lives in securing order far from their own borders.

Elements of both realism and idealism continue to characterize the European situation, although the balance between the two this time around is different from any other time this century. What makes Europe of the late twentieth century different from the Europe of 1918 to 1945 is the fact that it has become more politically homogeneous than at any time since the French Revolution, and this creates possibilities for international order that simply have not existed among European states with radically different approaches to domestic conflict resolution. The future of order on the continent depends very much on whether this homogeneity is consolidated, and it is unlikely to be traditional geostrategic considerations that will determine the outcome at this level. In all likelihood, it will be determined instead by whether Western states are willing to use the tools they have created to prevent and control conflicts in Central and Eastern Europe and to invest in the transitions to democracy there for as long as it takes for these countries to be successful, and thus to become full partners within an expanding Western institutional framework. That, in turn, may depend on Western democracies' ability to resolve the nagging social and economic contradictions they currently face. However, if the Western institutional framework that resolved Europe's traditional geostrategic dilemmas remains strong, and if democracy in Central and Eastern Europe is consolidated, then even a negative outcome in Russia will not necessarily inhibit the creation of a sturdy post–Cold War European order.

The International Financial System and the Nation-State

Diane B. Kunz

Writing just two years after the end of World War I, John Maynard Keynes observed, "the power to become habituated to his surroundings is a marked characteristic of mankind. Very few of us realize with conviction the intensely unusual, unstable, complicated, unreliable, temporary nature of the economic organization by which Western Europe has lived for the last half century. We assume some of the most peculiar and temporary of our late advantages as natural, permanent, and to be depended on, and we lay our plans accordingly."[1]

Keynes's analysis could easily be applied to our present circumstances; during the twentieth century we appear to have come full circle. Politically this historical phenomenon can be summed up simply by the phrase "from Sarajevo to Sarajevo." The twentieth century began with the First World War, triggered by the assassination of Archduke Franz Ferdinand in that city, while the siege of Sarajevo in the mid-1990s indelibly stamped the identity of the post–Cold War world. This circular pattern is equally true of the international financial order. The functioning gold-standard-based global financial system gave way in the wake of World War I. The ill-fated attempts to glue it back together during the interwar period collapsed in the Great Depression, ushering in a period of autarchy and an even more catastrophic war.

Nation-states walked into the abyss unrestrained by international controls. In the aftermath of World War II, the Anglo-American search for a repaired global financial system fell victim to a new kind of conflagration—the "Cold War." During this bipolar struggle, two separate economic systems competed, each dominated by a single nation-state. Only after the end of the Cold War did these two systems begin to merge. For the first time in nearly a century an integrated global financial system resembling the Edwardian-era structure functions again. The issue for the future is whether the stability of the current system will outlast that of its role model. And the best way to find clues to the orbit of the third incarnation of the international financial system in this century is to reexamine the earlier trajectories.

Versailles and After

The first total war in modern times created the landscape faced by diplomats and bankers in 1918. World War I, which caused nine million deaths among the combatants, completely altered the nature of domestic economies.[2] From wartime factory conversion to the entrance of numerous women into jobs previously reserved for men to rationing and the curbing of consumer expenditures on alcohol, the war altered every aspect of economic existence. Of crucial importance was the depletion of the treasuries of adversaries on both sides of the conflict caused by the enormous expense of more than four years of continuous fighting. The direct cost of the war was approximately $230 billion (in 1914 dollars), and the indirect cost added another $150 billion.[3] Equally important was the loss of foreign markets to upstart nations: chiefly the United States, but also Japan, India, Brazil, and South Africa.[4] At war's end, the great powers staggered

like punch-drunk prizefighters, clinging to each other to keep
from collapsing.

Two of the three chief Central Powers imploded at the end of
the conflict. The Ottoman Empire, perennial "Sick Man of Europe," had been on its deathbed for centuries. The war severed
the life-support system administered by the European great powers. The end of the Austro-Hungarian dual monarchy boded ill,
not only for its citizens but for the health of the European trading
system. In place of the integrated, polyglot Austro-Hungarian
Empire, numerous successor states attempted simultaneously to
carve independent economic and political existences. Germany,
now a fledgling republic, had escaped war damage to its territory
and appeared to be in better shape. But an enormous time bomb,
in the shape of recklessly funded war expenditures, lay buried
in the German economy.

The Allied nations were devastated as well. Imperial Russia
had vanished in 1917. Former allies branded its successor, the
Soviet Union, as an enemy and treated it accordingly. The
newly established communist government had already repudiated the czarist debts and showed little inclination to join the
world economic order.[5] France had borne much of the fighting;
after the war, broke and battle-scarred, it sought an answer
abroad to its economic woes. Great Britain at least escaped the
physical damage of the conflict, but the richest Allied state was
deeply in debt, to its own citizens as well as abroad. Britain's
huge foreign investments would have made financing of its
own war effort possible, but London also needed to bankroll its
allies. During the war Britain had borrowed £1,350 million, of
which over £1,000 million had come from the United States.
His Majesty's government had then lent more than £1,750 million to empire nations and European allies. But the one-third
that had gone to Russia was probably gone for good and the rest
would not be repaid quickly. As longtime British foreign minister Edward Grey put it:

> Some of us thought that economic disaster would make
> itself felt more quickly after the outbreak of war; that it

would rapidly become so acute as to bring war to an end. In that we were wrong, but we were wrong only in our estimate of the time and manner in which economic disaster would make itself felt. . . . The longer the war went on the greater the magnitude of the economic disaster was sure to be, and the more prolonged and enduring would be the effects of it. Those who had the worst forebodings of what war would mean did not over-estimate the human suffering or the economic distress that it has actually caused.[6]

All combatants had deserted the gold standard during the conflict, but Great Britain's lack of fealty struck deepest at the world financial system. The City of London, financial district to the nation and the world, had presided over a truly integrated global system. The resumption by the United States of specie payments in 1879 had inaugurated a forty-year period in which virtually all major countries followed "the rules of the game." Gold was the coin of the realm, either directly or by virtue of paper issued against gold. The privately owned Bank of England and City bankers, not the British government, ran this show. They were judge and jury, creditors but also facilitators. The checks and balances against overreaching or poor dealings did not lie in the political arena but derived from market forces as interpreted by the Bank of England and the City. The vast wealth of the British Empire made this feat possible. Almost 40 percent of British savings in the late nineteenth century were invested abroad each year, whereas immediately before the war foreign investment accounted for over 30 percent of accumulated British wealth.[7] If the British bankers abdicated, who would replace them?

The obvious answer was the United States. During the Great War the United States had come of age economically. At the beginning of the conflict it still depended on London for commodities financing as well as investment.[8] In 1914 the United States was a net debtor on foreign account of about $3.7 billion. At the war's end it was a net creditor in about the same amount, as well as banker to the Allied nations.[9] But Washington had stood apart from its confrères. While entering the fray on the side of the Allied powers, it insisted that it be an "associated" rather than "allied" power. This nomenclature revealed the deeper reality that the United States had no intention of abandoning the strictures of its founding fathers against entangling alliances. Uncle Sam may have lent more than $7 billion to the Allies, but now American officials expected to be repaid.[10]

These issues dominated much of the negotiations at the Paris Peace Conference that formally opened on January 18, 1919. The British and French governments looked to Germany for reparations that they could use to repay their debts to the United States. Both Prime Minister David Lloyd George of Britain and Premier Georges Clemenceau of France had encouraged their publics to imagine large sums coming from across the Rhine. Reparations were a time-honored postwar device, extracted by Germany after the Franco-Prussian War and the Brest-Litovsk Treaty. Moreover, as finally quantified in the London Schedule of 1921 the bill sent to Berlin was not outrageous.[11] But many Germans never accepted the legitimacy either of this obligation or of the Versailles settlement as a whole.

The result was the failure of the German government to pay reparations, which triggered the French and Belgian occupation of the Ruhr in January 1923 and the catastrophic hyperinflation that devastated the German middle and lower-middle classes.[12] As the stalemate continued, British officials, fast losing confidence in the Versailles Treaty, informed their French counterparts that their patience was up. Another way to enforce the financial obligations of the Versailles Treaty needed to be found.[13]

This time the Americans did come to the rescue, but in this case they came in the form of private bankers. Washington continued to stand aloof from international economic questions. The Coolidge government also maintained the fiction that war debts and reparations had nothing to do with each other. So in stepped the House of Morgan, following the precedent set by City bankers before the Great War. At that point the Morgan partnership controlled three banking houses: J. P. Morgan and Company in New York, Morgan, Grenfell and Company in London, and Morgan et

Compagnie in Paris.[14] Accustomed to working with the British
and French governments (they had acted as their bankers during
the First World War), Morgan partners provided the brains behind the 1924 Dawes Plan designed to fund reparations in a
sound and practical manner. Thomas Lamont and Russell Lef-
fingwell led the team, producing a settlement that appeared to
satisfy most of the participants.

The Morgan partners also collaborated with various central
bankers, especially Benjamin Strong and Montagu Norman, to
restabilize European currencies in the years that followed.
Strong, formerly the head of the Morgan-connected Bankers Trust
Company, commanded the Federal Reserve Bank of New York.
The fledgling Federal Reserve System (which had been created
only in 1913) virtually ignored the international aspects of central banking.[15] Strong happily took it upon himself to remedy this
gap. With no statutory authority, he made the Federal Reserve
Bank of New York the American central bank for foreign transactions. Using his contacts with the Morgan bank, he helped sell
the Dawes bonds and assisted as well in the return to the gold
standard by Britain in May 1925.[16]

The chief architect of the pound's return to gold at its prewar
parity of £1 = \$4.86 was the bizarre Montagu Norman, governor
of the Bank of England. Known for his sinister goatee and periodic nervous breakdowns, Norman presided over an institution
that was proud of its private status. Norman viewed the British
government as merely his largest client and treated Downing
Street accordingly.[17] But Norman was not alone in believing that
a gold-backed pound with a value fixed at its prewar parity was
essential if London was to regain its previous financial predominance. The embattled British industrial position militated in favor of this restoration: London's international accounts increasingly drew on invisibles for their sustenance. And how better to
snare international accounts than to prove that the pound was
once again as good as gold?[18] Equally important was the British
elite's long-standing confusion of the strength of the pound with
the power of the empire.

The success of these financial policies and the apparent diplomatic triumph of Locarno made 1925 seem a new dawn of peace and prosperity. Delegating the economic aspects of the peace to private entities had apparently worked well. Governments congratulated themselves on successfully avoiding hard choices. Norman's instruction to Chancellor of the Exchequer Philip Snowden—you handle the budgetary side of things and I'll do the monetary half—seemed to reflect a desirable division of labor. But half a decade later it all fell apart. The Wall Street crash, the abortive Young Plan, and the Great Depression wrecked the fragile European economic order. On September 18, 1931, the British government decided to sever the pound's connection to gold.[19] The slump had convinced London's bankers and government officials that the City could no longer run the world system by itself.

American private bankers were overwhelmed too, but President Herbert Hoover and Secretary of State Henry L. Stimson could do little to help Europe after the Great Depression had brought the United States to its knees. Yet the Republicans were a model of international fraternity compared with their successors. Franklin Roosevelt took office determined to put American economic interests first. That meant avoiding any entangling international financial commitments, such as those mooted at the World Economic Conference of June–July 1933. Roosevelt's message telling the conclave that its concern should be repayment of war debts has long been criticized, and rightly so. British and French leaders, however, not to mention the Nazi regime that had come to power at the same time as the Roosevelt administration, proved equally determined to go it alone.

Autarchy was the order of the day; cooperation had become a dirty word. The international system was dead. Nation-states now reigned supreme. The depression had defeated private and central bankers alike. In strode national governments amassing unheard-of power over foreign economic policy. Washington seized control of the Federal Reserve Bank of New York in 1935; the French government nationalized the Bank of France a year later.[20] Upon becoming chancellor of the exchequer in November

1931, Neville Chamberlain made it clear that he and the cabinet, not Norman, would determine British financial policy.[21] Each of the governments concluded that what central banks possessed (in British prime minister Stanley Baldwin's famous phrase) was "power without responsibility."[22] Accountability would be possible only if central banks were answerable to governments and, through them, to voters. Leaders as different as Roosevelt, Chamberlain, and Léon Blum believed that international finance was too important to be left to the bankers.

The Post–World War II Era

On the same day in 1931 that British leaders reached their painful decision to sever the pound from the gold standard, Japanese troops invaded Manchuria. Aggressive acts launched by Germany and Italy as well as Japan erupted throughout the 1930s, eventually leading to another global conflict. It began in September 1939 as a European war and became a truly worldwide conflagration in 1941, when the Soviet Union and the United States entered the fray. As the conflict ground on, American leaders pondered the nature of the postwar economic order. Much had changed during the depression decade. Of chief importance was the spread of "Hullism"—a gospel preached by U.S. secretary of state Cordell Hull, among others, that saw economic barriers as a central cause of the Great Depression and the Second World War. By this logic, increasing international economic cooperation was essential to the postwar world.[23] But structural changes wrought by the New Deal meant that American intervention would be led by Washington, not New York.

With this goal in mind American and British diplomats began working on the framework of an international financial order soon after the United States entered the war. The resulting Bretton Woods agreements, signed in July 1944, created the International Monetary Fund and the International Bank for Reconstruction and Development, known as the World Bank. The IMF would oversee the international financial system, attempting to avoid the disastrous devaluations that characterized the depression decade while allowing a return to currency convertibility and multilateral transactions.[24] The World Bank would provide capital to countries struggling to reconstruct their shattered infrastructure.

Given the other golden rule (he who has the gold, rules), it is not surprising that the United States largely determined the shape of these institutions. Despite the celebrated quip by Keynes about the Americans that "they have all the money-bags but we have all the brains," U.S. treasury secretary Henry Morgenthau and bureaucrat Harry Dexter White had their way on all important issues. The Second World War had transformed the U.S. economy from a basket case to the American dream. The U.S. government possessed one-third of the world's monetary gold in 1945, while the American gross national product accounted for one-half of the entire world's output. Clearly, the United States would determine the shape of the postwar economic order.

That the World War II production miracle was apparently born in the private sector significantly affected the conception of the world monetary order that Washington intended to orchestrate.[25] The depression-era doubts about bankers and businessmen had vanished. The growing resurgence of the Republican Party, always more oriented toward businessmen, mirrored this change. The Bretton Woods agreements therefore enshrined the private sector as the funding mechanism for the putative new world order. IMF currency stabilizations and World Bank loans would make the world safe for U.S. trade and financial expansion. The relatively small American appropriations for these institutions made sense only because government funding was intended as a beachhead for the private sector, not its replacement.[26]

This faith in private finance was a major distinguishing point between the United States and its grand-alliance partner the Soviet Union. The growing tension between the two nations found expression in dictator Josef Stalin's decision not to join the IMF in December 1945. This action dealt the U.S. dream of an integrated financial world a severe blow. During the next two years the disputes over German reparations, Turkey and Iran, and Eastern European governance led to a new state of being, the Cold War. One of the most successful American shots at the Soviet Union was economic.

The Marshall Plan, launched in June 1947, embodied the dual American response to the Soviet political threat as well as postwar European economic collapse.[27] Wartime destruction and the cruel winter of 1946–47 had made a mockery of the optimistic wartime prognostications of American policymakers. The Bretton Woods blueprints had not been designed for so massive a reconstruction task. As Europe lay economically paralyzed, American diplomats made the connections that poverty equals protest, protest brings chaos, and chaos leads to communism. At that point, it was less Soviet armies than Soviet siren songs that menaced the West.

The administration of Harry Truman proved willing to appropriate huge sums of money, but only on the condition that the United States be fully in charge of any aid program. Although Secretary of State George Marshall had framed his proposal as an invitation to Europeans to draw up a scheme for using American aid, that was a propaganda device intended to defuse Soviet charges of American imperialism. Equally, extending the invitation to all European countries to join the program was a public relations stunt. Fortunately, Stalin never called the American bluff, instead ordering his foreign minister, Vyacheslav Molotov, to leave the Paris negotiations in July 1947.

The eighteen countries that participated in the Marshall Plan enjoyed incredible prosperity in the next quarter century.[28] The Marshall Plan provided the United States with the first victory in the Cold War. Paradoxically, the invention of nuclear weapons virtually ruled out direct military confrontation between the superpowers at a very high price: the Soviet Union and the United States had to spend staggering sums to maintain the balance of power. Meanwhile both nations waged psychological warfare in the main battlefields and limited war on the periphery. Economic strength and economic successes proved crucial to these struggles.

The bipolar security division of the Cold War world had its echo in a concurrent economic division. For four decades two separate systems operated. The American sphere was predominantly capitalist, largely under the control of the private sector but secured by a government safety net. Central banks, all now owned by their governments, alone and in tandem worked to keep their domestic economies intact and the American-dominated international system spinning.

The size of the safety net varied from country to country. Many European nations created significant nationalized industries and provided large welfare subsidies. Free education through university level became a right for any child bright enough to take advantage of this unprecedented opportunity. Whole new towns arose, partially redeeming the post–World War I pledge of homes for heroes. In the United States the same process took place camouflaged as defense spending. Keynesianism, not to mention socialism, remained a dirty word to many Americans. But the domestic side effects of the national security state did as much to spread the wealth in the United States as state socialism did abroad.[29]

The capitalist economic system depended on the United States—as provider of gold, lender of last resort, and, crucially, military protector. Bretton Woods furnished the United States multilateral cover under which to run the Western economic order. The many paths of the interwar period had become one. At the same time the North Atlantic Treaty Organization committed the United States for the first time in its history to defend other nations. The American border was pushed as far east as Berlin. While military expenditures became a constant in U.S. budgets, providing allied defense allowed the United States to demand economic cooperation from other nations as well as to exact economic assistance.

Although the Bretton Woods agreements provided the framework for the Western economic system, they never actually worked as intended. Immediately after European currencies generally returned to convertible status in 1958, the system began to falter. A decade of stopgap measures followed. Then, in August 1971 Richard Nixon decided that even the modicum of international fealty paid by the United States to the gold-based financial order was too much. Ironically, severing the link between the dollar and gold and floating the dollar only increased Washington's power and influence. From a fixed-rate gold-exchange system, the Western world moved to a pure dollar standard based on a currency with nothing tangible to back it up. With dollars weighing down Western treasuries, allies found that they had no choice but to support the dollar. That the United States returned to debtor status in 1985 only further heightened foreign dependence on continued American financial well-being. The United States would prove the truth of the banking adage: a banker who lends a little has a borrower, a banker who lends a lot has a partner. With the Bretton Woods system gone, the dollar emerged as the foundation of the capitalist international order.

Periodic government bailouts of private-sector troubles, such as the oil shocks and the Third World debt crisis, did not shake the general faith in the efficacy of private enterprise as the engine of mass wealth. Indeed, beginning in the twilight years of the Cold War, the private sector made an unexpected comeback in states that had been dominated by social democratic economic models put in place in the 1940s. Government economic intervention became increasingly discredited. Margaret Thatcher's government set the tone by selling off government properties, including British Telecom, British Petroleum, and British Airways. The Socialist president of France, François Mitterrand, quickly abandoned his left-wing economic policies upon taking office in 1981; and from the Nordic bulwarks of the welfare state to Latin America's newly empowered democracies, the byword was: markets always fight and markets will be right.

The Soviet Union managed to match American defense spending throughout most of the Cold War. The communist economic system was also based on the nation-state. The Soviet Union dominated its Eastern European sphere of influence as effectively as the United States did in the West.[30] The price proved high: civilians in Russia and behind the Iron Curtain generally lived a gray, drab existence, devoid of consumer creature comforts. Not for them the cornucopia available to almost all classes on the other side of the divide. In his famous kitchen debate with Soviet premier Nikita Khrushchev in 1959, Nixon said: "We do not want our decisions made at the top by one government official that all houses should be the same. . . . [And] is it not far better to be talking about washing machines than machines of war, like rockets? Isn't this the kind of competition you want? . . . Let the people choose the kind of house . . . the kind of ideas they want. We have many different manufacturers and many different kinds of washing machines, so that the housewives may have a choice."[31] Nixon's way turned out to be not only the American way but the way of the future.

Then Is Now: The Post–Cold War Order

The post–Cold War era came upon us suddenly. We are again one world, at least financially. By the century's end, we had finally reestablished the pre–World War I global interconnections. In this reunited world, the capitalist way leads triumphantly. This resurgence of faith in market economics comes at a time when government control over capital markets has deteriorated significantly. The enormous technological changes of the past twenty years are partly responsible. Computers have made possible new forms of financial trading as well as twenty-four-hour markets. In this high-velocity, high-risk world, the executives of Barings are not the only ones asking, who's in charge here? The speed of electronic transfers combined with the sheer volume of dollars and other currencies now circulating around the globe threatens to overwhelm the control exercised by governments and central banks. Moreover, many of the new financial instruments, such as derivatives and asset-backed securities, have not been tested in a bear market, not to mention a depression. Neither do we know the social or political implications of a major slump when so great a proportion of citizens act as shareholders. These facts might inspire governments to seek greater control over their capital markets. Yet the opposite is occurring. Of great interest is the strong movement to privatize or depoliticize central banking. We have truly come full circle here: politicians again long for a Montagu Norman to serve as their straw man. Unwilling to directly disappoint constituents who simultaneously seek entitlements and reduced taxes, a growing number of office holders advocate independent central bankers to serve as their government's nanny.[32] Forgotten is the logic of the 1930s that led to nationalization of central banks in the first place. This desire is particularly understandable in countries formerly controlled by communists. While newly enfranchised voters lust after the goods capitalism offers, they understandably wish to retain the social security system that characterized communist states. That there is no such thing as a free lunch has not yet sunk in.

The United States, the only surviving superpower, continues to dominate the world financial order. When Washington sets a goal as a top priority, a majority of one still suffices. The Mexican crisis of 1994–95 provides a case study of Washington's economic decision making in the post–Cold War world.[33] Although the size of the Mexican economy roughly equals that of Los Angeles, the Clinton administration, through its successful push for the North American Free Trade Agreement (NAFTA), advertised Mexico as a fit partner for the United States. Through early 1994, the Mexican economy flourished. Among other things, the combination of low U.S. interest rates and the NAFTA agreement, whose chief importance was to guarantee Mexico immunity from any American protectionist impulses, lured massive foreign investment into the country.[34]

But the political uncertainty that dominated the 1994 Mexican election campaign, starting with the assassination of presidential candidate Luis Donaldo Colosio, undermined foreign confidence. At the same time Mexicans, understanding that the peso was overvalued against the dollar, took advantage of the unrealistic exchange rates to go on a consumption spree. The right economic solution would have been for the government to absorb the pain of a 20 percent peso devaluation. But the ruling Institutional Revolutionary Party (PRI), determined to win the upcoming presidential election, knew that any such action could have a bad result if cost-of-living increases or a recession caused voters to punish it at the polls.

After winning the election to maintain the PRI's hold on power, the new president, Ernesto Zedillo Ponce de León, inherited an economy with a severe short-term problem. That the Mexican economy was solvent and had good long-term prospects was little comfort to foreign investors who now fled the peso in droves. No one wanted to be the last one out. Mexican foreign-exchange reserves, around $30 billion in March 1994, plummeted to probably $5 billion. Worse still, the Mexican government had taken to upholding the stability of the peso by issuing short-term securities linked to the dollar known as Tesobonos. While the use of this financial instrument encouraged foreign investors to remain in Mexico, it meant that in the event of a steep devaluation the cost to the Mexican treasury would be that much higher.

Within weeks of taking office Zedillo had no choice but to announce a quick devaluation. The market took it badly and the peso dropped 50 percent. The spillover effects proved disastrous, as foreign investors shunned other emerging markets, both in Latin America and in Asia. With outstanding Tesobono obligations of $23 billion, Mexico faced a liquidity crisis of drastic proportions. In the United States, the Clinton administration found itself staring straight at an economic and political disaster. Much of the foreign investment in Mexico was American. Unlike the Latin American debt crisis of 1982, when banks were at risk, now ordinary Americans, through their pension and other funds, found their nest eggs at stake. Moreover, the Clinton administration, by making NAFTA a key part of its first-term agenda, had oversold the Mexican economy. Now, without U.S. help, that confederate would collapse. The specter of penniless Mexicans fleeing in large numbers to the United States also conjured political problems for a president reeling from his party's election debacle in 1994 but intent on winning a second term.

Clinton administration officials quickly prepared a $50 billion rescue package and sent it to Congress. Treasury Secretary Robert Rubin was apparently confident that because the rescue made economic sense it would be politically palatable. But Congress, under the gleeful control of Republicans for the first time in forty years, revolted. Very quickly the package became disparaged as merely a Wall Street bailout. Scheduled hearings would have dragged out any solution until far too late. Timeliness and certainty of outcome are the key elements of any financial rescue. Pontificating in the Senate and House threatened both.

Clinton and his team gave up on Capitol Hill and instead arranged their own executive-branch rescue. American money in the form of a $20 billion line of credit came from the Treasury's Exchange Stabilization Fund. Fortunately for the president, this money could be spent without congressional authorization. Yet while the action was technically legal, this fund, created in the wake of the devaluation of the dollar in 1933, was meant to prop up only the most secure currencies. No one could say that about the peso in early 1995. At the same time the U.S. government pressured the IMF into appropriating $17.8 billion. This sum far exceeded what the IMF's rules allowed and was opposed by European nations with far less at stake in Mexico.[35] But the United States got its way: the rescue went through, and it proved a great success. The Mexican economy, albeit after a severe recession, rebounded. Mexico repaid bailout monies early. And NAFTA remains in place.

What does the Mexican case say about international ability to manage financial crises? So much still depends on the United States, and especially on the American president. It is clear that Congress wants neither the power nor the responsibility for international financial decision making. And it is the inappropriate vehicle for action. Just as there can be only one hand on the nuclear trigger, so must the executive branch be in charge of international crisis management. When an economic storm hits, reaction must be quick and sure if panic and downward spiral into disaster are to be avoided.

Unlike in the nuclear field, however, effective U.S. responsibility for international economic management is two-headed. The Mexican rescue demonstrates the range of presidential power. But equally important is the role of the U.S. Federal Reserve Board. Under its two most recent chairmen, Paul Volcker and Alan Greenspan, the Fed has taken a major role in managing the various international economic crises of the past fifteen years. Both men have done an excellent job. Yet the notion that one appointed official can hold significant sway over the international economy as a whole gives pause. Delegating such power to one virtually unaccountable individual is not only antidemocratic but it may, in the future, be antithetical to good market operations, particularly as the international economy expands to include former communist states.

The many political and economic unknowns of these transitional times have injected a great deal of uncertainty into the economic outlook. The nature of the players and their respective amount of influence are central issues. American economic and financial leadership is certainly not a given over the long term— but for the moment it seems assured even though the United States' share of world output continues to shrink. This enduring power and influence stems in part from America's enormous domestic market, great natural resources, and large pool of educated workers. Moreover, no rival possessing the necessary economic power as well as political inclination to take over the role has yet emerged. Russia remains in a state of virtual collapse, with neither an effective central government nor a useful industrial base. The vaunted Japanese miracle has burst, and Germany is still absorbing the costs of reunification. Although a German-dominated European central bank might step up in the future, governments of both the right and the left in Germany have been determined to meet the strict economic criteria it had insisted on for joining the club of charter euro issuers and making sure that other European nations don't miss the euro bus.

In Asia, a major player waits on the sidelines. The expanding Chinese capitalist base rests on shaky political foundations. The outcome of the struggle for power in the People's Republic of China will greatly influence the world's financial markets. Yet there is no road map to its future structure. The death of Deng Xiaoping has opened a leadership vacuum at the highest levels of the PRC. With little true Marxist faith to hold this disparate nation together, it is not far-fetched to think that the Chinese leadership will use economic repression to keep the country intact. Moreover, uniquely among communist and former communist states, the PRC's army is heavily involved in business. With the People's Liberation Army currently the strongest structure in the PRC, what does it mean for the future of the Chinese government that a free market will directly threaten the military's power base? Does the Chinese leadership understand the importance of a free flow of business news to a successful capitalist market? Does it care?

These questions are important to us all. Not only does China possess the world's largest monetary reserves since its July 1997 takeover of Hong Kong, but with a population of 1.3 billion its domestic market dwarfs all others. Any economic decision made by Beijing can have enormous "knock-on" effects, in which the impact ripples from one country to another around the globe. If the Chinese government, for example, were to adopt Henry Ford's goal of a car in every family's garage, the consequences for world energy consumption could create a new oil shock. The received wisdom is that China's fully joining the world economy is obviously a good thing. That may be so, but the long-term ramifications of so large and rich an economy becoming fully integrated into the capitalist world are little understood.

Nation-states rose to preeminence in the twentieth-century financial order. Now their influence is under attack from two directions: on one hand, the markets are eating away at national control over financial institutions, and on the other the continued growth of supranational blocs may have the same effect. Will the nation-state become as extinct as state Marxism? Key here is the still ongoing push for a euro currency. Who joins the euro bloc and who makes the fiscal and monetary decisions for euro nations will greatly affect the international financial order. If the euro becomes the generally used European currency, it may indeed propel the United States to expand NAFTA both geographically and substantively. An Asian-based regional competitor, at this moment still an unlikely possibility, will then seem more attractive to Pacific Rim nations that feel excluded from large market sectors.

The euro, in time, may also become a rival to the dollar as the key reserve and trading currency. In the long run it is the strength of a nation's underlying economy that propels a currency to key status. The European Union generates about 31 percent of world output and 20 percent of world trade; the United States accounts for 27 percent of world output and 18 percent of global trade. Yet the dollar is used for between 40 and 60 percent of world finance.[36] These numbers indicate that the dollar's monopoly status will at some point end and be replaced by a dollar-euro duopoly. If that happens, the influence of the United States on international economic decision making will decline proportionately. Such shared power does not augur well for nation-state control over an ever larger, ever more complicated international economy.

Yet the dollar's singular role may not quickly end. While underlying fundamentals are important, a nation needs the requisite will to achieve international economic influence and key-currency status. The British government's decision that foreign economic power and influence were crucial to British foreign policy played a larger role in the pound's ability to carry more weight than it deserved for decades than did the existence of the empire, commonwealth, and sterling area. The United States had the requisite economic power in the interwar years but shunned any responsibility for the international financial system. It is hard to see the European Central Bank possessing the necessary impetus to dethrone the dollar rapidly.

Such delay may be all to the good. The evolving nature of international capital markets makes its essential that national and supranational bodies attempt to exert control over the markets before it is too late. Greater institutionalized efforts to cooperate across national and regional lines are essential. As the fallout in Malaysia and Singapore in the wake of the Mexican crisis illustrated, today there is no such thing as a local financial collapse. The first level of cooperation should be statutory and information-based. The successful American regulation of domestic securities markets is based on disclosure of all relevant information. The Securities Act of 1933 and the Securities Exchange Act of 1934 do not require issuers to sell good securities. They simply mandate that the sellers disclose the nature of what they are offering.

The internationalization of markets makes it imperative for securities laws to be extended globally. This task could be accomplished by each nation forbidding sales to its citizens of securities that lack underlying documentation meeting Securities and Exchange Commission standards. Each nation has the power to enact such legislation for its own citizens. Such regulation would limit the risk factor in national markets. At the same time the United States and fellow G-7 governments should consider encouraging major traders of foreign securities to form an entity such as the interwar-era Foreign Bondholders Protective Council. Such an industry group could require frequent reporting by issuers not bound by domestic securities laws and would act as a clearinghouse for information. Should a situation like Mexico reoccur, the bondholders group could also administer reschedulings and readjustments. Having a standing committee ready to cope with a major financial problem is an additional safeguard against serious disruptions of the world economic system. Issuers would cooperate if the alternative were to be priced out or shut out of the international securities markets.

Creating an international bankruptcy code would provide another buffer for capital markets. Chapter 9 of the U.S. Bankruptcy Code contains provisions for municipal bankruptcy.[37] It incorporates Chapter 11 "work-out" provisions that allow debtors to avoid liquidations. The intent is to allow debtors a breathing space; protected from their creditors, they can return to financial health. Using these provisions as a precedent, a legal framework designed to deal with sovereign issuer defaults could be promulgated that would do much to cure international defaults and keep them from spreading. Making acceptance of these provisions by sovereign borrowers a condition of IMF credits would ensure quick adoption by the most likely candidates. The code could be administered by the IMF as well.

The most serious disruption of the international system would be a world depression. In the twenty-five years since the last worldwide recession the global markets have expanded and mutated beyond all recognition. The stock market tumble of 1987 is the nearest thing we have to a precedent. At that point the Federal Reserve System, led by Alan Greenspan, acted quickly and wisely. Following Walter Bagehot's dictum, the Fed opened its spigot to all comers, avoiding the kind of credit crunch that followed the 1929 crash. As a result, the damage was contained, allowing stock markets to recover and then surpass their 1987 levels. In the succeeding decade, however, the number of players and the financial instruments available for trading have changed dramatically. Whether the Fed, alone or with other countries and central banks, can contain the next depression is a crucial question. In 1930, Keynes wrote, "we are suffering, not from the rheumatics of old age, but from the growing-pains of over-rapid changes, from the painfulness of readjustment between one economic period and another. The increase of technical efficiency has been taking place faster than we can deal with the problem of labour absorption; the improvement in the standard of living has been a little too quick."[38] Keynes and his contemporaries flunked their great test. We don't know how we will do.

11

Global Issues and the New Security Agenda

Paul Kennedy

When the statesmen of 1919 and 1945 confronted the altered strategic landscapes of their respective postwar worlds, they were increasingly aware of newer forces at work alongside their traditional great-power concerns. Calls for democracy, nationalist stirrings in the colonies, demands by labor movements and trade unions for greater social and economic justice, ideas about a new world order enhanced through international organization, new technologies and forms of communication, all made the task of statecraft more complex and challenging than in Talleyrand's day. Like most leaders brought up in the Western tradition, they saw their job essentially as a Burkean one: how to preserve the order and stability many of their peoples ached for while admitting reasonable demands for change and heading off calls for more revolutionary action. Although their desire to preserve essential national interests remained unchanged, and balance-of-power considerations could never be set aside, they could see that the security agenda was also affected by novel elements, including shifting economic balances, altered social expectations, and the arrival of new political actors, all of which required thoughtful handling.

Much the same set of challenges, though probably in intensified form, face today's policymakers as they grapple with global changes at our century's beginning. It would be foolish to deny that traditional balance-of-power and military security worries have disappeared with the end of the Cold War. As viewed from the Pentagon (to take but one obvious perspective), innumerable problems loom. How does one satisfactorily deal with a rising China, whose economic and military growth casts a shadow across Asia and threatens to reduce American regional influence? How does one handle a badly maimed and unpredictable Russia, especially in regard to the disposal of its nuclear materials and its relations with its unstable neighbors? How does one best keep the pressure upon "rogue states" and foil their efforts to damage American interests? How can a lasting Mideast peace accord be brought forward? How can one halt the spread of weapons of mass destruction, particularly across Asia?[1] How should peace-enforcement operations be carried out in future conflicts, if such actions should be pursued at all? And how does one prepare one's armed forces for so many different forms of military contingencies?

While recognizing that such a plethora of existing military and diplomatic tests face today's national leaderships, this chapter focuses on certain newer forces for change and instability as humankind moves into the new century. None of these would traditionally have been regarded as matters requiring the attention of a War Department or an Admiralty, and some scholars will argue that they ought not to be so regarded as "security" issues now. But if the West's strategic purpose is to establish lasting peace and prosperity worldwide in order to reduce the sources of conflict, then it seems unreasonable to exclude these matters from consideration and possible action.

What this entails, therefore, is a recognition that certain forces for change that have absolutely no military security aspect in their origin could and can produce consequences that affect international stability and security. Let us start with an obvious, indeed almost predictable, example. The financial and communications revolution so ably described in this volume by Diane Kunz originated in a historic conjuncture of Thatcher-Reagan market-liberalization measures, the coming of computerized trading in stocks and currencies, and an explosion in ways to access information about investment opportunities. The first and obvious result has been to create a global marketplace that rewards the players who accept Wall Street rules and punishes those (including national governments) who resist "harmonization" with these fast-flowing, pervasive market forces. Those punished can include developed countries—one thinks of the market's drubbing of the Mitterrand government, and therefore the franc, in the early 1980s because of its socialist policies—and, much more frequently, emerging-markets states from Belarus to Brazil.

But precisely because these private flows of capital are so much larger than the funds provided through multilateral financial institutions, and because individual investors are apt to withdraw their monies at the first sign of trouble, the system has great potential for instability. It also possesses an inherent capacity to create "knock-on" effects far from the place of the original breakdown: when a Mexican peso crisis can produce ripples throughout the Western Hemisphere, hurting the stock markets and currencies of nations that are performing well according to objective economic criteria, it is safe to say that few if any nations are secure against future turbulences of this sort.

The point here is not the sudden discovery that the free market system is naturally a volatile one—Schumpeter warned long ago about the "creative gales" of capitalism—but that there is no such thing as strictly economic flows of capital. When an emerging-market country such as Indonesia or Brazil experiences large currency outflows, followed by the devaluation of its currency (and loss of its international purchasing power), the closure of factories, and a surge in unemployment, then the social peace in that state—and thus its political stability—can be shaken, and the international scene can become troubled. This is hardly a matter that regular security forces are equipped and trained to handle. Yet who would deny that the precariousness or stability of Brazil and Indonesia—and, for that matter, of Turkey, India and Pakistan, Mexico, Ukraine, and other states—is not, ultimately, a security matter?[2]

If our traditional military security apparatus is not equipped—and it was of course never intended to be equipped—to deal with global financial instabilities, it is even less well prepared to understand let alone handle the sometimes explosive effects of dramatic population increases in so many parts of the world. In traditional strategic thought the population factor often played a large role in statesmen's calculations, but almost always in the favoring of demographic increases: more births translated into more men for the army, more inhabitants to carry the tax burdens, and so on. Even in the twentieth century this sort of thinking had a powerful influence in politics, as could be seen in the debates over the pre-1914 army increases in Europe or in the official campaigns in Japan, Nazi Germany, and the USSR in the 1930s to encourage greater family size. In other words, swift demographic growth was viewed as a strategic asset, not a liability, at least so long as that expansion took place among one's own kith and kin. And if this created a demand for lebensraum next door or across the seas, then that was simply part of the natural order of things. Few denizens of Alexander the Great's Macedonia, the Norwegian fjords in Viking times, Elizabethan England, or pre-1789 France—all of which experienced a population explosion, and contained large numbers of ambitious, unemployed young men eager to march to the wars—bemoaned this surge in numbers.[3]

It was therefore left to a non-military observer like Thomas Malthus—who composed his *Essay on Population,* among other reasons, in response to the turbulence of the French Revolution—to draw attention to the potential threats to stability and security that could flow from too-swift demographic change.[4] Before developing this argument further in today's contexts, how-

ever, it is important to stress that adjective "potential." It is simply not the case that a fast growth in human population
automatically produces social and economic instabilities, and
thus political convulsions, as can be witnessed by the impressive
achievements of the United States in the twentieth century despite great increases in its overall population. Provided the nation's resources are adequate and jobs are created and the environment is not badly damaged, demographic growth holds few
perils.

The real questions to be asked relate to the circumstances in
which a swift population expansion is taking place. Is it in lands
where poverty is already widespread and the teeming numbers
of young people have little prospect of obtaining satisfactory
jobs? Is it where there is insufficient nutrition for the fresh
mouths? Is it occurring in a weak state, or one torn by human
rights abuses? Does it witness the migration of millions into unhealthy, overcrowded, crime-ridden shanty cities that may become tinderboxes of human discontent, like Paris in 1789? Are
these migrations also spilling over international boundaries,
causing foreign anxieties and reactions?[5] Are the population increases occurring disproportionately among some of the ethnic
subgroups, causing fears among those peoples with lower fertility
rates that they will be swamped in the future, or that their present
majority will one day only be a minority? One need look at only
a few recent examples of violence and bloodshed—Rwanda and
Burundi, Kosovo, Haiti, Chiapas, the West Bank—to see where
most if not all of the above conditions prevailed and where the
youth population explosion interacted with these other factors to
produce threats to national and even international security.

If this trend is generally true—namely, that a Malthusian-like
mismatch in certain societies between human needs and available resources places strains that become unbearable and potentially threaten the common weal—then the current patterns of
population change in many parts of the world ought to give strategic planners pause for thought. We know that, while the pace

of increase in overall world population has been slowing significantly in recent years, the demographic pressures continue to mount in key regions.

References to only a few such cases will suffice to make this point. To take the most obvious example, in much of Africa the population explosion that followed immunization and the decline in infant mortality rates continues to have massive ripple effects, like the waves created by a giant ocean liner, despite the overall reduction in the annual percentage increases during the past decade. This continent, which had less than half the total population of Europe in the 1950s, will soon have double the number, with most of the inhabitants living in conditions of poverty and environmental decay, and suffering from vast deficiencies in nutrition, health care, and education. Add to this many traditional ethnic and tribal rivalries, weak governmental structures even in the revived African democracies, the largely artificial borders of most states, and widespread human rights abuses, and one is bound to wonder whether some recent signs of a recovery in economic growth will be enough to repair torn social fabrics and bring whole countries back to health. In this troubled context the "youth bulge" that is so prevalent across Africa will be extremely difficult to handle, with more and more frustrated young men being attracted to violence and war.

To be sure, any hard-nosed Western realist might ask what threat there is to our security even if a million Africans die, whether from the consequences of desperate poverty or in the ethnic wars of the Rwanda variety. But even that critic might concede that, as the youth population of North Africa explodes while that in the much richer countries of nearby southern Europe slowly ages and declines, the future of relations between those two continents looks troublesome. It might be said that Europe is protected by a demographic-technological "fault line" running through the Mediterranean, yet that fault line can be crossed in various ways, such as through illegal migration, drug trafficking, and terrorism; that Europe's nations, especially France, have too many North African inhabitants not to be affected by turmoil in Algeria and elsewhere; and that the efforts of North African regimes to acquire sophisticated weaponry, including nuclear devices, surely give reason for pause. Ideally, the West must hope for all of North Africa to be stable, peaceful, democratic, prosperous, and friendly both now and in the future. Yet how likely is that while severe demographic and environmental pressures work their course in this area through the next two decades?

The same remarks can be made about an even more volatile and troubled region, the Middle East, where the current surge in youth population and the forecast continuation of such swift increases due to cultural and religious reasons bodes ill for future peace and stability. Once again, it is not population increases per se, important though they are, that give cause for concern but, rather, the political and social and geographic circumstances in which they are taking place. The rivalries between various of the Arab states are legion, as are their always delicate and often hostile relations with important neighbors like Turkey and Iran. The Israeli-Palestinian-Arab vortex, the cause of serious Mideast wars this past half century, remains as difficult as ever. Nationalist and religious passions abound. Democracy as known in Western terms scarcely exists. Fanatical splinter groups are out to upset the existing order, usually through terrorist means. Some of the most heavily militarized states in the world inhabit this region and are striving to gain ever more sophisticated weaponry. If any area can claim to be the world's most complex and intractable trouble spot, this is probably it.

All this is well known to traditional realists, which is why many of them study the Mideast military and diplomatic balances. Less attention is paid, usually, to some other characteristics of this region. Because of Muslim disapproval of birth control and the general condition of women in society, it possesses among the highest fertility rates in the world. This in turn translates into a rapidly growing youth population, captured so well in television footage of crowds of teenage Palestinians in the West Bank or Gaza Strip, who represent a true demographic time bomb if their needs cannot be met. It is also represented in the large numbers of unemployed youth who have drifted from the countryside into all of the large cities of this region, and who are easily persuaded by fundamentalist preachers that the West is the cause of their plight. The pressures upon the land, especially in a country like Egypt, whose teeming populations have to live on a narrow strip on either side of the Nile, are persistent and daunting. The existing chronic shortages of water (discussed further below), now made more severe by the burgeoning population, the demands of agriculture, and the growing needs of industry, exacerbate relations between Turkey, Syria, and Iraq, and between Israel, Jordan, and the Palestinian Authority.[6]

Several other regions of our planet contain the same tinderbox materials. In the former Soviet republics of central and east-central Asia, there exists a similar mix of fast-growing populations, a religious-fundamentalist revival, ethnic and tribal rivalries, ecological disasters, widespread criminality, a rampant arms trade, and insecure governments. In parts of Central America the political scene is different but the demographic and population pressures—exacerbated by inequitable land-holding systems—continue to mount. But perhaps the most interesting further case is that of India, and of South Asia as a whole. India is by no means a weak state, and its military and policing capabilities are formidable. Yet its fertility rates remain high and, as it adds an extra 17 million to its population each year (equivalent to the entire population of Australia) and steadily catches up to China as the most populous country on Earth, it is fair to ask whether even its sturdy governing structures can bear the strain. How will it handle its 1.4 billion people in 2025, in place of the existing 900 million? Will its young people get jobs? Will its ecology buckle under? How, under such internal pressures, will a perhaps harassed Indian regime handle relations with its angry and suspicious neighbor, Pakistan, which is suffering from even faster demographic growth and has much less stable governance? What happens, also, when a power with nuclear capabilities weakens from within?[7]

Related to these demographic challenges, and in some ways (though not all) caused by them, are the environmental pressures building up in many stressed societies on our planet. Once again, one needs to make clear that there is no simple correlation between environmental change, political instability, and international security matters. The nations of the West horribly polluted their rivers, choked up their atmospheres with dangerously unhealthy substances, and blighted their landscapes for a century or more during their industrial revolutions before they realized the need to be more environmentally responsible. But there is no evidence that this ecological neglect caused a breakdown in the social fabric, produced alarming revolutionary movements, or instigated world wars. When those Western countries were rich enough, and concerned enough, to repair their damaged environments they found that Nature recovered swiftly. Similarly, some countries in the developing world today—Singapore, for example—are so advanced economically that they have not only made the demographic transition to lower fertility rates but also are beginning to pay serious attention to their environments. Finally, we know that there are certain forms of ecological damage—like the overfishing of the oceans—that are serious in and of themselves but cannot reasonably be said to constitute a security threat.

Environmental pressures that could produce threats to human well-being and social stability exist at two levels, the general and the particular. There is no doubt that if the more gloomy forecasts about the effects of global warming are accurate, then mankind will face atmospheric turbulence and environmental hazards in the future that will cause great distress: melting of the polar ice caps, rise in sea levels, more extreme weather conditions, greater storm damage, crop displacement, and habitat changes are all on the list of dangers to come should the Earth's average temperatures rise even a few degrees. Still, viewed from a security perspective, these all remain vague, generic, in a way intangible concerns; or, alternatively, physical problems that can be dealt with through regular means. Thus, increased coastal flooding can be answered by additional seawalls or relocating people from where they probably shouldn't have established homes to begin with. The northward movement of the corn belt from the United States into central Canada might be an economic blow to American agriculture in the Midwest, but it is scarcely a security issue; some regions will benefit positively from crop displacement, just as others lose. Perhaps if we had unrelentingly hotter summers, or a new ice age, we would find those newer conditions so invasive that we might regard it as a threat to our general well-being. But that will probably come upon us so gradually, and episodically, that we are unlikely to be moved to drastic actions. Gently rising flood waters will never seem as alarming as Soviet ICBMs targeted on one's country.

At the regional and local levels, however, environmental damage could indeed destabilize things. For example, so much of Bangladesh lies only a few feet above sea level that even a modest rise in the ocean's height would displace millions of people, turning them into refugees and increasing the flow of migrants across the Indian border. Local ecocides, as in the slash-and-burn deforestation in Brazil and Indonesia, are driving hundreds of thousands of peasants to the margins of society and cannot bode well for their countries' future stability. The unrest in the Chiapas region of Mexico does have special and particular roots, but it is also a manifestation of the demographic and environmental pressures common to much of Central America and may also be a harbinger of other, nearby uprisings and disturbances in a region that the United States simply cannot ignore. For many of the same environmental and socioeconomic reasons, North Africa trembles in the balance and Europe, too, must tremble at the possible consequences. While parts of south China suffocate under industrial smog, the inland provinces grapple with tens of millions of indigent, footloose workers in search of proper employment. In all these cases, a population explosion is under way that is simultaneously depleting the natural resources and putting pressure upon a weak social fabric.

Water shortages constitute an even more direct link between

environmental changes and security concerns. With the construction of the Ataturk Dam, Turkey has a stranglehold on the
water supplies of both Syria and Iraq, and it is by no means certain that the two states will tolerate this dependency: were the
United States so dependent upon a foreign country for its own
water supply, it probably would have deployed the Marines to
secure those sources. The same problem of water shortages af-
fects relations between Israel, the Palestinian Authority, and Jordan and is exacerbated year by year because of population growth
and the establishment of new settlements in arid and semi-arid
lands. Among the Central Asian republics that once were part of
the USSR, an equitable distribution of the waters from the great
rivers—which used to be controlled by a central ministry in Moscow—also becomes ever harder to achieve as economies revive
and populations grow. Every so often, Egypt reacts nervously, and
threateningly, to the prospect that upriver states might reduce the
flow of the Nile. Just as the West gets neuralgic at the thought
that its oil supplies might be reduced, so do many states in arid
regions regard a secure water supply as a vital security issue.[8]

It is argued by some scholars studying new global issues that
there are many other non-traditional threats, both to Western interests in particular and to international stability more generally,
such as the rise of organized crime groups in Russia and Belarus,
the power of drug cartels in Bolivia and elsewhere in Latin America, and such like. I would not deny their impacts, or their menace. Crime and drugs can have transnational consequences. Yet
they manifest themselves in local forms and appear to lack the
truly larger processes of, say, global warming or migration pressures into shanty cities all over the world.

Those latter forces, that is to say, the increasing impact of humankind on our habitats that produces demographic and environmental stress and brings some societies ever closer to worrying thresholds, are a threat to national and international stability
that should be taken seriously.[9] Yet it surely is not enough to
describe the problem, and wait passively for events to unfold.
The evidence suggests that many countries, including some of

great strategic significance as measured by traditional military criteria, are coming closer to the brink of social collapse, more because of internal transformations than traditional external dangers. This is not something that the international community can walk away from with impunity. More proactive policies are needed.

Yet, and this is the conundrum, these broad-based, non-military changes that may undermine whole societies are not something that can be easily dealt with through our existing state structures and by our traditional ways of thinking of what constitutes a "security threat." Most reasonable people would agree that today's policymakers, officials, and thinkers, like the statesmen of 1917–23 and 1943–48, are also obligated to come up with proposals to deal with the challenges that worry humankind. They would also probably agree that the solutions will be only partial ones, complicated by life's frictions, the messiness of local situations, human intransigence, and general ineptitude. So far as we know, for example, the Polish boundary settlements of 1919–22 and 1945 satisfied few completely, and dissatisfied many a great deal. How much more will that be the case in negotiating a global emissions-control pact that will really work? All alliances involve servitude, and all diplomacy involves compromises, but implementing the "new" diplomacy on environmental, demographic, and development issues is likely to be much tougher because these sorts of compromises (agreeing to reduce petroleum consumption, for example) directly infringe upon domestic ways of life in a way that settling distant colonial boundaries did not.

In other words, for all the similarities in our three postwar periods, there is a character to the new global challenges at the onset of the twenty-first century that distinguishes them from the problems that faced the Allied leaders at Versailles and Potsdam. To begin with, there is the question of timing or, perhaps better put, of deadlines. Decisions on the disposal of the German colonies in 1919, or on the western border of Poland in 1945, simply had to be made at the end-of-war conference itself by a few victorious great powers meeting in private and then in plenary session and committing those decisions to international treaty. At present, decisions on world population targets, even assuming such could be made by nation-states with any relevance for ordinary peoples' lives, lack all such sense of deadline and decisiveness. Again, does it matter all that much to people driving gas-guzzling sport-utility vehicles in Wyoming—a long way from the sea—that their emissions contribute to a global warming process that will erode the polar icecaps by the year 2040?

Shortly after the First World War, the British geopolitician Sir Halford Mackinder complained that it was hard to get a democracy to act strategically in peacetime, yet he was thinking only of such traditional and easily recognizable matters as the military balance of power.[10] How much more difficult is it to get democracies to take action when the perceived dangers are no longer ballistic missiles aimed at one's own country but vaguer, less tangible "threats" like global warming or the changing demographic balances between rich and poor countries—especially when there exists a cacophony of expert voices disputing whether these are threats at all?[11] Furthermore, the calls for decisive national and international action during the Cold War would always be echoed, and sometimes initiated, by powerful economic interest groups and their allies in the Congress, and it must be conceded that the environmentalist lobby, although articulate, simply lacks that amount of power and influence.

Yet another difficulty in galvanizing peoples and governments into decisive action to deal with the newer global challenges lies in the language that may or may not be used to appeal to one's fellow citizens. This is a particularly awkward problem in respect to global population increases and the shifting demographic balances between North and South. Hinting that developing nations need to take steps to cut their fertility rates and control their trace-gas emissions, as happened at the 1993 U.N. Conference on the Environment at Rio de Janeiro, simply provokes the retort that the richer countries are being "racist" and trying to prevent the developing world from catching up. Calling attention to the shrinking total populations of Europe and Japan, and contrasting that with the still burgeoning populations of Africa, Asia, and Latin America, risks the charge that the real but unexpressed concern is that the white peoples of the globe will be eclipsed by those of black, brown, or yellow hue.[12]

The final challenge relates to agency, that is, to how the sovereign governments of the world might come together to handle these newer forces for change and direct them along fruitful channels. Simply because such forces are transnational in scope, no single state can deal with them alone (although each of course can take localized actions like clearing up their rivers and cutting gas emissions). The need to create and use international structures and agencies in these matters is therefore overwhelming, always assuming that such bodies will be adequately empowered and effectively run. Here, surely, the examples of 1917–23 and 1943–48 merit emulation, for in both cases leading statesmen and their advisers recognized that international challenges could not be dealt with unless agencies with an international reach (the League of Nations and its related bodies, the United Nations, the Bretton Woods organizations) were established and authorized to work for the common weal.

A variety of proposals exist already for greater investment of attention and resources by the governments of the world in international cooperation to meet global challenges. Very few of them actually involve brand-new structures, although many existing bodies, especially those at the core of the United Nations Organization, would be significantly amended.[13] What is lacking at present, particularly in the United States, is the political willingness to reinforce and empower international structures to achieve what are clear international public goods.[14] Perhaps this American mood will change to a more favorable one as the global pressures themselves intensify and politicians come to realize that, in John Donne's words, "no man is an island, entire unto himself." But it would be infinitely preferable to take international proactive measures earlier, rather than be forced to respond to future crises and catastrophes.

However the political leaderships of our planet decide to handle or neglect the newer security challenges, one thing is certain. No longer, as in 1917–23 and 1943–48, can the package of policies to deal with our own altered strategic landscape simply be a "northern" or "Western" thing. Real progress in managing our Earth's demographic and environmental pressures will need to be part of a larger North-South deal, because without the cooperation of at least the major players in the developing world no significant advances can be made toward the common purpose of bringing prosperity and stability to a far larger share of our globe's population than presently obtains.[15] And in that need for improved North-South cooperation lies, of course, the biggest hurdle, since it will obviously involve a significant amount of power sharing. One cannot help wondering whether the leaders of the richer and most powerful countries of the world are ready for that, or ever will be. In sum, while we lack neither the resources nor the structures nor (probably) the personnel to tackle the issues discussed in this chapter, it is far from clear that we possess the political ingredients necessary—that is, leadership, imagination, and intelligence—to handle the novel strategic circumstances we are likely to confront in the early decades of the twenty-first century.

Afterword   Michael Howard

The chapters in this volume concentrate not so much on the actual alterations in the "landscapes" of international politics and their causes as on the way statesmen and peoples adjusted to the consequent changes in the international environment. In this afterword I shall therefore try to say something about the alterations themselves, and set the question in a broader historical context.

All the changes considered here have been the result of wars, with the remarkable exception of the events of 1989. Then, within a few tumultuous months, the Soviet Union abandoned its acquisitions, its aspirations, and its very ideology without a shot being fired: a defeat certainly, but a bloodless one, and no less far-reaching in its consequences than the defeat of Germany in both world wars, or that of Napoleonic France during the previous century. We might consider these transformations as seismic events, the political equivalent of earthquakes, except that they were manmade. Perhaps we should think of them as the collapse of edifices that had been erected a generation or more earlier, whose downfall was brought about by inherent instability, external pressures, or a combination of the two.

We should notice, however, that such attempts to build edifices of "peace"—that "architecture" so beloved by contemporary American statesmen—have been of comparatively recent date. Until the seventeenth century the peoples of Europe were accustomed to living in conditions of constant volcanic eruption, continuous small-scale wars in which peace was local and temporary where it existed at all. The great princes of the continent might conclude periodic peace treaties when they had temporarily exhausted their resources, but these were little more than truces within an ongoing Hobbesian state of continual armed conflict. Not until the Peace of Westphalia in 1648, which was some five years in the making, did the statesmen of Europe consciously try to create a stable system, a cultivatable landscape that would provide a peaceful environment in which common trade and civilization could flourish and war could be, if not abolished, then at least constrained within recognizable limits of legitimacy both in its occasion and its conduct.

The systems created by the statesmen at Westphalia and their successors all had at their root the concept of "balance," the creation of an order that would not be threatened by a hegemonic power. At the Peace of Utrecht in 1713 this concept became explicit. Wars were seen as having arisen from necessary resistance to a hegemonic power—Habsburg power before 1659, French power thereafter—which had now been humbled by coalitions of their adversaries. Peace settlements consisted in the redistribution of power, largely in terms of territorial reallocation and guarantees of inheritance, that would preserve an equitable balance in the future.

The combined wisdom of European statesmen could not, however, preserve the peace if secondary states like Prussia were determined to thrust themselves into the first rank, or if first-rank states like France saw themselves in danger of being reduced to the second; and no "system" could have survived the joint impact of the French Revolution and Napoleon Bonaparte. The statesmen at Vienna in 1814 accepted that mechanistic concepts of balance were not enough: there had to be the will and the machinery to enforce them. The Vienna settlement thus involved not simply the usual redistribution of territory, to reward the victors and penalize the vanquished, but a setting forth of principles for the maintenance of international order and the creation of a rudimentary mechanism for doing so. The Treaty of Chaumont that created the Quadruple Alliance laid down that the signatories would combine not only to fight the war but thereafter to maintain the peace, and in that maintenance the restored regime in France was enrolled as a necessary partner.

The "Vienna system" worked reasonably well. It did, by territorial redistribution, recreate a balance among the European powers; it laid down generally acceptable rules of behavior; and it created a crude mechanism in the "Congress system" for operating them. It worked as well as it did, however, because its operators were culturally homogeneous, sharing core values; and central to those values (except in the marginal case of England) was a well-founded suspicion of the disruptive effects of national sentiment and democratic institutions. The structure of the Vienna settlement was based as much on the suppression of democratic nationalism as on the balance of power between states. When, after 1848, the European powers could no longer suppress nationalism, they accepted its consequences in Western Europe with the unification of Germany and Italy, and tried to manage it farther east. There they cooperated in ensuring that the birth of new states should upset as little as possible the balance between the Habsburg, Romanov, and Ottoman empires on which the peace of the region depended. In 1914 their efforts finally collapsed. There followed a huge war that devastated a landscape that had been unchanged in essentials for 250 years.

By 1919 all the familiar landmarks in Europe had disappeared as completely as had those on the battlefields of the Western Front. There was no longer any balance of power, or any effective balancers. The Romanov, Habsburg, and Ottoman empires whose rivalries had occasioned the war no longer existed. Germany had been defeated, but far from destroyed. The European victors, France and Britain, were exhausted and economically dependent on the United States. President Wilson appeared as a deus ex machina to impose his own peace on Europe. His new system sought to embody the best features of the old by setting forth rules of behavior and creating a far more elaborate mechanism, the League of Nations, to implement them; but it decisively broke with the old system by regarding "national self-determination" as the basic criterion of international legitimacy rather than a disruptive element to be quarantined where it could not be suppressed. In doing so Wilson was perhaps making a virtue of necessity; the genie of nationalism could not be put back in the bottle. But where he erred, and erred disastrously, was in abandoning the concept of balancing power that had preserved stability, even if it had failed to prevent war, in Europe since the eighteenth century.

Balance had been the fundamental condition of European stability, as arguably it is of international stability in general. The only alternative is hegemony, and that the United States was not yet prepared to exert. The British, absorbed in the digestion of their new imperial possessions, showed themselves uninterested in cooperating to maintain any postwar balance in Europe. France did its best, single-handed, to create one, but against a power with Germany's territorial, demographic, and economic advantages it was an impossible task for any lone European power, perhaps even for any combination of European powers that excluded the Soviet Union. France's efforts to do so, by territorial redistribution (the quasi-annexation of the Rhineland), the creation of a network of alliances in Eastern Europe, and the permanent impoverishment of Germany through reparations, only embittered the Germans and antagonized former allies.

The Versailles settlement indeed revealed one of the most sinister aspects of twentieth-century diplomacy: the negative impact of public opinion on peacemaking. Wilsonian expectations that public opinion would not only support but insist on a "reasonable" peace were most cruelly belied. For the best part of a decade the French electorate understandably demanded a Carthaginian peace. The British and even more the American electorates refused to accept any commitments to participate in maintaining a peaceful European structure, while the Germans nursed a grievance that nothing short of massive revision of the Versailles settlement and the restoration of their status as a great power would be able to appease. The fundamental difference between the Vienna and the Versailles settlements was that the leaders who concluded the latter were responsible to democratic electorates. Their predecessors were not.

But was the perceived "injustice" of the peace treaties, or even the impotence of the victorious allies to maintain them, the fundamental reason for the instability of the postwar settlements? The essential paradox of Versailles was that it tried simultaneously to legitimize the autarchic nation-state and to construct an international "civil society" whose rules of behavior, especially with respect to the treatment of minorities and the labor force, would overrule that autarchy. Even more fundamental were the pressures of the international capitalist "system" on national economies and the blessings and curses it distributed with an uneven hand: the benefits of free capitalistic flows for "modernization," the curses of the internal conflicts this modernization set in motion, and, even worse, the miseries of the depression that nearly broke even a society as wealthy as the United States. The statesmen of the 1920s tried to create and maintain a socioeconomic system that would preempt the appeal of both the revolutionary left and the radical right. The first threat was successfully warded off; the second was not. Fascism in its various forms emerged as a backlash not only against the forces of international capital, and the pains of modernization it brought in its wake, but against all the values of the Enlightenment with which it was associated—not least those professing racial equality and human rights. It is a reaction that even now we have not learned to control.

It was the collapse of the Versailles settlement that jolted the United States into awareness of its vulnerability. It was not so much the fear of the power of the Fascist states that did this: physical conquest by Nazi Germany and Japan did not figure even in the most nightmarish of American interwar scenarios. The fear was that, in order to survive in such a world, the United States would have to abandon its own values and transform itself into a "garrison state" indistinguishable from its adversaries. The seeds of such a culture, indeed, have never been entirely extirpated from American society. Wilson's slogan, that the world must be made "safe for democracy," was not just a slogan: it was a perception that the values of the United States could not survive in isolation, and that unless the world could be transformed into the image of America, Americans would have to conform to the values of the world they hoped to transform. It was the mirror image of the Trotskyite belief that unless the Soviet Union could spark a universal proletarian revolution, the capitalistic world would sooner or later destroy it. Indeed it proved easier to believe that communism might exist in one country than that capitalism could.

So for the United States—or at least the pre-Kissingerian United States—there could be no settlement based on a balance between equal, collegiate powers. Those powers who had disturbed the peace by planning and launching aggressive war were simply criminals who had to be punished. The victors—democracies or honorary democracies—would then police the world. Such a policing regime resembled benevolent hegemony rather than the "collective security" of the Wilsonian dream. It might be masked under the title of "cooperative security." But it still contained no element of balance.

These were the ideas with which the United States emerged from World War II and confronted a yet more desolate landscape. Germany and Japan had ceased to exist as powers at all. The remaining European states, France and Britain included, survived only as pensioners of the United States where they were not occupied by a triumphant and hostile Soviet Union. The scene might have looked yet bleaker had the United States not possessed, however briefly, a monopoly of the atomic bomb. The

American attempt to bring the Soviet Union into a Western-dominated political and economic system failed, but half a loaf was better than no bread, and the frontiers of the American sphere of influence were rapidly drawn. West Germany was absorbed with the rest of Western Europe as an American protectorate, and the Soviet Union responded in kind.

We may well ask why this postwar landscape was not poisoned, like that of 1919, by general detestation of Germany, to say nothing of Japan. In the case of Germany, three reasons can be suggested. First, it is difficult to detest for very long people who are living amid ruins, many of them refugees with nowhere to go, all faced with the prospect of starvation and lethal pandemics. Second, there was the rational appreciation of the need to restore the German economy if there was to be any hope of economic recovery for Europe as a whole. And third there was the necessary acceptance, on both sides, of the Germans as allies in the confrontation of the Cold War. As for the Japanese, the shock of Hiroshima and Nagasaki acted as an effective antidote to the worst excesses of Allied revanchism. Nonetheless, it was to be decades before the visceral loathing of the Germans and Japanese by the peoples who had suffered under their occupation was to be eradicated; and a necessary condition of that eradication—and indeed for the defeated powers to accept the new order—was the total subjugation, disarmament, and, so far as possible, reeducation of their populations. The sharing of core values, which had been a necessary condition of the preservation of peace after the Napoleonic wars, now had to extend beyond elites to entire populations.

Nuclear weapons made it easier to create and maintain a balance between the two rival hegemons who, after 1945, attempted to divide the world between them; while the division of Europe made it possible to create a Western European system in which the shrunken German Federal Republic could be accepted as a partner as easily as the powers at Vienna had accepted a chastened post-Napoleonic France. Within that system, capitalism brought prosperity, as it had failed to do a quarter century earlier, and its success brought about political stability. But again, we must not forget how uncertain it appeared in the 1940s that it *would* succeed, and how attractive was the appeal of communism to a generation that had known only the miseries inflicted by a free market or by Fascist oppression. A full decade was to pass before the seismic eruptions that had distorted the European landscape finally died down.

It took much longer for them to die down elsewhere. In a world-historical perspective, the most important consequence of World War II was the destruction of the global hegemony exercised by European empires—a process simultaneous with, and reciprocally affecting, the development of the confrontation between the United States and the Soviet Union. When it became clear that the European frontiers of their hegemonies were unalterable, the competition between the superpowers moved to the Third World, where it was handled by both sides with a singular lack of finesse. Third World nationalism was underestimated by powers who believed that they could control it or, more important, that their adversaries could control it; on the other hand, the capacity of these newly independent states to affect the global balance, even those so potentially wealthy as India or so strategically placed as Egypt, was greatly overrated. The problems of dealing with these new states were huge. Should one accept them, whatever their political complexion? Cooperate with them? Confront them? Subvert them? The learning process was slow—in the case of Vietnam, disastrously so—and the impact of the Cold War usually counterproductive. But there were no easy choices. It took over a decade for the leaders of the new countries to realize that the West had infinitely more to offer them than had the Soviet Union. By then, ironically, the West was beginning to wonder whether it was worth offering them anything at all.

Meanwhile, in Europe itself, a generation of peace brought about by the nuclear balance of terror made it possible for the superpowers and their associates to recognize the existence of a common interest in stability and to accept, however tacitly, rules of conduct for maintaining it. Henry Kissinger, a statesman trained in the subtleties of diplomatic history rather than in the far more inflexible discipline of law, began to treat the Soviet Union as a partner in maintaining global stability rather than as an adversary bent on subverting it. More important, a regime came to power in the German Federal Republic prepared to accept and legitimize the *status quo post bellum* in return for a normalization of relations with Eastern Europe, which these leaders shrewdly realized could only work to the advantage of the West. The foundation of the new structure remained the division of Germany, the balance between the superpowers, and their commitment to the security of their associates in Europe; but on that foundation a superstructure could now be constructed within which the peoples of Europe need no longer regard one another as enemies. The treaties of 1970–73 marked the true conclusion of the Second World War. After a period of uncertainty in the early 1980s, when the Soviet Union appeared to be testing the limits of the new détente, the international landscape at last seemed stable.

But it wasn't. The collapse of the Soviet Union meant the disappearance of one of the main pillars on which the entire edifice had been erected, and again the landscape was transformed. Within a few months Germany was reunited, the Soviet Union withdrew its forces to its own borders, and the states of Eastern Europe recovered their freedom of action. A few months later the Soviet Union itself was dissolved. Before this happened, however, Soviet leaders cooperated in easing the transition to a new order in which the good will and sheer common sense displayed by all the participants recalled the palmiest days of the Vienna Congress. Western leaders understood very well that, although the Soviet Union—and, even more, its successor regime in Russia—was impotent for the time being to prevent the West from imposing its preferred settlement, that impotence would not last forever, and that any lasting settlement had to be predicated on enduring Russian good will.

Yet the Paris settlement of 1990 was in an important sense the polar opposite of the Vienna settlement of 1814–15. The latter gave the powers a collegiate responsibility for maintaining order—if necessary by direct intervention to suppress the new phenomenon of liberalism wherever it appeared. The Paris settlement, on the contrary, opened formerly closed and protected economies to all the disruptive impact of the global market economy, often with traumatic results. For the more mature states of Eastern Europe the effect was on the whole benign; for the successor states of the Soviet Union, it was not. Modernization and stability do not go hand in hand. Even if social disruption does not occur on the massive scale that played so significant a part in causing the two world wars, it can create regional instabilities—especially evident in southeastern Europe, Indonesia, South Asia, and central Africa—that constantly threaten escalation. We are today faced with problems comparable to those that confronted the European powers throughout the nineteenth century, except that ours are on a global scale. A central dilemma all statesmen face now is to determine whether, in the interests of overall stability, we have the right, or the capability, to intervene in these regional conflicts whose implications may ultimately be worldwide.

Finally, who are the "we" who claim that right? In the nineteenth century it was a genuine college of powers. Today no such college exists, or is likely to do so. Russia is a great power by courtesy, China still a regional power. Japan shrinks from global responsibilities. The states of Europe can individually exert no more than marginal influence and have yet to learn how to exercise any collectively. We are left with the United States, militarily and economically without any rival. It is a reluctant hegemony, but hegemony it is. Today, the United States enjoys the power and bears the obligations of the great empires of the past. Americans do not like the word "empire." I myself, somewhat naturally, have no objection to the concept—the exercise of power by a people confident in the superiority of their own value system and possessing the capacity to defend and where possible to extend it. This system may be camouflaged under the title of "Commonwealth," although that did not do Britain much good.

But that is what the United States has at present—unchallenged military, economic, and cultural supremacy in the world (and much as some of us may dislike that culture, we cannot deny the power of its appeal). That global supremacy entails global responsibilities that now must be embraced. The United States may not be very good at managing the affairs of the world, but there is no one else who can manage the task better.

Notes

Chapter 1. The Great Powers and the New International System, 1919–1923

1. Edward Hallett Carr, *The Twenty Years' Crisis, 1919–1939* (1939; reprint, New York: Harper & Row, 1964), p. 21: "The utopian sets up an ethical standard which purports to be independent of politics, and seeks to make politics conform to it. The realist cannot logically accept any standard value save that of fact."

2. "The human will will continue to seek an escape from the logical consequences of realism in the vision of an international order which, as soon as it crystallizes itself into concrete political form, becomes tainted with self-interest and hypocrisy and must once more be attacked with the instruments of realism." Ibid, p. 93.

3. Max Günzenhäuser, *Die Pariser Friedenskonferenz 1919 und die Friedensverträge 1919–1920: Literaturbericht und Bibliographie* (Frankfurt: Bernard & Graefe, 1970), ably covers the literature, but should be supplemented by the bibliography in Alan Sharp, *The Versailles Settlement: Peacemaking in Paris, 1919* (New York: St. Martin's, 1991), pp. 220–30.

4. William R. Keylor, *The Twentieth-Century World: An International History*, 2d ed. (New York: Oxford University Press, 1992), p. 74. It was estimated that in France some eight million acres (an area the size

of Holland) had been destroyed. For slightly different figures, see Paul Kennedy, *The Rise and Fall of the Great Powers* (New York: Random House, 1987), pp. 278–79.

5. David Stevenson, *The First World War and International Politics* (Oxford: Clarendon, 1991).

6. Quotation is from Lloyd George's Fontainebleau memorandum, *Memorandum Circulated by the Prime Minister on 25 March 1919, House of Commons Papers*, Cmd. 1614 (1922), p. 23.

7. Denise Artaud, *La réconstruction de l'Europe, 1919–1929* (Paris: Presses Universitaires de France, 1973), pp. 6–9.

8. N. Gordon Levin, Jr., *Woodrow Wilson and World Politics* (London: Oxford University Press, 1968), p. 5.

9. Wilson's program, presented in his Fourteen Points speech to Congress on January 8, 1918, and supplemented by the "Four Principles" on February 11, the "Four Ends" on July 4, and the "Five Particulars," on September 27, prompted Clemenceau's famous quip regarding the "inflationary pressures" on utopian programs since the Old Testament ("the good Lord himself required only ten points"). It nevertheless produced a "rapturous reception . . . by intellectual elites and vast crowds" when Wilson arrived in Europe in December 1918. Sharp, *Versailles Settlement*, p. 14. In the period between January 15 and February 15, 1918, French postal censors reported: "While criticisms of our own diplomacy . . . are frequent, the approbation given President Wilson is without reserve." Quoted in David Stevenson, *French War Aims Against Germany, 1914–1919* (New York: Oxford University Press, 1982), p. 101.

10. On Wilson's partners, see Anthony Lentin, *Lloyd George, Woodrow Wilson, and the Guilt of Germany* (Leicester, U.K.: Leicester University Press, 1984), and David R. Watson, *Georges Clemenceau: A Political Biography* (London: Methuen, 1974).

11. U.S. preparations are discussed in Lawrence E. Gelfand, *The Inquiry: American Preparations for Peace, 1917–1919* (New Haven: Yale University Press, 1963); Britain's in Erik Goldstein, *Winning the Peace: British Diplomatic Strategy, Peace Planning, and the Paris Peace Conference, 1916–1920* (Oxford: Clarendon, 1991); France's in Stevenson, *French War Aims Against Germany*.

12. "The confusion in Paris before and during the deliberations . . . contributed considerably to the erratic course of events." Sally Marks, *The Illusion of Peace* (New York: St. Martin's, 1976), p. 4.

13. F. S. Marston, *The Peace Conference of 1919: Organization and Procedure* (London: Oxford University Press, 1944), pp. 111–19; also Isaiah Bowman in Edward M. House and Charles Seymour, eds., *What Really Happened at Paris* (New York: Scribner's, 1921), pp. 158–59.

14. The Council of Four became responsible for Germany's frontiers; the Council of Five, a body of foreign ministers, was responsible for the other boundaries as well as for some economic matters. Strong criticism of these procedures appears in Gerhard Schulz, *Revolutions and Peace Treaties, 1917–1920,* trans. Marian Jackson (London: Methuen, 1972), pp. 164–66.

15. The remaining peacemaking process between July 1919 and July 1923 was divided between governments and a variety of inter-Allied agencies. Sharp, *Versailles Settlement,* pp. 39–41.

16. See Ernest May, "Public Opinion," in Samuel F. Wells, Jr., and Paula Bailey Smith, eds., *New European Orders: 1919 and 1991* (Washington, D.C.: Woodrow Wilson Center Press, 1996), pp. 18–40. Also, Ronald B. McCallum, *Public Opinion and the Last Peace* (London: Oxford University Press, 1944); Pierre Miquel, *La paix de Versailles et l'opinion publique française* (Paris: Flammarion, 1972). On the chaotic nature of diplomacy among the great powers, Harold Nicolson remarked: "We were never for one instant given to suppose that our recommendations were absolutely final. And thus we tended to accept compromises, and even to support decisions, which we ardently hoped would not, in the last resort, be approved." Harold Nicolson, *Peacemaking, 1919* (New York: Grosset & Dunlap, 1965), pp. 122–23, 128–29.

17. Sandi Cooper, *Patriotic Pacifism: Waging War on War in Europe, 1815–1914* (New York: Oxford University Press, 1991); Verdiana Grossi, *Le pacifisme européen, 1889–1914* (Brussels: Emile Bruylant, 1994).

18. Speech by Socialist deputy Albert Thomas, January 11, 1918, in *Journal Officiel de la République Française, Chambre des Députés, Débats Parlementaires,* Session Ordinaire, 1917–18, pp. 38–39.

19. G. W. Egerton, *Great Britain and the Creation of the League of Nations* (Chapel Hill: University of North Carolina Press, 1978), pp. 57–62.

20. Egerton, *Great Britain and the Creation;* Peter Yearwood, " 'On the Safe and Right Lines': The Lloyd George Government and the Origins of the League of Nations," *Historical Journal* 32, no. 1 (March 1989): 131–55; David Hunter Miller, *The Drafting of the Covenant* (New York: Putnam's, 1928), 1:3–7.

21. Miller, *Drafting of the Covenant,* 2:231–37.

22. Ten seats were held by the great powers; the rest were occupied by Belgium, Brazil, China, Portugal, Serbia, Czechoslovakia, Greece, Poland, and Romania. Sharp, *Versailles Settlement,* p. 56. Miller's informal notes are useful for the candid tenor of the discussion: see Miller, *Drafting of the Covenant,* 1:450; 2:123–26, 143; also Arthur Walworth, *Wilson and His Peacemakers* (New York: Norton, 1986), pp. 115–16.

23. When America absented itself from the League, the Council consisted

of four major powers and four minor powers, all with a veto. With the expansion of Council membership in 1926, there was a permanent numerical preponderance of smaller powers, although in practice the great powers still dominated the League Council. The founders of the United Nations took the precaution of giving only permanent members a veto on the Security Council.

24. *Foreign Relations of the United States: The Paris Peace Conference*, 3: 286–315.

25. Walworth, *Wilson and His Peacemakers*, pp. 119–20.

26. Sharp, *Versailles Settlement*, p. 62.

27. "Vox populi, vox diaboli," he said. Sharp, *Versailles Settlement*, p. 62. Significantly, British intellectuals never followed up their early enthusiasm for the League with as firm a support for collective security as they gave to the far vaguer principle of disarmament.

28. Marianne Brink, "Deutschlands Stellung zum Völkerbund in den Jahren 1918/19 bis 1922" (Ph.D. diss., Free University Berlin, 1962).

29. Egerton, *Great Britain and the Creation*, pp. 147–49; Walworth, *Wilson and His Peacemakers*, pp. 307–9; Seth Tillman, *Anglo-American Relations at the Paris Peace Conference of 1919* (Princeton: Princeton University Press, 1961), pp. 281–97; Miller, *Drafting of the Covenant*, 2:370–72.

30. R. S. Baker, *Woodrow Wilson and the World Settlement* (Garden City, N.Y.: Doubleday, Page, 1922), 1:93.

31. Stevenson, *The First World War and International Politics*, pp. 253–54.

32. See F. P. Walters, *A History of the League of Nations* (London: Oxford University Press, 1952).

33. In Article 1 of his first draft of the Covenant, Colonel House wrote in July 1918: "The same standards of honor and ethics shall prevail internationally and in affairs of nations as in other matters. The agreement or promise of a power shall be inviolate." Charles Seymour, ed., *Intimate Papers of Colonel House* (Boston: Houghton Mifflin, 1926–28), 4:28.

34. H. R. Cummings, head of the League's Information Section, wrote the following after spending five weeks at the Genoa Conference in the spring of 1922: "I find it a salutary experience to move . . . in a distinctly non-League atmosphere and to realize, painfully, close at hand, that in the really first-class problems of the world, the League has not taken its proper place." "Genoa and the League," May 24, 1922, League of Nations Archive, Special Circular 184. Cf. Carlo Schanzer, "L'equivoco fondamentale della Società delle Nazioni," *Nuova Antologia* 232 (Nov. 1923): 3–16.

35. Sharp, *Versailles Settlement*, p. 64; Levin, *Woodrow Wilson and World*

Politics, pp. 250–51; Marks, *The Illusion of Peace,* pp. 14–15; cf. Inis L. Claude, Jr., *Swords into Plowshares: The Problems and Progress of International Organization,* 4th ed. (New York: Random House, 1971), chapter 12.

36. For historical background, Alfred Cobban, *The Nation State and National Self-Determination* (London: Collins, 1969). The post–Cold War search for a new world order has produced a spate of critical studies: Daniel Patrick Moynihan, *Pandaemonium: Ethnicity in International Politics* (New York: Oxford University Press, 1993); Walker Connor, *Ethnonationalism: The Quest for Understanding* (Princeton: Princeton University Press, 1994); Henry Kissinger, *Diplomacy* (New York: Simon & Schuster, 1994); Derek Heater, *National Self-Determination: Woodrow Wilson and His Legacy* (New York: St. Martin's, 1994).

37. The "lessons" of the Civil War had marked the Southerner Wilson: "*Because* I love the South," he stated in 1880, "I rejoice in the failure of the Confederacy," and "[he] thanked God that the union *still* binds us together." Woodrow Wilson, *The Public Papers of Woodrow Wilson,* eds. Ray Stannard Baker and William E. Dodd (New York: Harper & Brothers, 1925–27), 1:43–59. Wilson later opposed the Filipino peoples' desire for independence on the basis of their need for tutelage in the ways of democracy: "You cannot call a miscellaneous people, unknit, scattered, diverse of race and speech and habit, a nation, a community. . . . No people can form a community or be wisely subjected to common forms of government who are as diverse and as heterogeneous as the people of the Philippine Islands." Ibid, 1:416–42. See Tony Smith, *America's Mission: The United States and the Worldwide Struggle for Democracy in the Twentieth Century* (Princeton: Princeton University Press, 1994), pp. 37–65.

38. Wilson, *Public Papers,* 5:155–62. Point 10 called for "autonomy for minorities within the Habsburg monarchy."

39. "A Draft of a Note to the Austro-Hungarian Government," October 19, 1918, ibid., 5:383.

40. David Foglesong, *America's Secret War Against Bolshevism: U.S. Intervention in the Russian Civil War, 1917–1920* (Chapel Hill: University of North Carolina Press, 1995); Georg Schild, *Between Ideology and Realpolitik: Woodrow Wilson and the Russian Revolution, 1917–1921* (Westport, Conn.: Greenwood, 1995).

41. "Certain Phrases of the President Contain the Seeds of Trouble," December 20, 1918, Herbert Hoover, Pre-Commerce File, Box 10, "Lansing," Herbert Hoover Library, West Branch, Iowa.

42. Wilson on March 27: "Everywhere we are compelled to change boundaries and national sovereignties. Nothing involves greater danger, for these changes run contrary to long-established customs and change

the very life of populations whilst, at the same time, they affect their feelings." *Deliberations of the Council of Four (March 24–June 28, 1919): Notes of the Official Interpreter Paul Mantoux* [hereinafter referred to as Mantoux], trans. and ed. Arthur Link and Manfred F. Boemeke (Princeton: Princeton University Press, 1992), 1:31.

43. Harold I. Nelson, *Land and Power: British and Allied Policy on Germany's Frontiers, 1916–19* (London: Routledge & Paul, 1963).

44. Gelfand, *The Inquiry,* and Goldstein, *Winning the Peace.*

45. See "Outline of Tentative Report and Recommendations, prepared . . . for the President and the Plenipotentiaries," January 21, 1919, Woodrow Wilson Papers, Library of Congress.

46. Klaus Schwabe, *Woodrow Wilson, Revolutionary Germany, and Peacemaking, 1918–1919: Missionary Diplomacy and the Realities of Power,* trans. Robert and Rita Kimber (Chapel Hill: University of North Carolina Press, 1985), pp. 109–11.

47. Wilson did agree on the Austrians' right to unite *voluntarily* with Germany, with the consent of the League of Nations. Mantoux, 1:144–45, 234, 458–60; 2:392, 422.

48. Wilson finally agreed to a compromise whereby the Saar, remaining nominally under German sovereignty, was placed for fifteen years under a League administration dominated by France, after which a plebiscite would be held. Mantoux, 1:55–68, 83–85, 185–86, 195–99, 204–8, 210–17.

49. Sharp, *Versailles Settlement,* pp. 106–13.

50. Ibid., pp. 119–23.

51. Mantoux, 2:82.

52. Only eleven days after the armistice, a huge pogrom erupted in Lemberg (Lwów), newly liberated by the Poles. Carole Fink, "The Paris Peace Conference and the Question of Minority Rights," *Peace and Change* 21, no. 3 (July 1996): 277–78.

53. This principle applied, however, only to whites. During his first administration Wilson issued a federal order establishing segregation for federal employees and phased most African Americans from the civil service. John Hope Franklin [and Alfred A. Moss, Jr.], *From Slavery to Freedom: A History of African Americans,* 7th ed. (New York: Knopf, 1994), pp. 324–25.

54. Mantoux, 1:439–41.

55. Miller, *Drafting of the Covenant,* 2:387–92.

56. The committee met sixty-four times between May and December 1919, producing treaties with Poland, Czechoslovakia, Romania, Yugoslavia, and Greece and drafting the articles that were inserted in the peace treaties with Austria, Hungary, Bulgaria, and Turkey. Texts in League

of Nations, *Protection of Linguistic, Racial, and Religious Minorities* (Geneva: League of Nations, 1927).

57. The best printed source is by the British committee member, Sir James Headlam-Morley, *A Memoir of the Paris Peace Conference, 1919* (London: Methuen, 1972).

58. *Foreign Relations of the United States: The Paris Peace Conference,* 3: 395–410.

59. Except for special provisions for the partitioned province of Upper Silesia, Germany was not forced to sign a minority treaty; and Italy (thirty years younger than Greece, and about to acquire some half million Slavs) was exempt.

60. See Paderewski to Lloyd George, June 15, 1919, Lloyd George Papers, House of Lords Record Office, London, F57/5/2.

61. David Lloyd George, May 17, 1919: "We cannot allow propagandist associations and societies from all over the world to flood the League of Nations with their complaints." Mantoux, 2:91.

62. Carole Fink, "The League of Nations and the Minorities Question," *World Affairs* 157, no. 4 (Spring 1995): 197–206.

63. Michael Burns, "Disturbed Spirits: Minority Rights and New World Orders, 1919 and the 1990s," in Wells and Smith, eds., *New European Orders,* pp. 41–61.

64. Artaud, *La réconstruction de l'Europe,* pp. 37–38.

65. Details in Bernadotte E. Schmitt and Harold C. Vedeler, *The World in the Crucible, 1914–1919* (New York: Harper & Row, 1984), pp. 455–62.

66. Etienne Mantoux, *La paix calomniée* (Paris: Gallimard, 1946), pp. 74–76.

67. On April 8, 1919, Lloyd George received a sharply worded telegram from 233 members of Parliament reminding him that they expected a bill to be presented to Germany with nothing less than the full imperial claim. Cf. David Lloyd George, *The Truth About the Peace Treaties* (London: Gollancz, 1938), 2:374–84.

68. Sharp, *Versailles Settlement,* pp. 77–101.

69. See Lloyd George's statement to the London Conference on March 3, 1921: *Documents on British Foreign Policy, 1919–1939,* 1st ser., vol. 15, pp. 258–59.

70. Above all John Maynard Keynes, *The Economic Consequences of the Peace* (London: Macmillan, 1919).

71. Lloyd George to Wilson, April 23, 1919, Lloyd George Papers, House of Lords Record Office, F/60/1/13; "Scheme for the Rehabilitation of European Credit and for Financing Relief and Reconstruction," *Activities 1914–1919: The Treasury and Versailles,* ed. Elizabeth Johnson,

vol. 16 of *The Collected Writings of John Maynard Keynes* (London: Macmillan, 1971), pp. 429–37.

72. Keynes, Minutes, May 4 and May 10, 1919, *Activities 1914–1919,* pp. 440–42.

73. With its permanent members applying their veto nearly three hundred times, the Security Council was virtually paralyzed. The Korean conflict, a U.S.-controlled collective security effort, was the exception. Clark Eichelberger, *The UN: The First Twenty-Five Years* (New York: Harper & Row, 1970), pp. 21–26.

74. Carole Fink, "The United Nations After Fifty Years," *Global Justice* 2, no. 1 (Winter 1996): 6–8.

75. The number of U.N. peacekeeping missions since 1989 has been identical to those of the entire Cold War but have involved far more costly, complex, and dangerous operations than ever before. Peacekeeping expenses rose from $300 million in 1987 to $3 billion in 1993, which does not include the budgets for the health, refugees, and human rights agencies. Ibid., pp. 8–9.

76. Boutros Boutros-Ghali, *An Agenda for Peace* (New York: United Nations, 1992), pp. 1–2; Ian Williams, "Letter from the United Nations," *New Statesman & Society* (April 1, 1994): 11.

77. John Isaacs, "Strengthening the World Policeman," *Bulletin of the Atomic Scientists* 49, no. 10 (Dec. 1993): 14–15; and Kosta Tsipis and Philip Morrison, "Arming for Peace," *Bulletin of the Atomic Scientists* 50, no. 2 (Mar. 1994): 38–43, recommend a U.N. force to control the non-proliferation of nuclear weapons.

78. Richard K. Betts, "The Delusion of Impartial Intervention," *Foreign Affairs* 73, no. 6 (Nov.–Dec. 1994): 20–33; Gayle Kirshenbaum, "Who's Watching the Peacekeepers?" *Ms.* 4, no. 6 (May–June 1994): 10 ff.

79. Joseph Schechtman, *European Population Transfers, 1939–1945* (New York: Oxford University Press, 1946); see also Chaudrhi Muhyammad Ali, *The Emergence of Pakistan* (New York: Columbia University Press, 1967), and Benny Morris, *The Birth of the Palestinian Refugee Problem, 1947–1949* (Cambridge: Cambridge University Press, 1987).

80. "One must assume that Wilson, Lloyd George, and probably even old Clemenceau, would have been astonished and dismayed at the extent to which the noble principle that had guided their efforts at peacemaking three quarters of a century ago had been so thoroughly discredited by virtue of this tragic truism: moving frontiers is unlikely to reduce the prevalence of warfare and bloodshed in multi-cultural, multi-ethnic, or multi-religious societies, at least for very long. But moving people might." William R. Keylor, "The Principle of National Self Determination as a Factor in the Creation of Postwar Frontiers in Europe, 1919 and 1945," in Christian Baechler and Carole Fink, eds.,

*L'établissement des frontières en Europe après les deux guerres mon-
diales* (Bern: Peter Lang, 1996), pp. 53–54.

81. John W. Young, *Cold War Europe, 1945–1991,* 2d ed. (London: Arnold,
1996).

82. Although the European Bank for Reconstruction and Development has
some links to schemes of the early 1920s, nothing like a Marshall Plan
was proposed. See John Feffer, *Shock Waves: Eastern Europe After the
Revolutions* (Boston: South End, 1992).

83. See Anthony Lewis, Op-Ed page, *New York Times,* June 16, 1997.

Chapter 2. International Associationalism: The Social and Political Premises of Peacemaking After 1917 and 1945

1. For a modern reformulation of the Kantian or Wilsonian claim, see
Michael Doyle, "Liberal Institutions and International Ethics," in Ken-
neth Kipnis and Diana T. Meyers, eds., *Political Realism and Inter-
national Morality* (Boulder, Colo.: Westview, 1987); also Michael
Doyle, "Liberalism and World Politics," *American Political Science
Review* 98 (1986): 1151–70; Bruce Russett and Harvey Starr critically
evaluate the claim in *World Politics,* 2d ed. (New York: Freeman,
1985), pp. 409ff. See also among many specialized studies Stuart A.
Bremer, "Democracy and Militarized Interstate Conflict, 1916–1965,"
International Interactions 18 (1993): 231–49, and Stuart A. Bremer,
"Dangerous Dyads: Conditions Affecting the Likelihood of Interna-
tional War, 1816–1965," *Journal of Conflict Resolution* 36, no. 2 (June
1992): 309–41; also Henry Farber and Joanne Gowa, "Common Interests or Common Polities? Reinterpreting the Democratic Peace," *Journal of Politics* 59, no. 2 (May 1997): 393–417; Zeev Maoz and Bruce
Russett, "Normative and Structural Causes of Democratic Peace,"
American Political Science Review 87, no. 3 (Sept. 1993): 624–38, and
Zeev Maoz, *Domestic Sources of Global Change* (Ann Arbor: University of Michigan Press, 1996).

2. There is another, more encompassing claim: namely, that as states
modernize and industrialize they are less likely to resort to war, not
because of their politics, but because of their internal socioeconomic
development and the needs of the international economy. This is a
descriptive, not prescriptive law. It essentially predicts that over time
war should disappear as an outmoded human institution as societies
become industrialized. It borrowed from the great sociological differentiation between agricultural, hierarchic, priestly, and military societies, on one hand, and peaceable, civilian, and industrial societies
on the other. As industry prevailed, nations would beat their swords
into steam engines. We can find this sociologically grounded expec-

tation in Saint Simon and John Stuart Mill, Veblen and Schumpeter, Norman Angell, and many other writers. It presupposes that conflict is pre-modern, non-rational, and destined to wither away. There is finally the argument that societies evolve morally and will abandon war as once they abandoned slavery and later colonialism. See James Lee Ray, "The Abolition of Slavery and the End of International War," *International Organization* 43, no. 3 (Summer 1989): 405–40.

3. See Arno J. Mayer, *Political Origins of the New Diplomacy* (New Haven: Yale University Press, 1959), and Arno J. Mayer, *Politics and Diplomacy of Peacemaking: Containment and Counterrevolution at Versailles, 1918–1919* (New York: Knopf, 1967); also N. Gordon Levin, Jr., *Woodrow Wilson and World Politics* (New York: Oxford University Press, 1968). For an alternative view of Wilson's diplomacy, see Klaus Schwabe, *Woodrow Wilson, Revolutionary Germany, and Peacemaking, 1918–1919,* trans. Robert and Rita Kimber, (Chapel Hill: University of North Carolina Press, 1985).

4. For the ILO, see among the many works, Francis Graham Wilson, *Labor in the League System: A Study of the International Labor Organization in Relation to International Administration* (Stanford, Calif.: Stanford University Press, 1934), James T. Shotwell, ed., *The Origins of the International Labor Organization,* 2 vols. (New York: Carnegie Endowment for International Peace and Columbia University Press, 1934); Antony Evelyn Alcock, *History of the International Labor Organization* (New York: Octagon, 1971); and, from the viewpoint of functional theory, the treatment of the ILO in Ernst B. Haas, *Beyond the Nation-State: Functionalism and International Organization* (Stanford, Calif.: Stanford University Press, 1964), pp. 126–68.

5. For the minorities treaties see Julius Stone, *International Guarantees of Minority Rights: Procedure of the Council of the League of Nations in Theory and Practice* (London: H. Milford, Oxford University Press, 1932); Arthur Balogh, *Der internationale Schutz der Minderheiten* (Munich: A. Dresler, 1928); C. A. Macartney, *National States and National Minorities* (New York: Russell & Russell, 1968); Christoph Gutermann, *Das Minderheitenschutzverfahren des Völkerbundes* (Berlin: Duncker & Humblot, 1979); Bastiaan Schot, *Nation oder Staat? Deutschland und der Minderheitenschutz: zur Völkerbundspolitik der Stresemann-Ära* (Marburg/Lahn: J.G. Herder-Institut, 1988); and Peter Babej, "Weimar Revisionism and the League Minorities System: An Analysis of the Interplay Between National Objectives and International Institutions," (Ph.D. diss., Harvard University, 1994). From the viewpoint of Jewish organizations, cf. Jacob Robinson et al., *Were the Minorities Treaties a Failure?* (New York: Institute of Jewish Affairs of

the American Jewish Congress and the World Jewish Congress, 1943). Carole Fink is currently researching the history of the paradigm minorities treaty that Poland acceded to.

6. On this theme see Haas, *Beyond the Nation-State*, pp. 3–85; and the discussion of interwar corporatism in Charles S. Maier, *Recasting Bourgeois Europe: Stabilization in France, Germany, and Italy in the Decade After World War I* (Princeton: Princeton University Press, 1975).

7. See Hurst Hannum, "Contemporary Developments in the International Protection of the Rights of Minorities," *Notre Dame Law Review* 66 (1990): 1431–48; also Hurst Hannum, *Autonomy, Sovereignty, and Self-Determination: The Accommodation of Conflicting Rights*, rev. ed. (Philadelphia: University of Pennsylvania Press, 1996). Richard B. Bilder, "Can Minorities Treaties Work?" in Yoram Dinstein, ed., *The Protection of Minorities and Human Rights* (Dordrecht: Martinus Nijhoff, 1992), pp. 61–82, offers an optimistic assessment and defense of the treaties.

8. See among the numerous treatments written since archival accessibility, Stephen V. O. Clarke, *Central Bank Cooperation, 1924–1931* (New York: Federal Reserve Bank of New York, 1967); Barry Eichengreen, *Golden Fetters: The Gold Standard and the Great Depression, 1919–1939* (New York: Oxford University Press, 1992), with extensive bibliography and references to particular national experiences; Donald Moggridge, *British Monetary Policy, 1924–1931: The Norman Conquest of $4.86* (Cambridge: Cambridge University Press, 1972); Diane B. Kunz, *The Battle for Britain's Gold Standard in 1931* (London: Croom Helm, 1987); Stephen A. Schuker, *The End of French Predominance in Europe* (Chapel Hill: University of North Carolina Press, 1976); Kenneth Mouré, *Managing the Franc Poincaré: Economic Understanding and Political Constraint in French Monetary Policy, 1928–1936* (Cambridge: Cambridge University Press, 1991).

Chapter 3. American Grand Strategy from World War to Cold War, 1940–1950

1. See especially Robert Dallek, *Franklin D. Roosevelt and American Foreign Policy, 1932–1945* (New York: Oxford University Press, 1979), pp. 171–313; Warren F. Kimball, *Forged in War: Roosevelt, Churchill, and the Second World War* (New York: William Morrow, 1997); Waldo Heinrichs, *Threshold of War: Franklin D. Roosevelt and American Entry into World War II* (New York: Oxford University Press, 1988).

2. For the classic governmental study, see U.S. Department of Commerce,

The United States in the World Economy (Washington, D.C.: Government Printing Office, 1943); Lloyd C. Gardner, Economic Aspects of New Deal Diplomacy (Madison: University of Wisconsin Press, 1964).

3. Acheson testimony, June 12, 1945, U.S. Senate, Committee on Banking and Currency, Bretton Woods Agreements Act, 79th Cong., 1st sess., (Washington, D.C.: Government Printing Office, 1945), 2:20–22, 33, 49.

4. Harley A. Notter, Postwar Foreign Policy Preparation, 1939–1945 (Washington, D.C.: Government Printing Office, 1949), p. 128; see also Stephen D. Krasner, "State Power and the Structure of International Trade," World Politics 28 (April 1976): 317–47.

5. Dean G. Acheson, "The War, Rehabilitation, and Lasting Peace," Department of State Bulletin 9 (December 18, 1943), p. 421.

6. See, for example, Notter, Postwar Foreign Policy Preparation, pp. 23–61; Robert D. Schulzinger, The Wise Men of Foreign Affairs: The History of the Council on Foreign Relations (New York: Columbia University Press, 1984), pp. 59–112; David G. Haglund, Latin America and the Transformation of U.S. Strategic Thought, 1936–1940 (Albuquerque: University of New Mexico Press, 1984), pp. 164–222; Foreign Relations of the United States, 1940, 5:1–257, 353–79 [hereinafter cited as FRUS].

7. In addition to the citations in note 6, see Eugene Staley, "The Myth of the Continents," Foreign Affairs 19 (April 1941): 481–95; National Foreign Trade Council, Report of the Twenty-seventh National Foreign Trade Convention (New York: National Foreign Trade Council, 1940), pp. 13–16; Beatrice Bishop Berle and Travis Beal Jacobs, eds., Navigating the Rapids, 1918–1971: From the Papers of Adolf A. Berle (New York: Harcourt Brace Jovanovich, 1973), pp. 318–47.

8. Samuel I. Rosenman, ed., The Public Papers and Addresses of Franklin D. Roosevelt, 1940 (New York: Macmillan, 1941), pp. 261, 281–82; Frank Ninkovich, Modernity and Power: A History of the Domino Theory (Chicago: University of Chicago Press, 1994), p. 120.

9. For analyses along similar lines, see Ninkovich, Modernity and Power, pp. 112–22; John Lamberton Harper, American Visions of Europe: Franklin D. Roosevelt, George F. Kennan, and Dean G. Acheson (New York: Cambridge University Press, 1994), pp. 63–76.

10. Dean G. Acheson, This Vast External Realm (New York: Norton, 1973), p. 19.

11. Public Papers of the Presidents of the United States: Harry S. Truman, 1952–1953 (Washington, D.C.: Government Printing Office, 1966), pp. 194–95, 189.

12. Mark Skinner Watson, Chief of Staff: Prewar Plans and Preparations (Washington, D.C.: Office of the Chief of Military History, 1950); Russell F. Weigley, The American Way of War: A History of United States

Military Strategy and Policy (New York: Macmillan, 1973), pp. 242–359.

13. Dallek, *Roosevelt and American Foreign Policy*, pp. 282–84; Theodore A. Wilson, *The First Summit: Roosevelt and Churchill at Placentia Bay, 1941*, rev. ed. (Lawrence: University Press of Kansas, 1991); Townsend Hoopes and Douglas Brinkley, *FDR and the Creation of the U.N.* (New Haven: Yale University Press, 1997), pp. 26–42; Randall Bennett Woods, *A Changing of the Guard: Anglo-American Relations, 1941–1946* (Chapel Hill: University of North Carolina Press, 1990), pp. 51–54; Georg Schild, *Bretton Woods and Dumbarton Oaks: American Economic and Political Postwar Planning in the Summer of 1944* (New York: St. Martin's, 1995), pp. 33–37.

14. See, for example, Dean G. Acheson, *Present at the Creation: My Years in the State Department* (New York: Norton, 1969), pp. 27–34; Acheson testimony, 3 February 1943, House of Representatives, Committee on Foreign Affairs, *Extension of the Lend-Lease Act*, 78th Cong., 1st sess. (Washington, D.C.: Government Printing Office, 1943), pp. 86–89.

15. See, for example, Alfred E. Eckes, Jr., *A Search for Solvency: Bretton Woods and the International Monetary System, 1941–1947* (Austin: University of Texas Press, 1975); Woods, *A Changing of the Guard;* Schild, *Bretton Woods and Dumbarton Oaks;* Susan Ariel Aaronson, *Trade and the American Dream: A Social History of Postwar Trade Policy* (Lexington: University Press of Kentucky, 1996).

16. Amos Perlmutter, *FDR and Stalin: A Not So Grand Alliance, 1943–1945* (Columbia: University of Missouri Press, 1993); Robert Nisbet, *Roosevelt and Stalin: The Failed Courtship* (Washington, D.C.: Regnery Gateway, 1988); Frederick W. Marks, III, *Wind Over Sand: The Diplomacy of Franklin Roosevelt* (Athens: University of Georgia Press, 1988); Remi Nadeau, *Stalin, Churchill, and Roosevelt Divide Europe* (New York: Praeger, 1990).

17. Dallek, *Roosevelt and American Foreign Policy*, pp. 317–528; Warren F. Kimball, *The Juggler: Franklin Roosevelt as Wartime Statesman* (Princeton: Princeton University Press, 1991); Kimball, *Forged in War;* Lloyd C. Gardner, *Spheres of Influence: The Great Powers Partition Europe, from Munich to Yalta* (Chicago: Ivan R. Dee, 1993); Harper, *American Visions of Europe*, pp. 77–131.

18. Mark A. Stoler, *The Politics of the Second Front: American Military Planning and Diplomacy in Coalition Warfare, 1941–1943* (Westport, Conn.: Greenwood, 1977).

19. Melvyn P. Leffler, *A Preponderance of Power: National Security, the Truman Administration, and the Cold War* (Stanford, Calif.: Stanford University Press, 1992), pp. 56–59.

20. Robert A. Divine, *Second Chance: The Triumph of Internationalism in America During World War II* (New York: Atheneum, 1967); Hoopes and Brinkley, *FDR and the Creation of the U.N.;* Robert C. Hildebrand, *The Origins of the United Nations and the Search for Postwar Security* (Chapel Hill: University of North Carolina Press, 1990); Thomas M. Campbell, *Masquerade Peace: America's UN Policy, 1944–1945* (Tallahassee: Florida State University Press, 1973).

21. Harper, *American Visions of Europe,* pp. 107–12; Kimball, *The Juggler,* pp. 83–105; Kimball, *Forged in War,* pp. 220–21, 279–80, 329–30; Martin J. Sherwin, *A World Destroyed: The Atomic Bomb and the Grand Alliance* (New York: Knopf, 1975).

22. "A Security Policy for Postwar America," Naval Historical Center, Strategic Plans Division, series 14, box 194, A1–2.

23. Fred Kaplan, *The Wizards of Armageddon* (New York: Simon & Schuster, 1983), p. 22.

24. *FRUS, The Conferences of Malta and Yalta, 1945,* pp. 1077–78.

25. Leffler, *Preponderance of Power,* pp. 60–99.

26. Memorandum by the Joint Strategic Survey Committee, no date, *FRUS, Potsdam,* 1:596; Department of State, June 27 and 28, 1945, ibid., 587–88, 258.

27. Expanded Draft of Letter from Secretary of War to Secretary of State, "U.S. Position re Soviet Proposals on Kiel Canal and Dardanelles," July 8, 1945, National Archives (NA), Record Group (RG) 165, American-British Conversations (ABC) 093 Kiel (July 6, 1945), sec. 1-A.

28. Robert L. Messer, *The End of an Alliance: James F. Byrnes, Roosevelt, Truman, and the Origins of the Cold War* (Chapel Hill: University of North Carolina Press, 1982); Alonzo L. Hamby, *Man of the People: A Life of Harry S. Truman* (New York: Oxford University Press, 1995), pp. 312–86.

29. Memorandum for the President, by John McCloy, April 26, 1945, Harry S. Truman Papers (HSTP), Presidential Secretary's File (PSF), box 178 (Harry S. Truman Library, Independence, Missouri); Henry L. Stimson to Truman, May 16, 1945, ibid., box 157; Joseph Grew to Truman, June 27, 1945, *FRUS, Potsdam,* 1:279; *Presidential Papers of the Presidents: Harry S. Truman, 1945,* p. 61.

30. *Presidential Papers of the Presidents: Harry S. Truman, 1947,* pp. 167–72; United Nations, Economic Commission for Europe, *Economic Survey of Europe (1947)* (Geneva: United Nations, 1948), pp. 31–74; Fred L. Block, *The Origins of International Economic Disorder: A Study of United States International Monetary Policy from World War II to the Present* (Berkeley: University of California Press, 1977), pp. 70–86;

Alan S. Milward, *War, Economy, and Society, 1939–1945* (Berkeley: University of California Press, 1977), pp. 345–61.

31. JCS 1769/1, "United States Assistance to Other Countries from the Standpoint of National Security," April 29, 1947, *FRUS, 1947*, 1:739–41.

32. George F. Kennan, "Russia's National Objectives," April 10, 1947, box 17, George F. Kennan Papers (Mudd Library, Princeton University); Kennan, "Comments on the National Security Program," March 28, 1947, ibid.

33. Minutes of the Meetings of the Policy Planning Staff, August 25 and September 4, 1947, NA, RG 59, Policy Planning Staff, box 32; Kennan, "Problems of Far Eastern Policy," January 14, 1948, box 17, Kennan Papers; Kennan, "Where We Are Today," December 21, 1948, ibid.; Central Intelligence Agency (CIA), "Strategic Importance of the Far East to the US and the USSR," May 4, 1949, HSTP, PSF, box 256.

34. Walter Millis, ed., *The Forrestal Diaries* (New York: Viking, 1951), pp. 350–51.

35. Memorandum by Chief of Staff, no date [July 1947], NA, RG 165, ABC 471.6 Atom (17 August 1945), sec. 6-A; Leffler, *Preponderance of Power*, pp. 147–50.

36. President's Committee on Foreign Aid, *European Recovery and American Aid* (Washington, D.C.: Government Printing Office, 1947), pp. 18–22.

37. Chiarella Esposito, "Marshall Plan Lessons for Contemporary Aid Donors," in Barry Eichengreen, ed., *Europe's Post-war Recovery* (Cambridge: Cambridge University Press, 1995), p. 77.

38. Lucretia Reichlin, "The Marshall Plan Reconsidered," ibid., p. 50; Barry Eichengreen, "Mainsprings of Economic Recovery in Post-War Europe," ibid., pp. 16–32; Michael J. Hogan, *The Marshall Plan: America, Britain, and the Reconstruction of Western Europe, 1947–1952* (New York: Cambridge University Press, 1987).

39. Memorandum of Conversation, by George C. Marshall, July 21, 1947, *FRUS, 1947*, 2:1003.

40. Meeting of the Secretaries of State, War, and Navy, July 3, 1947, NA, RG 107, Robert P. Patterson Papers, Safe File, box 3.

41. Lewis Douglas to Marshall, March 2, 1948, *FRUS, 1948*, 2:111.

42. Acheson to Truman, April 8, 1949, *FRUS, 1949*, 3:175–76; see also Leffler, *Preponderance of Power*, 207–18, 277–86.

43. Albert Wedemeyer to Omar Bradley et al., "Coordination of United States–Western European Military Resources to Counter Soviet Communism," March 20, 1948, NA, RG 319, Plans & Operations, 381 Europe Top Secret; Joint Strategic Plans Committee 876, "United States

Military Alliances with Nations of Western Europe," n.d. [early April 1948], ibid., 092 Top Secret.

44. Kennan to Robert Lovett, October 6, 1947, NA, RG 59, Policy Planning Staff, box 33; Charles Bohlen, "Preliminary Analysis of Announcement of Revival of the European Comintern," October 7, 1947, NA, RG 59, Charles Bohlen Papers, box 6.

45. For the views of Kennan and Bohlen, see *FRUS, 1948,* 3:152–54, 157–58, 177, 186.

46. See, for example, CIA, "Special Evaluation No. 27," March 16, 1948, NA, RG 319, Plans & Operations, 350.05 TS; Intelligence Staff Study, "Cumulative Effects of United States Actions Upon USSR, Western Europe, and USA," attached to S. J. Chamberlin to Albert C. Wedemeyer, April 14, 1948, ibid., 092 TS; Memorandum of Information, by Thomas Browning Inglis, March 16, 1948, Naval Historical Center, Strategic Plans Division, A8.

47. Jean Edward Smith, ed., *The Papers of General Lucius D. Clay: Germany, 1945–1949* (Bloomington: Indiana University Press, 1974), 2: 650.

48. Testimony, by Lovett, June 3, 1948, in U.S. Senate, Committee on Foreign Relations, *The Vandenberg Resolution and the North Atlantic Treaty,* vol. 6 of *The Legislative Origins of American Foreign Policy* (New York: Garland, 1979), pp. 76–79.

49. Bradley to Eisenhower, "NME Views on Situation in Germany," June 30, 1948, NA, RG 319, Plans & Operations, 092 TS.

50. Steven L. Rearden, *History of the Office of the Secretary of Defense: The Formative Years, 1947–1950* (Washington, D.C.: Government Printing Office, 1984), pp. 335–51.

51. Précis of Conversation, October 18, 1948, *FRUS, 1948,* 3:886.

52. Department of State, Office of Intelligence and Research, "Soviet Internal Situation," July 1, 1949, NA, RG 330, Office of the Secretary of Defense, box 3, CD 2-2-38.

53. Geir Lundestad conceived this interpretive framework, but it has been widely adopted, especially in the work of John Lewis Gaddis. See Lundestad, "Empire by Invitation? The United States and Western Europe, 1945–1952," *Journal of Peace Research* 23 (September 1986): 263–77; and, most recently, John Lewis Gaddis, *We Now Know: Rethinking Cold War History* (Oxford: Clarendon, 1997).

54. Norman Naimark, *The Russians in Germany: A History of the Soviet Zone of Occupation, 1945–1949* (Cambridge: Harvard University Press, 1995); Jan T. Gross, *Revolution from Abroad: The Soviet Conquest of Poland's Western Ukraine and Western Belorussia* (Princeton: Princeton University Press, 1988).

55. This point is developed persuasively in Gaddis, *We Now Know.*

56. Testimony, by Acheson, March 8, 1945, U.S. Senate, Committee on Banking and Currency, *Bretton Woods Agreements Act,* 79th Cong., 1st sess. (Washington, D.C.: Government Printing Office, 1945), 1:35.

Chapter 4. Reversal of Fortune: Britain, France, and the Making of Europe, 1945–1956

1. David Reynolds, "Great Britain," in David Reynolds, ed., *The Origins of the Cold War in Europe: International Perspectives* (New Haven: Yale University Press, 1994), pp. 77–95.
2. For a general assessment of French diplomacy and national strategy in this period, see William I. Hitchcock, *France Restored: Cold War Diplomacy and the Quest for Leadership in Europe, 1944–1954* (Chapel Hill: University of North Carolina Press, 1998).
3. On the Suez crisis, see in particular Keith Kyle, *Suez* (New York: St. Martin's, 1991); and on the economic dimension, Diane Kunz, *The Economic Diplomacy of the Suez Crisis* (Chapel Hill: University of North Carolina Press, 1990).
4. Maurice Vaisse, "Post-Suez France," in Wm. Roger Louis and Roger Owen, eds., *Suez, 1956: The Crisis and its Consequences* (Oxford: Oxford University Press, 1989), p. 335.
5. Memorandum by Sir O. Sargent, "Stocktaking After VE-Day," July 11, 1945, in *Documents on British Policy Overseas,* series 1, vol. 1, ed. R. Butler and M. Pelly (London: HMSO, 1984), pp. 181–92. Foreign Minister Anthony Eden and Foreign Office adviser Alexander Cadogan both minuted their endorsement of the paper.
6. Randall Woods explains that the nominal interest rate was 2 percent, but "given the fact that payments were to be deferred until 1951, the actual rate was 1.62 percent." Woods, *A Changing of the Guard: Anglo-American Relations, 1941–1946* (Chapel Hill: University of North Carolina Press, 1990), p. 359. See also Kenneth Morgan, *Labour in Power, 1945–1951* (Oxford: Oxford University Press, 1984), pp. 144–50. The Keynes memorandum is reprinted in Donald Moggridge, ed., *The Collected Writings of John Maynard Keynes,* vol. 24, *Activities 1944–1946, The Transition to Peace* (London: Macmillan, 1979), pp. 398–411.
7. Victor Rothwell, *Britain and the Cold War, 1941–1947* (London: Macmillan, 1987), pp. 46–64.
8. John Darwin, *The End of the British Empire: The Historical Debate* (London: Blackwell, 1991), pp. 43–47; and A. N. Porter and A. J. Stockwell, *British Imperial Policy and Decolonization, 1938–1964,* vol. 1, *1938–1951* (London: Macmillan, 1987), pp. 46–64.
9. An earlier line of attack on Bevin, captured in Anthony Nutting, *Europe Will Not Wait* (London: Praeger, 1960), has been superseded by

a more nuanced assessment of Bevin's strategy. For a good survey of the debate see Bert Zeeman, "Britain and the Cold War: An Alternative Approach—The Treaty of Dunkirk Example," *European Historical Quarterly* 16 (1986): 343–67; Martin Folly, "Breaking the Vicious Circle: Britain, the United States, and the Making of the North Atlantic Treaty," *Diplomatic History* 12, no. 1 (Winter 1988): 59–77; and John Baylis, *The Diplomacy of Pragmatism: Britain and the Formation of NATO, 1942–1949* (Kent, Ohio: Kent State University Press, 1993). For the mackerel quip, see Avi Shlaim, Peter Jones, and Keith Sainsbury, *British Foreign Secretaries Since 1945* (London: David and Charles, 1977), p. 48.

10. For a sympathetic view of Bevin's policy—one that sees the Treasury as the real opponent of European ties—see Geoffrey Warner, "The Labour Government and the Unity of Western Europe, 1945–1951," in Ritchie Ovendale, ed., *The Foreign Policy of the British Labour Governments, 1945–1951* (Leicester: Leicester University Press, 1984), pp. 61–82.

11. Alan S. Milward, *The European Rescue of the Nation-State* (London: Routledge, 1992), p. 426.

12. George Peden, "Economic Aspects of British Perceptions of Power," in *Power in Europe?* vol. 2, ed. Ennio Di Nolfo (Berlin: De Gruyter, 1992), pp. 156–57; and Roger Bullen, "Britain and Europe, 1950–1957," ibid., pp. 499–504. See also John Young, "The Parting of the Ways? Britain, the Messina Conference and the Spaak Committee, June–December 1955," in John Young and Michael Dockrill, eds., *British Foreign Policy, 1945–1956* (London: Macmillan, 1989), pp. 197–224; and John Young, "Towards a New View of British Policy and European Unity, 1945–1957," in R. Ahmann, A. M. Birke, and M. Howard, eds., *The Quest for Stability: Problems of West European Security, 1918–1957* (London: Oxford University Press, 1993), pp. 435–62.

13. For a strong, and perhaps overstated, assessment of British industrial decline, see Correlli Barnett, *The Audit of War* (London: Macmillan, 1986).

14. Anthony Adamthwaite, "Britain and the World, 1945–1949: The View from the Foreign Office," in *International Affairs* 61, no. 2 (Spring 1985), p. 232. Also see his "Overstretched and Overstrung: Eden, the Foreign Office, and the Making of Policy," in *Power in Europe?* pp. 19–42. For a similarly critical view of British long-term strategic thinking—deemed "rambling and alarmingly ignorant"—see Alan S. Milward, *The Reconstruction of Western Europe, 1945–1951* (Berkeley: University of California Press, 1984), p. 501; and Milward, *European Rescue,* pp. 430–33.

15. Victor H. Feske, "The Road to Suez: The British Foreign Office and the Quai d'Orsay, 1951–1957," in Gordon A. Craig and Francis L. Lowenheim, eds., *The Diplomats: 1939–1979* (Princeton: Princeton University Press, 1994), 167–200.

16. Ambassador Jefferson Caffery to State Department, February 7, 1947, *Foreign Relations of the United States, 1947*, 2:154.

17. The best recent work on the French economy in this period is Frances Lynch, *France and the International Economy: From Vichy to the Treaty of Rome* (London: Routledge, 1997). For the earlier period, see Kenneth Mouré, *Managing the Franc Poincare: Economic Understanding and Political Constraint in French Monetary Policy, 1928–1936* (London: Cambridge University Press, 1991); and Julian Jackson, *The Politics of Depression in France, 1932–1936* (London: Cambridge University Press, 1985).

18. Charles S. Maier, *In Search of Stability: Explorations in Historical Political Economy* (London: Cambridge University Press, 1987), pp. 121–52. An excellent study of the transformation of French economic thinking across the era of the Second World War is Michel Margairaz, *L'état, les finances et l'économie: Histoire d'une conversion, 1932–1952* (Paris, 1991). On the Monnet Plan and its origins, see Philippe Mioche, *Le plan Monnet: genèse et élaboration, 1941–1947* (Paris: Publications de la Sorbonne, 1987), pp. 35–72.

19. On the motives of the Monnet Plan, see especially Milward, *Reconstruction of Western Europe*, pp. 126–67; and Frances Lynch, "Resolving the Paradox of the Monnet Plan: National and International Planning in French Reconstruction," *Economic Historical Review* 37, no. 2 (May 1984): 229–43.

20. "Memorandum de Jean Monnet pour G. Bidault sur la conférence de Paris," July 22, 1947, Monnet Papers (microfiche) AMF 14/1/4, French National Archives, Paris.

21. Office of Economic and Financial Affairs in the French Foreign Ministry to Jean Monnet, August 9, 1948, Y-Internationale, 1944–49, Archives of the Ministry of Foreign Affairs, Paris.

22. Minutes of a discussion of senior Treasury officials, January 5, 1949, published in Richard Clarke, *Anglo-American Economic Collaboration in War and Peace, 1942–1949* (Oxford: Clarendon, 1982), pp. 208–10.

23. For the origins of the Schuman Plan, see William I. Hitchcock, "France, the Western Alliance, and the Origins of the Schuman Plan, 1948–1950," *Diplomatic History* 21, no. 4 (Fall 1997): 603–30; Pierre Gerbet, "La genèse du Plan Schuman: Des origines à la déclaration du 9 mai 1950," *Revue française de science politique* 6 (1956): 525–53;

and Gérard Bossuat, *La France, l'aide américaine et la construction européenne, 1944–1954* (Paris: Comité pour l'Histoire Economique et Financière de la France, 1992), 655–75, 735–45.

24. Works that deal with the origins of the EDC include Armand Clesse, *Le projet de CED du Plan Pleven au "crime" du 30 août* (Baden-Baden: Nomos, 1989); Robert McGeehan, *The German Rearmament Question: American Diplomacy and European Defense After World War Two* (Chicago: University of Illinois Press, 1971); Thomas A. Schwartz, *America's Germany: John J. McCloy and the Federal Republic of Germany* (Cambridge: Harvard University Press, 1991); and David Clay Large, *Germans to the Front: West German Rearmament in the Adenauer Era* (Chapel Hill: University of North Carolina Press, 1996).

25. See especially the letter from Alexandre Parodi to Prime Minister Pierre Mendès-France, August 21, 1954, in Pierre Mendès-France, *Oeuvres complètes*, vol. 3, *Gouverner c'est choisir, 1954–1955* (Paris: Gallimard, 1954), pp. 816–17; and Jean Lacouture, *Pierre Mendès-France*, trans. George Holoch (New York: Holmes and Meyer, 1984), pp. 268–76.

26. For the final text of the London Conference, see *Documents Diplomatiques Français, 1954* [hereinafter cited as *DDF*], Annexes (Paris: Imprimerie nationale, 1987), pp. 329–51.

27. The adverse effects of the Korean War were the more regretable in that France by 1950 had stabilized its economy. The trade deficit had shrunk to a postwar low; prices had stabilized; unemployment was low; and the counterpart aid from the Marshall Plan helped cover the budget deficit. Warren Baum, *The French Economy and the State* (Princeton: Princeton University Press, 1958), pp. 66–67. The rearmament program, however, led to budget deficits larger than anything seen since the end of the war. See Frances Lynch, "The Economic Effects of the Korean War in France, 1950–1952," European University Institute Working Paper no. 86/253, December 1986.

28. Jean Monnet takes a certain amount of credit for "la relance européenne" in his memoirs, but Spaak had much more to do with it. Monnet, *Mémoires* (Paris: Fayard, 1976), pp. 467–504.

29. *DDF 1955*, 1 (January–June), Rivière to Pinay, April 1, 1955, doc. 163, pp. 377–78; Spaak to Pinay, April 4, 1955, doc. 171, pp. 399–400; Garnier to Pinay, April 26, 1955, doc. 228, pp. 517–18.

30. *DDF 1955*, 1, Note du Département, April 7, 1955, doc. 181, pp. 418–21; and note 2, p. 418. Foreign Minister Antoine Pinay, meeting with his British counterpart Harold Macmillan, made precisely the same point: in light of the Austrian treaty, it was important to give the Germans the idea that European integration was not dead; the West had

to have something to offer. On the other hand, Pinay said that new initiatives must be not "utopian" but concrete, and limited to such areas as energy and transport. *DDF 1955, Annexes,* 1 (January–June), Pinay-Macmillan talks, April 21, 1955, p. 28–29.

31. *DDF 1955,* 1, Note de la Direction des Affaires Economiques et Financières, May 18, 1955, doc. 288, pp. 665–70.

32. *DDF 1955,* 1, Note du Département, n.d. [beginning of May 1955], doc. 239, pp. 546–51.

33. *DDF 1955,* 1, François-Poncet to Pinay, May 25, 1955, doc. 297, pp. 683–86.

34. *DDF 1955,* 1, Note de la Direction des Affaires Economiques et Financières, May 18, 1955, doc. 288, pp. 665–70; and Note du Département, May 26, 1955, doc. 301, pp. 692–93.

35. *DDF 1955,* 1, Pinay to major embassies, June 10, 1955, doc. 332, pp. 756–58. Adenauer was always a strong backer of the Common Market, though the German economics minister, Ludwig Erhard—a vigorous advocate of free trade—fought a stiff rearguard action against it, arguing that it would merely extend protectionism to the member states. For a full discussion of German views and policy toward both Euratom and the Common Market, see the work of Hanns Jürgen Küsters, *Die Gründung der europäische Wirtschaftsgemeinschaft* (Baden-Baden: Nomos, 1982).

36. See for example the instructions delivered to the French delegation to the Brussels talks. These were strongly in favor of Euratom, and cautious—but not opposed—to the Common Market idea. *DDF 1955,* 2 (July–December), Note du Service de Coopération Economique, July 5, 1955, doc. 13, pp. 19–23.

37. *DDF 1956,* 1, Note de la Direction Générale des Affaires Economiques et Financières, April 6, 1956, doc. 222, pp. 526–28. A European atomic agency was "eminently desirable," this memo concluded.

38. *DDF 1955,* 2, Note de la Direction des Affaires Economiques et Financières, September 7, 1955, doc. 179, pp. 437–39; and *DDF 1956,* 1, Rivière to Pineau, February 6, 1956, doc. 87, p. 178.

39. *DDF 1955,* 2, Note de la sous-direction d'Europe centrale, November 21, 1955, doc. 379, pp. 836–39.

40. *DDF 1956,* 1, Christian de Margerie to Pineau, March 23, 1956, doc. 199, pp. 478–80. "Every day," de Margerie wrote, "ever more aware of the strength of their country, a good number of [German] politicians . . . are turning away from the European idea. They think it more profitable for their country not to submit to new supranational authorities and to try its luck on the plane of free, open competition."

41. *Foreign Relations of the United States, 1955–1957,* 27, Memorandum

of Conversation, Dulles, Eden, et al., January 30, 1956, pp. 619–20. Foreign Minister Selwyn Lloyd described the British view as "hostile" to the Common Market.

42. *DDF 1955,* 2, Note du Service de Coopération Economique, July 5, 1955, doc. 13, pp. 19–23. On British policy and the origins of the EEC, see Young, "Towards a New View of British Policy," pp. 435–62; and Milward, *European Rescue,* pp. 424–33.

43. *DDF 1956,* 2, Pineau to major embassies summarizing Mollet-Adenauer talks, October 2, 1956, doc. 235, pp. 493–96; and Couve to Pineau, October 10, 1956, doc. 261, pp. 553–54. Adenauer's criticisms of the United States sound much like de Gaulle's, and shed much light on the origins of the 1963 Franco-German Treaty of Friendship. Milward argued that the French and the Germans were already poised to compromise by November 6, and therefore the impact of Suez should not be overestimated. Milward, *European Rescue,* pp. 214–15. But their willingness to compromise can itself be ascribed to the series of international pressures visible throughout the 1955–56 period, which have been outlined in this chapter.

44. *DDF 1956,* 3 (October–December), Mollet to Adenauer, October 31, 1956, doc. 75, 121–22; and on the reasons for the blocked talks, see Notes pour le Président du Conseil, November 3 and 5, doc. 123, pp. 197–202.

45. The French *procès-verbal* includes only the first part of the Adenauer-Mollet conversation; the exchanges after Eden's call are not included. *DDF 1956,* 3, November 6, 1956, doc. 138, pp. 231–38. But Christian Pineau gives a lively rendering of the meeting: Christian Pineau and Christiane Rimbaud, *Le Grand Pari: L'Aventure du Traité de Rome* (Paris: Fayard, 1991), pp. 221–23.

46. Pineau and Rimbaud, *Le Grand Pari,* pp. 223–26. On the French assessment of the German concessions, *DDF 1956,* 3, Pineau to major posts, November 8, 1956, doc. 146, pp. 249–51. Another factor in making the French still more favorable to Euratom than ever before was that the Suez crisis had dramatically underscored French dependence on imported Middle Eastern oil. Suddenly, atomic energy appeared to be a prerequisite to national independence. Mollet to Adenauer, November 13, 1956, doc. 165, pp. 288–89.

47. Fernand Braudel and Ernest Labrousse, *Histoire économique et sociale de la France,* vol. 4, part 3 (Paris: Presses Universitaire de France, 1982), p. 1012.

Chapter 5. The Making of a Political System: The German Question in International Politics, 1945-1963

1. Rusk-Gromyko meeting, October 2, 1963, POL GER (Office of German Affairs), State Department Central Files for 1963, Record Group 59, U.S. National Archives, College Park, Maryland. The arguments in this chapter have been elaborated upon, with far greater evidence, in my book, *A Constructed Peace: The Making of the European Settlement, 1945-1963* (Princeton: Princeton University Press, 1999).

2. Policy Planning Staff meeting, October 18, 1949, pp. 6-7, Policy Planning Staff Records, 1947-53, box 32, RG 59, U.S. National Archives.

3. Ibid., p. 9.

4. Douglas to Marshall, May 20, 1948, *Foreign Relations of the United States, 1948*, 2:263 [hereinafter cited as *FRUS*].

5. Kennan paper, March 8, 1949, *FRUS, 1949*, 3:98.

6. George Kennan, *American Diplomacy, 1900-1950* (Chicago: University of Chicago Press, 1951), p. 69.

7. Hans-Peter Schwartz, *Adenauer: Der Staatsmann, 1952-1967* (Stuttgart: Deutsche Verlags-Anstalt, 1991), pp. 299, 396.

8. American and German officials understood the point at the time. One high State Department official, Foy Kohler, pointed out to the top permanent official in the German Foreign Office that including a provision on nuclear non-proliferation—meaning essentially a guarantee of Germany's non-nuclear status—in an agreement that would settle the Berlin crisis would serve to "hold the Russians" to the agreement. The German official had to admit that he was "impressed by this argument." Meeting between Carstens, Kohler, et al., March 11, 1962, and Schröder, Rusk, Carstens, and Kohler, March 11, 1962, National Security Archive, Berlin File, Washington, D.C. The Americans also made it quite clear to the Soviets that if they took too aggressive a line on Berlin, this might well lead to the Germans getting control of nuclear weapons. See Kennedy-Adzhubei meeting, January 31, 1962, and Kennedy to Khrushchev, February 15, 1962, *FRUS, 1961-1963*, 14: 782, 821, and Kennedy-Dobrynin meeting, July 17, 1962, *FRUS, 1961-1963*, 15:224. Note also Rusk's comment in a meeting with the British and French on February 13 that by "pressing on Berlin too hard," the Russians "might force the Western Powers to allow Germany to acquire a national nuclear capability and thus cause a major change in Power relationships." Ormsby Gore to Foreign Office, February 14, 1963, Public Record Office, London, FO 371/163567. For the U.S. account, see *FRUS, 1961-1963*, 14:809.

9. Hickerson-Inverchapel meeting, January 21, 1948; Hickerson in U.S.-

U.K.-Canada talks, March 23, 1948; Douglas to Lovett, April 17, 1948, in *FRUS, 1948,* 3:11, 64, 91.

10. Interdepartmental meeting, August 30, 1947, *FRUS, 1947,* 1:762–63. On "third force" thinking at this time, see also the quotation from an unpublished State Department history of the Marshall Plan in Max Beloff, *The United States and the Unity of Europe* (Washington, D.C.: Brookings Institution, 1963), p. 28.

11. Acheson to Bruce, June 28 and July 16, 1951, and Acheson memorandum, July 6, 1951, *FRUS, 1951,* 3:802, 804, 816, 835.

12. National Security Council [NSC] meeting, November 21, 1955, *FRUS, 1955–1957,* 19:150–51.

13. NSC meeting, June 15, 1956, *FRUS, 1955–1957,* 26:128. NSC meetings, December 11, 1958 and March 26, 1959; Eisenhower-Herter meeting, December 12, 1958; Eisenhower-Spaak meeting, November 24, 1959, in *FRUS, 1958–1960,* 7(1):367, 370–71, 445, 521, 524. Extract from Dulles's press conference of July 16, 1957, quoted in Dulles to Perkins, July 16, 1957, U.S. National Archives, RG 59, 740.5611/7–1657.

14. Eisenhower to Bermingham, February 28, 1951, *Eisenhower Papers,* 12:76–77. Emphasis in original.

15. See especially the Eisenhower–de Gaulle meeting, December 19, 1959, *Documents Diplomatiques Français* 1959, 2:761.

16. Eisenhower-Macmillan meeting, March 28, 1960, *FRUS, 1958–1960,* 9:260.

17. NSC meetings, July 16 and 30, 1959, *FRUS, 1958–60,* 3:261, 289. Note also that the president's listing of Germany (along with Britain, France, and Italy) as a candidate for nuclear assistance in Eisenhower-Norstad meeting, August 3, 1960, *FRUS, 1958–1960,* 7(1):610.

18. See especially Schwartz, *Adenauer,* pp. 299, 396. Also Adenauer's comments at a December 1956 cabinet meeting, quoted in Christian Greiner, "Zwischen Integration und Nation: Die militärische Eingliederung der BRD in die NATO, 1954 bis 1957," p. 276, in Ludolf Herbst, ed., *Westdeutschland, 1945–1955: Unterwerfung, Kontrolle, Integration* (Munich: Oldenbourg, 1986).

19. Schwarz, *Adenauer,* 2:178, 299; Adenauer in Günter Buchstab, ed., *Adenauer: "Wir haben wirklich etwas geschaffen": Die Protokolle des CDU-Bundesvorstands, 1953–1957* (Düsseldorf: Droste, 1990), September 20, 1956, pp. 1029, 1073, 1079. He was still talking along these lines in 1963. See for example, Adenauer–de Gaulle meeting, January 22, 1963, *Akten zur Auswärtigen Politik der Bundesrepublik Deutschland 1963,* 1:141.

20. State-Defense meeting, June 17, 1958, Declassified Documents Reference Service (microfiche), 1982/1578.

21. Bundy to Kennedy, April 24, 1962, *FRUS, 1961–1963*, 13:1068.
22. De Gaulle–Adenauer meeting, January 21, 1963, *Akten zur Auswärtigen Politik der Bundesrepublik Deutschland 1963*, 1:117; and Bohlen to Kennedy and Rusk, January 4, 1963, *FRUS, 1961–1963*, 13:745.

Chapter 6. The Trials of Multilateralism: America, Britain, and the New Economic Order, 1941–1947

1. Paul Kennedy, *The Rise and Fall of the Great Powers* (New York: Random House, 1987), p. 357.
2. Ibid., p. 359, and Melvyn P. Leffler, *A Preponderance of Power: National Security, the Truman Administration, and the Cold War* (Stanford: Stanford University Press, 1992).
3. Winant memo, undated, Department of State, *Foreign Relations of the United States, 1945*, 6:22–24; *Anglo-American Financial Agreement: Hearings Before the Committee on Banking and Currency*, U.S. Senate, 79th Cong., 2d session (Washington, D.C., 1946), pp. 177–78, 193; "Some Economic Problems Raised by the Joint Declaration of August 14, 1941," Files of Harvey A. Notter, RG 59, National Archives (NA); U.S. Draft Memo of Understanding of Financial Matters, October 30, 1945, 611.4131/5–746, RG 59, NA; Joan Hoff Wilson, *American Business and Foreign Policy, 1920–1933* (Lexington: University Press of Kentucky, 1971) pp. 2–5; N. Gordon Levin, Jr., "Woodrow Wilson and World Politics," in N. Gordon Levin, Jr., ed., *Woodrow Wilson and the Paris Peace Conference*, 2d ed. (Lexington, Mass.: Heath, 1972), pp. 93–117; Hawkins to Grady, October 18, 1940; and "The Place of the Trade Agreements Act in Our Present and Future Commercial Policy," undated, RG 353, Intra- and Interdepartmental Committee Files, NA. For a thoroughgoing defense of the multilateralists and a refutation of the Williams-Kolko thesis, see Alfred Eckes, Jr., "Open Door Expansionism Reconsidered: The World War II Experience," *Journal of American History* 59, no. 4 (March 1973): 910–45.
4. "Questions and Answers Concerning the British Loan," no date, box 27, Papers of Dean Acheson, and Edelsberg to Blaisdell, no date, box 6, Papers of Thomas C. Blaisdell, Jr., Harry S. Truman Library, Independence, Missouri; Conference Report for Rosenman, November 15, 1943, Papers of Samuel Rosenman, Franklin D. Roosevelt Library, Hyde Park, New York; and "The Anglo-American Economic Agreement," January 17, 1946, FO 371/52950, Foreign Office Records, Public Record Office (henceforth PRO), London.
5. Acheson to Winant, September 14, 1945, 740.00119 Council/9-1945, RG 59, NA; and Warren F. Kimball, *The Most Unsordid Act: Lend-*

Lease, 1939–1941 (Baltimore: Johns Hopkins University Press, 1969), pp. 119–50. See also Alan P. Dobson, *U.S. Wartime Aid to Britain, 1940–1946* (London: Croom Helm, 1986).

6. See David Reynolds, *The Creation of the Anglo-American Alliance, 1937–1941: A Study in Competitive Co-operation* (London: Europa, 1991).

7. Keynes to Henderson, April 5 and 9, 1942, and May 9, 1942, and Comments from Keynes, January 29, 1942, and Comments on the "Treasury Note on External Monetary and Economic Policy," undated, T247/67, Papers of John Maynard Keynes, Records of the Treasury, PRO.

8. Keynes to Cohen, October 9, 1941, T247/69, Keynes Papers, Treasury Records, PRO.

9. See Armand van Dormael, *Bretton Woods: Birth of a Monetary System* (New York: Holmes & Meier, 1978), pp. 7–8; and Keynes to Henderson, September 5, 1942, T247/67, Keynes Papers, Treasury Records, PRO.

10. Comments of Keynes on British Financial Policy, January 29, 1942, and Keynes to Caine, April 29, 1942, T247/67, Keynes Papers, Treasury Records, PRO; van Dormael, *Bretton Woods,* pp. 34–37; and Richard N. Gardner, *Sterling-Dollar Diplomacy: Anglo-American Collaboration in the Reconstruction of Multilateral Trade* (Oxford: Clarendon, 1956), p. 77.

11. The State-Treasury rivalry was perhaps the most intense in wartime Washington because these two agencies displayed more organizational cohesiveness than other bureaucracies. H. G. Nicholas observed that while State and Treasury officials continually referred to the attitude of the department, others had as their frame of reference their "boss"—Ickes, Nelson, Crowley, and so forth. See H. G. Nicholas, ed., *Washington Dispatches, 1941–1945: Weekly Political Reports from the British Embassy* (Chicago: University of Chicago Press, 1981), xi; James MacGregor Burns, *Roosevelt: The Soldier of Freedom* (New York: Harcourt Brace Jovanovich, 1970), pp. 354–55; John Morton Blum, *From the Morgenthau Diaries,* vol. 3, *Years of War, 1941–1945* (Boston: Houghton Mifflin, 1967), p. 279; Kimball, *The Most Unsordid Act,* p. 225; and Roy F. Harrod, *The Life of John Maynard Keynes* (New York: Harcourt, Brace, 1951), pp. 537–38.

12. Batt to Hopkins, July 7, 1944, box 9, Papers of Harry Hopkins, FDR Library.

13. Currie to Hopkins and Currie to John S. Fischer, July 20, 1944, box 5, Papers of Assistant Secretary for Economic Affairs (Clayton-Thorp), HST Library; "Foreign Capital Position of the U.S. and G.B.," September 2, 1943, box 82, Notter Files, RG 59, DOS Records, NA; and Taft memo on "Phase II Lend-Lease," August 25, 1944, box 10, Papers of Charles P. Taft, Library of Congress (LC), Washington, D.C.

14. See Richard E. Darilek, *A Loyal Opposition in Time of War: The Republican Party and the Politics of Foreign Policy from Pearl Harbor to Yalta* (Westport, Conn.: Greenwood, 1986).

15. Ibid., pp. 125–26.

16. *New York Times,* February 16, 1944.

17. Conference Report for Rosenman, November 15, 1943, Papers of Samuel Rosenman, FDR Library.

18. Van Dormael, *Bretton Woods,* pp. 36–37, 44–46; Keynes to Caine, April 29, 1942, T247/67, Keynes Papers, Treasury Records, PRO; and Gardner, *Sterling-Dollar Diplomacy,* pp. 73–74.

19. "Morgenthau Opens Conference," *New York Times,* July 3, 1944; van Dormael, *Bretton Woods,* pp. 78–79, 173–74.

20. A. G. Kenwood and A. L. Lougheed, *The Growth of the International Economy, 1820–1960* (Albany: State University of New York Press, 1960), pp. 23–36; Gardner, *Sterling-Dollar Diplomacy,* p. 261; Delegation meeting, and Instructions to American Delegation-Fund, July 1, 1944, book 749, Diaries of Henry Morgenthau, Jr., FDR Library; and Memo on Bretton Woods, June 30, 1944, Files of Dean Acheson, RG 59, NA.

21. Blum, *Morgenthau Diaries,* pp. 274, 276; U.S. Delegation meeting, July 2, 1944, book 749, HM Diaries, FDR Library.

22. U.S. Congress, *Hearings on the 1945 Extension of the Reciprocal Trade Agreements Act,* House Ways and Means Committee (Washington, D.C., 1946), p. 11; Acting Secretary of State to Winant, March 5, 1945, 840.50/3–545, RG 59, NA.

23. *The 1945 Extension of RTAA,* pp. 10–14.

24. During lunch with Raymond Buel of *Fortune* magazine a month after renewal, Charles Taft admitted as much. Luncheon Meeting with Raymond L. Buel and James Agnell, June 25, 1945, box 10, C. Taft Papers, LC.

25. Keynes to Hopkins, July 22, 1944, T247/45, Keynes Papers, Treasury Records, PRO.

26. C. J. Bartlett, *A History of Post-War Britain, 1945–1974* (London: Longman, 1977), p. 17; and "The Real Issue," *Economist,* June 23, 1945.

27. Michael Foot, *Aneurin Bevan: A Biography* (London: Macgibbon and Key, 1962), p. 25.

28. Matthew A. Fitzsimons, *The Foreign Policy of the British Labour Government, 1945–1951* (Notre Dame, Ind.: University of Notre Dame Press, 1953), pp. 26–27.

29. Keynes memo, "Overseas Financial Policy in Stage III," April 17, 1945, D/150, Beaverbrook Papers, House of Lords Record Office, London; R. W. Ashton-Gwatney to Eady, March 5, 1945, T236/436, Eady Papers,

Treasury Records, PRO; and Beaverbrook to Keynes, April 17, 1945, T247/50, Keynes Papers, Treasury Records, PRO.

30. Wayne S. Knight, "The Nonfraternal Association: Anglo-American Relations and the Breakdown of the Grand Alliance, 1945–1947," (Ph.D. diss., American University, 1979), pp. 119–20; and Statement by the President, July 15, 1946, box 802, Official File Harry S. Truman Papers, HST Library.

31. For an excellent survey of U.S. economic foreign policy during the period of the early Cold War, see Diane B. Kunz, *Butter and Guns: America's Cold War Economic Diplomacy* (New York: Free Press, 1997).

32. Randall Bennett Woods, *A Changing of the Guard: Anglo-American Relations, 1941–1946* (Chapel Hill: University of North Carolina Press, 1990).

33. Michael S. Hogan, "The Marshall Plan," in Charles S. Maier, ed., *The Cold War in Europe* (New York: M. Wiener, 1991), p. 204. The best and most recent histories of America's efforts to aid in the reconstruction of Europe following World War II are Michael Hogan, *The Marshall Plan: America, Britain, and the Reconstruction of Western Europe, 1947–1952* (Cambridge: Cambridge University Press, 1987), and Alan S. Milward, *The Reconstruction of Western Europe, 1945–1951* (Berkeley and Los Angeles: University of California Press, 1984).

34. Marshall's original invitation had included all of Europe, including the Soviet satellites and European Russia. American officials believed that for a variety of reasons they could not exclude the communist powers. Aside from wanting the United States to appear magnanimous, Marshall and his aides feared that if the Eastern-bloc nations were not invited, French and Italian communists would prevent participation by their countries. What Washington hoped was that the prospect of integrating their economies with those of the West would ensure that Russia and its client states would never join. As it turned out, they were right.

35. For a concise summary of the Marshall Plan's goals and achievements, see Randall B. Woods, "The Marshall Plan: A Forty Year Perspective," German Marshall Fund of the United States (Washington, D.C., 1987).

36. Hogan, "Marshall Plan," p. 215.

37. Ibid., p. 206.

38. Alan S. Milward, "The Reconstruction of Western Europe," in Maier, ed., *The Cold War in Europe,* pp. 245–46.

Chapter 7. Third World Nationalism and the Great Powers

1. Churchill cited in Akira Iriye, *The Cold War in Asia: A Historical Introduction* (Englewood Cliffs, N.J.: Prentice-Hall, 1974), 87.

2. *Foreign Relations of the United States, 1945: The Conferences of Malta and Yalta* (Washington: Government Printing Office, 1955), 884.

3. *The Complete War Memoirs of Charles de Gaulle,* trans. Jonathan Griffin and Richard Howard (New York: Simon & Schuster, 1967), p. 573.

4. Republic of France, Ministère des Colonies, *Brazzaville: 30 janvier–8 fevrier 1944,* p. 32.

5. Tony Smith, *The Pattern of Imperialism: The United States, Great Britain, and the Late Industrializing World Since 1815* (Cambridge: Cambridge University Press, 1981), chapter 3; see also John Darwin, *Britain and Decolonisation: The Retreat from Empire in the Post-war World* (New York: St. Martin's, 1988); Anton Andereggen, *France's Relationship with Subsaharan Africa* (Westport, Conn.: Praeger, 1994).

6. See the four articles on French-African relations by Eric Fottorino in *Le Monde,* July 22–26, 1997.

7. On Soviet and American thinking about the Third World, see Tony Smith, *Thinking Like a Communist: State and Legitimacy in the Soviet Union, China, and Cuba* (New York: Norton, 1987), chapter 4.

8. John Lewis Gaddis, *We Now Know: Rethinking Cold War History* (New York: Oxford University Press, 1997); and Andrzej Korbonski and Francis Fukuyama, eds., *The Soviet Union and the Third World: The Last Three Decades* (Ithaca: Cornell University Press, 1987).

9. See the documentation gathered in the Woodrow Wilson Center's Cold War International History Project *Bulletin,* no. 8/9, 1996–97.

10. Tony Smith, *America's Mission: The United States and the Worldwide Struggle for Democracy in the Twentieth Century* (Princeton: Princeton University Press, 1994), chapter 5.

11. Ibid., pp. 14, 90, 114, 163, 327.

12. John Lewis Gaddis, *Strategies of Containment: A Critical Appraisal of Postwar American National Security Policy* (New York: Oxford University Press, 1982).

13. For example, see Thomas Risse-Kappen, *Cooperation Among Democracies: The European Influence on U.S. Foreign Policy* (Princeton: Princeton University Press, 1995).

Chapter 8. The United States, the Cold War, and the Post–Cold War Order

1. That system arose out of the Napoleonic wars and, though its norms had eroded by the late nineteenth century, it survived the upheaval of German and Italian unification, guided by the underlying conservatism of British and German policy. As that conservatism eroded, especially in Berlin, Paris, and St. Petersburg, and as the horror of general war dissipated and alliance rivalry intensified, the ingredients for collapse fell into place. An outline of the nineteenth-century system during its efflorescence, contrasting it with its eighteenth-century

predecessor, is offered in Paul W. Schroeder, *The Transformation of European Politics, 1763–1848* (Oxford: Clarendon, 1994).

2. For an overview see Abbott Gleason, *Totalitarianism: An Inner History of the Cold War* (New York: Oxford University Press, 1995).

3. The best glimpses of the thinking in the Soviet Foreign Ministry in 1945–46 are afforded by Vladimîr O. Pechatnov, "The Big Three After World War II: New Documents on Soviet Thinking About Post-War Relations with the United States and Great Britain," Cold War International History Project [hereinafter CWIHP] Working Paper no. 13, July 1995; and the Novikov (Molotov) telegram of September 1946 reproduced in Kenneth M. Jensen, ed., *Origins of the Cold War: The Novikov, Kennan, and Roberts "Long Telegrams" of 1946*, rev. ed. (Washington, D.C.: U.S. Institute of Peace, 1993), taking particular note of the commentary by Steven Merritt Miner. For a discussion of Roosevelt's postwar vision that charitably emphasizes its coherence, see John Lamberton Harper, *American Visions of Europe* (Cambridge: Cambridge University Press, 1994), pp. 77–121.

4. John Lewis Gaddis, *We Now Know: Rethinking Cold War History* (Oxford: Clarendon, 1997), pp. 51–53. For example: "One empire arose, therefore, by invitation, the other by imposition." My quarrel with this formulation is only that Gaddis, trying to find common ground with other scholars, has been too generous in adopting others' usage of the term "empire." Voluntary associations of nations that have no "emperor" or equivalent office, that select their own rulers, that have few or no common laws, and no imperial or supranational policing are not empires. Too elastic usage of "empire" is directly akin to Johan Galtung's description of unrealized social potential as "violence" (indirect, structural), thus equating economic disadvantage or subordination with being shot dead. Philosophically we must be wary, when stumbling upon such surreal use of the language, to prevent "an encroachment of coherence considerations upon standards of truth." Willard V. Quine, *Pursuit of Truth*, rev. ed. (Cambridge: Harvard University Press, 1990), p. 98.

5. See, for example, the portraits of how American and British officials perceived their choices in William Stueck, *The Korean War: An International History* (Princeton: Princeton University Press, 1995), pp. 132–38, 148–51.

6. On this last point see, in particular, Gordon Chang and He Di, "The Absence of War in the U.S.-China Confrontation over Quemoy and Matsu in 1954–1955: Contingency, Luck, Deterrence?" *American Historical Review* (December 1993): 1500–1524.

7. See Marc Trachtenberg, *History and Strategy* (Princeton: Princeton University Press, 1991), pp. 100–152.

8. See Nikita S. Khrushchev, *Khrushchev Remembers*, trans. and ed. Strobe Talbott (Boston: Little, Brown, 1970), pp. 434–36; Adam B. Ulam, *Expansion and Coexistence: The History of Soviet Foreign Policy, 1917–1967* (New York: Praeger, 1968), pp. 586–89; and Adam B. Ulam, *The Rivals: America and Russia Since World War II* (New York: Viking, 1971), pp. 253–66.

9. McGeorge Bundy has a persuasive portrait of Eisenhower's attitudes in *Danger and Survival: Choices About the Bomb in the First Fifty Years* (New York: Random House, 1988).

10. See Vladislav Zubok and Constantine Pleshakov, *Inside the Kremlin's Cold War: From Stalin to Khrushchev* (Cambridge: Harvard University Press, 1995). A good portrait of the renewed confidence in Soviet power, amid a well-researched picture of the subjective tilts and veers in Soviet as well as American perceptions of the strategic balance, is in William Curti Wohlforth, *The Elusive Balance: Power and Perceptions During the Cold War* (Ithaca: Cornell University Press, 1993).

11. See Qiang Zhai, *The Dragon, the Lion, and the Eagle* (Kent, Ohio: Kent State University Press, 1994), pp. 178–207; Shu Guang Zhang, *Deterrence and Strategic Culture: Chinese-American Confrontations, 1949–1958* (Ithaca: Cornell University Press, 1992), pp. 225–67; and the convenient synthesis in Gaddis, *We Now Know*, pp. 250–53.

12. See the discussion and sources cited in Ernest May and Philip Zelikow, *The Kennedy Tapes: Inside the White House During the Cuban Missile Crisis* (Cambridge: Harvard University Press, 1997), pp. 34–35, 38–39, 678–80. One reason Kennedy's decisions during the missile crisis seemed so difficult was because he thought he was choosing not simply between war and peace but in effect, between an immediate nuclear confrontation over Cuba or a later nuclear confrontation, under even worse circumstances, over Berlin. See, e.g., his summary of the discussion on the night of October 18 and his explanation of the matter to the Joint Chiefs of Staff on October 19, ibid., pp. 172, 175–76.

13. See Qiang Zhai, "Beijing and the Vietnam Conflict, 1964–1965: New Chinese Evidence," CWIHP *Bulletin*, no. 6–7 (Winter 1995–96): 233–43.

14. On the Soviet invasion of Czechoslovakia, see the new information in Anatoly Dobrynin, *In Confidence* (New York: Random House, 1995), pp. 183–88.

15. Ibid., p. 617.

16. Timothy Garton Ash, *In Europe's Name: Germany and the Divided Continent* (New York: Random House, 1993), p. 178.

17. Ibid., pp. 152–76, 188–89; A. James McAdams, *Germany Divided:*

From the Wall to Reunification (Princeton: Princeton University Press, 1993), p. 176.

18. Quoted in David Marsh, *The Germans: A People at the Crossroads* (New York: St. Martin's, 1990), pp. 115–18.

19. Helmut Kohl, *Ich Wollte Deutschlands Einheit,* ed. Kai Diekmann and Ralf Georg Reuth (Berlin: PropylSen, 1996), p. 33.

20. Willy Brandt, *Erinnerungen* (Zurich: PropylSen, 1989), p. 55. The language in Reagan's speech reportedly originated with a White House speechwriter, Peter Robinson. Lou Cannon, *President Reagan: The Role of a Lifetime* (New York: Simon & Schuster, 1991), p. 774.

21. For background, see Jonathan Valdez, *Internationalism and the Ideology of Soviet Influence in Eastern Europe* (Cambridge: Cambridge University Press, 1993).

22. Don Oberdorfer, "Thatcher: Gorbachev Has Ended Cold War," *Boston Globe,* November 18, 1988, p. 7; George Shultz, *Turmoil and Triumph: My Years as Secretary of State* (New York: Charles Scribner's, 1993), pp. 1131, 1138.

23. In their memoir, *A World Transformed* (New York: Knopf, 1998), George Bush and Brent Scowcroft call their perspective one of "gentle rollback." For evidence that this is not just a retrospective gloss, and evidence on the related arguments in the new administration, see Philip Zelikow and Condoleezza Rice, *Germany Unified and Europe Transformed: A Study in Statecraft,* rev. ed. (Cambridge: Harvard University Press, 1997), pp. 24–32; Robert L. Hutchings, *American Diplomacy and the End of the Cold War* (Baltimore: Johns Hopkins University Press, 1997), pp. 35–40, 54–71. For Mandelbaum's views, see his "Ending the Cold War," *Foreign Affairs* 68 (Spring 1989): 19.

24. On this framing of the problem and the vital judgments, see Zelikow and Rice, *Germany Unified and Europe Transformed,* pp. 81–92; on the internal dynamics in East Germany see generally Elizabeth Pond, *Beyond the Wall: Germany's Road to Unification* (Washington, D.C.: Brookings Institution, 1993); Charles S. Maier, *Dissolution: East Germany from the Crisis of Communism to the Trials of Unity* (Princeton: Princeton University Press, 1997).

25. See Zelikow and Rice, *Germany Unified and Europe Transformed,* esp. chapters 4 and 5.

26. Ibid., pp. 128–29 (at Malta summit meeting of December 1989).

27. Ibid., p. 115 (to Bush in a phone conversation on November 17, 1989).

28. For a sampling of many relevant Mitterrand quotations see Jacques Attali, *Verbatim, 3, Chronique des années 1988–1991* (Paris: Fayard, 1995), pp. 241, 313, 337, 369, 416, 495.

29. See Hutchings, *American Diplomacy and the End of the Cold War,* pp. 190–96, 273–300; Vojtech Mastny, ed., *The Helsinki Process and the*

Reintegration of Europe, 1986–1991: Analysis and Documentation (New York: New York University Press, 1992); John Fry, *The Helsinki Process: Negotiating Security and Cooperation in Europe* (Washington, D.C.: National Defense University Press, 1993); and Zelikow and Rice, *Germany Unified and Europe Transformed,* pp. 303–14, 443n.105.

30. Anatoly Chernyayev, interview, in Zelikow and Rice, *Germany Unified and Europe Transformed,* p. 332.

31. On the July 1990 party congress, see Robert Kaiser, *Why Gorbachev Happened: His Triumphs, His Failure, and His Fall,* rev. ed. (New York: Simon & Schuster, 1991), pp. 336–56.

32. See Ed Hewett, "The New Soviet Plan," *Foreign Affairs* 69 (Winter 1990–91): 146.

33. An appropriately vivid account of the August 1991 events is in Michael Dobbs, *Down with Big Brother: The Fall of the Soviet Empire* (New York: Knopf, 1997), pp. 371–421.

34. See James A. Baker, III, with Thomas M. DeFrank, *The Politics of Diplomacy: Revolution, War, and Peace, 1989–1992* (New York: Putnam's, 1995), pp. 525–26.

35. Ibid., p. 583. During a fluid and pivotal period from December 15–19, 1991, just after the Brest declaration was announced but before the Alma-Ata meeting, Baker flew to and met with the key players in Moscow, Bishkek (Kyrgyzstan), Alma-Ata (Kazakhstan), Minsk (Belarus), and Kiev (Ukraine).

36. On the arduous negotiations leading up to the Lisbon accord, the best available source is ibid., pp. 658–65.

37. See Zelikow and Rice, *Germany Unified and Europe Transformed,* pp. 258–60, 325–27, 337–38, 349–52.

38. For a more generous but still balanced summary see Hutchings, *American Diplomacy and the End of the Cold War,* pp. 196–212, 333–34; see also Baker with DeFrank, *The Politics of Diplomacy,* pp. 613–19, 654–58.

39. Joseph S. Nye, Jr., *Bound to Lead: The Changing Nature of American Power* (New York: Basic, 1990); C. John Ikenberry and Charles A. Kupchan, "Socialization and Hegemonic Power," *International Organization* 44 (Summer 1990): 283, 284.

40. These points are elaborated in Philip Zelikow, "The New Concert of Europe," *Survival* 34 (Summer 1992): 12–30.

41. See Philip Zelikow, "The Masque of Institutions," *Survival* 38 (Spring 1996): 6–18.

42. Frank Ninkovich, *Modernity and Power: A History of the Domino Theory in the Twentieth Century* (Chicago: University of Chicago Press, 1994), p. 248.

Chapter 9. Europe After the Cold War: Realism, Idealism, and the Search for Order Without Empire

I wish to thank the many government officials in Bonn, Paris, and Washington who have generously shared their time and their insights into the policies and events under consideration in this chapter, with a special thanks to Dr. Martin Ney. I would also like to acknowledge the research assistance of Henry Farrell and Gregory Caplan, whose careful minds have greatly improved this work.

1. For insight into these two strands of thinking in the new Bush administration during the first half of 1989, see James A. Baker, III, *The Politics of Diplomacy: Revolution, War, and Peace, 1989–1992* (New York: G. P. Putnam's, 1995), chapters 5 and 6.

2. Numerous accounts of the diplomacy and politics of the process that brought about German unity have been written. The most authoritative, given its unparalleled access to confidential archives in the United States, West Germany, and the Soviet Union (specifically the personal papers of Mikhail Gorbachev) is Philip Zelikow and Condoleezza Rice, *Germany Unified and Europe Transformed* (Cambridge: Harvard University Press, 1995). See also Horst Teltschik, *329 Tage: Innenansichten der Einigung* (Berlin: Siedler, 1991), and Elizabeth Pond, *Beyond the Wall: Germany's Road to Unification* (Washington, D.C.: Brookings Institution, 1993).

3. Indeed, that was what was reportedly toasted by the foreign ministers of the four powers on September 12, 1990, when they signed the act that ended their rights and responsibilities for Germany. Zelikow and Rice, *Germany Unified*, p. 2.

4. It may well be that after Helmut Kohl's ten-point plan was announced, no one was in control of the process of German unity. Kohl, however, still maintains the plan was not intended to produce anything more than a framework for German unity, which he believed at the time would make the process more controllable rather than accelerate it. Teltschik, *329 Tage*, pp. 42–86. In any case, the United States was the only one of the four powers to understand that trying to inhibit the process rather than channel it would likely produce security losses rather than gains. Baker, *The Politics of Diplomacy*, pp. 58–68.

5. For a full discussion of the strategies for reassuring the Soviet Union while moving steadfastly toward the goal of German unity within NATO, see Baker, *The Politics of Diplomacy*, pp. 230–60. See also Zelikow and Rice, *Germany Unified*, pp. 251–85.

6. The most important of these steps prior to German unity was taken in the July 1990 NATO summit. The "London Declaration of a Transformed North Atlantic Alliance" issued on July 6 offered to establish

a fundamentally new relationship between the alliance and its former adversaries, including the creation of liaison missions by members of the Warsaw Pact at NATO's military strategy, with a movement away from "forward defense" and "flexible response," and relegation of nuclear forces to weapons of last resort. For detailed description of the U.S. position leading up to the summit, see Zelikow and Rice, *Germany Unified,* pp. 303–24. See also Robert Hutchings, *American Diplomacy and the End of the Cold War* (Baltimore: Johns Hopkins University Press, 1997), chapter 3.

7. It presumably became unavoidable when it became clear that the only alternative available to unity was a reassertion of Soviet control in East Germany. To have pursued this path would have had dramatic consequences for Soviet relations with the West, and thus for the entire range of Soviet reform policies begun under Gorbachev.

8. One of the key strands was clearly the reevaluation by the Soviet military of the ways wars might occur that could threaten the Soviet Union, which had apparently reached a critical point already in the early 1980s. For a summary of the arguments, see Michael MccGwire, "Rethinking War: The Soviets and European Security," *Brookings Review* 6, no. 2 (Spring 1988): 3–12, and for a more complete exploration, Michael MccGwire, *Perestroika and Soviet National Security* (Washington, D.C.: Brookings Institution, 1991). The completion of the nuclear revolution in Soviet doctrine that occurred at that time was a precondition for the reevaluation of the costs and benefits of Moscow's Eastern European empire and, ultimately, the collapse of the buffer zone. But if a reduction of the empire's geostrategic significance can provide the basis for accepting a fundamentally different relationship between Moscow and the capitals of Eastern Europe, it alone surely could not have made German unity acceptable on its own. On the meeting in the Caucasus, see Teltschik, *329 Tage,* pp. 316–42; Hans-Dietrich Genscher, *Erinnerungen* (Berlin: Siedler, 1995), pp. 833–41; and Zelikow and Rice, *Germany Unified,* pp. 333–42.

9. There is actually no way to prove that the Soviet Union saw Germany as any less of a threat specifically because of its integration in the European Community. For a broader assessment of changing Soviet attitudes toward the threat from Germany, and more precisely the roles of Western integration and Ostpolitik in helping facilitate reunification, see Timothy Garton Ash, *In Europe's Name: Germany and the Divided Continent* (New York: Random House, 1993), particularly chapter 8. For a general analysis of the Soviet approach to Germany, see F. Stephen Larrabee, "Moscow and the German Question," in D. Verheyen and C. Søe, *The Germans and Their Neighbors* (Boulder, Colo.: Westview, 1993), pp. 201–29.

10. Hannes Adomeit, "Gorbachev, German Unification, and the Collapse of Empire," *Post-Soviet Affairs* 10, no. 3 (July–September 1994): 197–233, and Hannes Adomeit, "Gorbachev and German Unification: Revision of Thinking, Realignment of Power," *Problems of Communism* 39, no. 4 (July–August 1990): 1–23.

11. Quote from Alexander Bessmertnykh in a 1991 interview in Michael Beschloss and Strobe Talbott, *At the Highest Levels: The Inside Story of the End of the Cold War* (Boston: Little, Brown, 1993), p. 240.

12. The July 1990 London Declaration seems to have been important in convincing the Soviet leadership that the NATO into which a united Germany would be integrated was indeed a new NATO. Washington was careful to provide both Gorbachev and Shevardnadze with details of the declaration before and immediately after the summit, allowing them to use the material in their internal battle against opposition to German unity within NATO. Hutchings, *American Diplomacy*, pp. 135–37.

13. Zelikow and Rice, *Germany Unified*, pp. 360–63, provides ample evidence for the various maneuvers of both Thatcher and Mitterrand in their respective attempts to impede German reunification. The Germans even believed that the British consciously risked the entire outcome of the 2 + 4 negotiations when they raised last-minute concerns about the types of NATO maneuvers that could be conducted on the former territory of the GDR after unification.

14. Much of the French effort beginning in spring 1990 was directed toward strengthening the European integration process, which Paris saw as a way to bind a Germany newly strengthened by reunification into a framework that would control its power, and give France a stronger voice in European affairs than it would otherwise have. Claire Tréan, "La France et la nouvelle ordre européen," *Politique Etrangère* 50, no. 1 (Spring 1991): 81–90.

15. For a different interpretation of these same events, see Robert J. Art, "Why Western Europe Needs the United States," *Political Science Quarterly* 111, no. 1 (1996): 1–39. Art focuses on the differences among the allies over the appropriate institutional framework for European security, and he finds these to be proof that security concerns and relative power positions remained strong motivations in Western Europe after the Cold War. He also believes that they threatened to create a destructive security competition among the allies that might have called into question European integration had they not been successfully resolved. My interpretation ascribes more importance to the strength and durability of institutional frameworks than to the fact that differences arose over how best to adapt these frameworks. The outcome of the disputes and the absence of a serious security competition

among the allies certaily speaks in favor of the present analysis. Security and relative power were clearly of concern, but the institutional framework within which the competition for influence was sorted out was more important than the existence of the competition—a historically new phenomenon among Europe's powers.

16. The difference between the approaches of the two men are well known, but there was convergence on this key issue of the role of the CSCE in Soviet acceptance of German unity. Confirmed in conversations with Jürgen Chrobog (at the time political director of the German Foreign Office) and Martin Ney (legal adviser in the West German Foreign Office to the 2 + 4 talks, and subsequently personal assistant to State Secretary Dieter Kastrup), May 1996.

17. The meeting was hastily arranged on the edge of the meeting of the U.N. General Assembly specifically for this purpose. Conversation with Martin Ney, May 1996.

18. Early in the unification process, Genscher in fact did not believe that unity within NATO would be an achievable goal, and spoke of the need for developing within a newly constituted CSCE "cooperative security structures—in which the alliances could later be absorbed." Hans-Dietrich Genscher, "Zur deutschen Einheit im europäischen Rahmen," speech before the Tutzing Protestant Academy on January 31, 1990 (*Der Bundesminister des Auswärtigen informiert, Mitteilung für die Presse*, No. 1026/1990).

19. Although this was not widely understood by Germany's allies, Genscher was reportedly preoccupied with the importance of this ratification by the Duma. His fear was that the Soviet Union would conclude that the West was moving to take advantage of a period of Soviet weakness, and to use this as an excuse to forestall ratification of the treaty. Conversations with German Foreign Office officials, June 1996.

20. This is all the more true, given that the original German government preferences were for a strong commitment to political union to accompany economic and monetary union, an objective for which it was unable to achieve adequate support. That Germany signed the Maastricht Treaty in the absence of this commitment signifies the importance it attached to strengthening European integration in the wake of the collapse of the Berlin Wall. For the evolution of German policy toward European integration during this period, see David Schoenbaum and Elizabeth Pond, *The German Question and Other German Questions* (New York: St. Martin's, 1996), pp. 174–229.

21. For more complete analysis of French policy during this period, see Anne-Marie LeGloannec, "Mitterrand et l'Allemagne," *French Politics and Society* 9 (Summer–Fall 1991): 121–29; Steven Philip Kramer, "The French Question," *Washington Quarterly* 14, no. 4 (Autumn

1991): 83–96; and Stanley Hoffmann, "French Dilemmas and Strategies in the New Europe" (Cambridge: Minda de Gunzberg Center for European Studies, Harvard University, n. d. [1992]).

22. Hoffmann, "French Dilemmas," pp. 140–41; and Kramer, "The French Question," pp. 87–88.

23. This was widely reputed to be the opinion of National Security Adviser Brent Scowcroft. It was the case regularly made by Robert Blackwill, special adviser to the president for Europe, in numerous private working groups around Washington during this period.

24. For further details on the controversy over a European security identity, see Art, "Why Western Europe Needs the United States."

25. The specific event that seems to have triggered the U.S. response was a "Joint Initiative on Establishing a Common Foreign and Security Policy," by French foreign minister Roland Dumas and German foreign minister Genscher on February 4, 1991. The initiative asserted that a European Union would be incomplete without a defense dimension, and concentrated on ways to transform the WEU into the nucleus of a European defense identity. Kramer, "The French Question," pp. 91–92.

26. Steven Greenhouse, "U.S. and France Are at Odds over a NATO Army," *New York Times,* May 28, 1991, p. 1.

27. A good summary of the arguments between particularly the French and the Americans during spring 1991 can be found in Edward Mortimer, "Europe's Teetering Pillar," *Financial Times,* May 1, 1991, p. 19.

28. Alan Riding, "U.S. Wary of European Corps, Seeks Assurance on NATO Role," *New York Times,* October 20, 1991, p. 12.

29. Conversation with Jürgen Chrobog, May 1996.

30. Alan Cowell, "Bush Challenges Partners in NATO over Role of U.S.," *New York Times,* November 8, 1991, p. 1.

31. This is the problem that Pierre Hassner had already identified as the core dilemma of the Atlantic alliance back in the late 1960s. See his classic *Change and Security in Europe: Part I,* Adelphi Paper 45 (London: International Institute for Strategic Studies, 1967).

32. The importance of Kantian ideals to thinking about the new European order was explicit during this period. For example, Helmut Kohl, in his opening speech to the CSCE foreign ministers gathering in Berlin on June 19, 1991, referred directly to Kant's *Perpetual Peace* and spoke of the uniting of Europe through the validation of human rights embodied in the French Revolution. The speech clearly articulated the importance of democracy and domestic order to securing the international order that Europe was attempting to create. Speech repro-

duced in *Bulletin,* Presse- und Informationsamt der Bundesregierung, no. 72, June 22, 1991, pp. 577–79.

33. For a detailed and not uncritical assessment of American policy toward Yugoslavia in the period leading up to its collapse, see Warren Zimmermann, *Origins of a Catastrophe: Yugoslavia and Its Destroyers* (New York: Times, 1996).

34. While one might argue that the recognition of Slovenia may have helped to limit the territorial reach of the immediate crisis, there can be little doubt that Western recognition of Croatia provided the excuse for the war in the Krajina, and subsequently led directly to the Bosnian declaration of independence, followed by the tragedy that unfolded there.

35. Susan Woodward makes a powerful case for this point in her analysis of the Yugoslav situation in *Balkan Tragedy: Chaos and Dissolution After the Cold War* (Washington, D.C.: Brookings Institution, 1995).

36. This was eventually symbolized by the creation of the contact group, which helped ensure that differences of perspective among the major powers on how to deal with the ongoing crisis could be more or less kept under control.

37. For a careful summary of the evolution of CSCE efforts in the area of conflict resolution during this period, see Gregory Flynn and Henry Farrell, "Piecing Together the Democratic Peace: The CSCE, Norms, and the 'Construction' of Security in Post–Cold War Europe," *International Organization* 53, no. 3 (Summer 1999): 505–35. The best summary of the overall institutional evolution of the CSCE can be found in Arie Bloed, *The Conference on Security and Cooperation in Europe: Analysis and Basic Documents, 1972–1993* (Dordrecht: Kluwer Academic, 1993).

38. The Valletta mechanism marked an important step forward in the development of the CSCE because it limited the principle of unanimity. But it was essentially stillborn and has never been used. It was saddled with a substantial number of escape clauses, which excluded key categories of disputes from consideration, and the commissions of international experts that could be created under its aegis were only empowered to make non-binding recommendations.

39. Although the emergency mechanism could be invoked by less that unanimous consent, and the Committee of Senior Officials of the CSCE could make recommendations on how to resolve a situation, these recommendations had to be reached by consensus.

40. This was a substantial innovation because it established the N-1 principle for members taking action. At the same time, any subsequent decisions by the CSCE about how to deal with the situation after re-

ceiving the report of a mission would still have to be taken by consensus.

41. For a comprehensive review of the negotiations that led to the Helsinki II Agreements, see Arie Bloed, ed., *The Challenge of Change: The Helsinki Summit of the CSCE and Its Aftermath* (Dordrecht: Martinus Nijhoff, 1994).

42. Members of the Bush administration argued forcefully that the preservation of NATO while some Cold War structures were collapsing, and while there was significant pressure for strengthening pan-European institutions and for creating a framework for a European defense identity, was a defining element of the new European context. There is no doubt that Europe would have looked very different by 1992 had NATO collapsed. However, NATO may never have been in as much danger as was frequently thought in Washington during this period. In any case, the most important adaptation of NATO to the new security environment, in terms of adjustments to its force posture as well as how it would relate as an institution to the states of Central and Eastern Europe, was largely undertaken in the period following that being considered here.

43. Flynn and Farrell, "Piecing Together the Democratic Peace."

Chapter 10. The International Financial System and the Nation-State

1. John Maynard Keynes, *The Economic Consequences of the Peace* (New York: Harcourt, Brace and Howe, 1920), p. 3.

2. J. M. Winter, *The Experience of World War I* (New York: Cambridge University Press, 1989), p. 206.

3. Rondo Cameron, *A Concise Economic History of the World: From Paleolithic Times to the Present,* 2d ed. (New York: Oxford University Press, 1993), p. 347.

4. One example will suffice. In 1913 the United Kingdom's exports of cotton piece goods stood at 7.075 billion linear yards. The yearly average for the years 1920–23 fell to 4.072 billion, and for 1924–25 it only reached 4.611 billion. See Trevor Wilson, *The Myriad Faces of War: Britain and the Great War, 1914–1918* (Cambridge, Eng.: Polity, 1986), p. 794. Also see Winter, *The Experience of World War I,* p. 216.

5. The Soviet Union finally made an appearance on the world economic stage at the 1922 Genoa Conference. Soviet dictator Vladimir Ilyich Lenin's intentions are now clear. As he wrote to Georgy Vasilievich Chicherin on February 10, 1922, "It suits us that Genoa be wrecked but *not by us,* of course" (emphasis in original). Richard Pipes, ed., *The Unknown Lenin: From the Secret Archive* (New Haven: Yale University Press, 1996), p. 145. Also see Carole Fink, *The Genoa Confer-*

ence: *European Diplomacy, 1921–1922* (Chapel Hill: University of North Carolina Press, 1984).

6. Wilson, *Myriad Faces of War*, p. 792. Also see William Ashworth, *An Economic History of England, 1870–1939* (London: Methuen, 1960), pp. 264–302; and Sidney Pollard, *The Development of the British Economy 1914–1980*, 3d ed. (London: Edward Arnold, 1983), pp. 1–50.

7. David M. Kennedy, *Over Here: The First World War and American Society* (New York: Oxford University Press, 1980), p. 297.

8. That the New York Stock Exchange closed for almost four months following the outbreak of the war is proof positive of this symbiotic relationship.

9. Kennedy, *Over Here*, p. 338.

10. On British borrowing in the United States, see Kathleen Burk, *Britain, America, and the Sinews of War, 1914–1918* (Boston: Allen & Unwin, 1985).

11. The Supreme Allied Council set the German obligation at 132 milliard (billion) gold marks ($33 billion). But this sum was theoretical: the Weimar government was held responsible to pay interest and amortization immediately on the "A" and "B" bonds only—a total of 50 milliard marks. Stephen A. Schuker, *The End of French Predominance in Europe: The Financial Crisis of 1924 and the Adoption of the Dawes Plan* (Chapel Hill: University of North Carolina Press, 1976), p. 14.

12. On German inflation, see Gerald D. Feldman, *The Great Disorder: Politics, Economics, and Society in the German Inflation, 1914–1924* (New York: Oxford University Press, 1993).

13. On the reparations imbroglio and Ruhr invasion see Melvyn P. Leffler, *The Elusive Quest: America's Pursuit of European Stability and French Security, 1919–1933* (Chapel Hill: University of North Carolina Press, 1979); Stephen A. Schuker, *American "Reparations" to Germany, 1919–1933: Implications for the Third World Debt Crisis* (Princeton: International Finance Section, Department of Economics, Princeton University, 1988); Schuker, *The End of French Predominance in Europe*; Marc Trachtenberg, *Reparation in World Politics: France and European Economic Diplomacy, 1916–1923* (New York: Columbia University Press, 1980).

14. The Morgan bank indeed began in Britain. American banker Junius Morgan started the family fortune by going into partnership with fellow expatriate George Peabody. From their London headquarters the two men dealt in "Yankee bonds": American securities sold abroad. Junius's son J. P. Morgan brought the firm back to the United States and concentrated on becoming the most important American financier

of the industrial age. Junius also took into the firm Peabody's distant relative S. Endicott Peabody, whose son, also named Endicott, founded the Groton School, which later numbered Franklin Roosevelt among its distinguished alumni. See Vincent P. Carosso, *The Morgans: Private International Bankers, 1854–1913* (Cambridge: Harvard University Press, 1987); Ron Chernow, *The House of Morgan: An American Banking Dynasty and the Rise of Modern Finance* (New York: Atlantic Monthly Press, 1990).

15. Lester Chandler, *Benjamin Strong, Central Banker* (Washington: Brookings Institution, 1958).

16. On the activities of the Federal Reserve Bank of New York, see Stephen V. O. Clarke, *Central Bank Cooperation, 1924–1931* (New York: Federal Reserve Bank of New York, 1967).

17. On Norman's career, see Andrew Boyle, *Montagu Norman* (London: Cassell, 1967); Henry Clay, *Lord Norman* (London: Macmillan, 1957); R. S. Sayers, *The Bank of England, 1891–1944* (Cambridge: Cambridge University Press, 1976).

18. Unfortunately the necessity to keep interest rates high to protect gold reserves had the effect of further damaging British industry.

19. See Diane B. Kunz, *The Battle for Britain's Gold Standard in 1931* (London: Croom Helm, 1987).

20. The president of the New York bank, George Harrison, was stripped of power and influence by the changes to the Federal Reserve Act in 1935. He went on to serve as a key civilian official on the Manhattan Project.

21. On international financial relations during the depression, see Barry Eichengreen, *Golden Fetters: The Gold Standard and the Great Depression, 1919–1939* (New York: Oxford University Press, 1992); Charles P. Kindleberger, *The World in Depression, 1929–1939* (Berkeley and Los Angeles: University of California Press, 1973).

22. Baldwin used this quote when speaking of the English press barons' campaign in favor of imperial free trade. He added that what Lord Beaverbrook and Lord Rothermere sought was the prerogative of the harlot throughout the ages.

23. On the Anglo-American negotiations, see Richard N. Gardner, *Sterling-Dollar Diplomacy in Current Perspective: The Origins and the Prospects of Our International Economic Order* (New York: Columbia University Press, 1980); Randall Bennett Woods, *A Changing of the Guard: Anglo-American Relations, 1941–1946* (Chapel Hill: University of North Carolina Press, 1990).

24. Concerning the Bretton Woods agreements, see Kenneth W. Dam, *The Rules of the Game: Reform and Evolution in the International Monetary System* (Chicago: University of Chicago Press, 1982); Harold

James, *International Cooperation Since Bretton Woods* (Washington: International Monetary Fund, 1996).

25. Forgotten was the fact that these miracles were midwifed by the "cost-plus contract." Essentially a blank check drawn on the U.S. Treasury, it enabled businessmen to utilize the trial-and-error method of production, to become profligate spenders, and to be generous to their workers, all without ever sacrificing any profits.

26. As Woods points out, the United States spent $8 billion a month on the war, and the total capitalization of the World Bank was $9.1 billion. Woods, *Changing of the Guard,* p. 144.

27. For a full account of American Cold War economic diplomacy, see Diane B. Kunz, *Butter and Guns: America's Cold War Economic Diplomacy* (New York: Free Press, 1997).

28. On the Marshall Plan, see Michael J. Hogan, *The Marshall Plan: America, Britain, and the Reconstruction of Western Europe, 1947–1952* (Cambridge: Cambridge University Press, 1987); and Alan S. Milward, *The Reconstruction of Western Europe, 1945–1951* (Berkeley and Los Angeles: University of California Press, 1984).

29. If we look at the two sectors mentioned in the text, education and housing, the comparison is exact. Defense appropriations enriched universities throughout the Cold War while the massive system of military bases spread throughout the United States built more housing than all American public housing programs combined.

30. The Soviets had to cope with competition from another nation-state—the People's Republic of China—a fate largely avoided by the United States.

31. Karal Ann Marling, *As Seen on TV: The Visual Culture of Everyday Life in the 1950s* (Cambridge: Harvard University Press, 1994), p. 276.

32. On the role of central banks, see Marjorie Deane and Robert Pringle, *The Central Banks* (New York: Viking, 1994); David Marsh, *The Bundesbank: The Bank that Rules Europe* (London: Heinemann, 1992).

33. The above account of the Mexican crisis comes largely from Bradford de Long, Christopher de Long, and Sherman Robinson, "The Case for Mexico's Rescue," *Foreign Affairs* 75, no. 3 (May–June 1996): 8–14.

34. Neither small investors nor fund mangers had apparently stopped to think why Mexican interest rates bore so large a risk premium.

35. Zanny Minton-Beddoes, "Why the IMF Needs Reform," *Foreign Affairs* 74, no. 3 (May–June 1995): 128.

36. C. Fred Bergsten, "The Dollar and the Euro," *Foreign Affairs* 76, no. 4 (July–August 1997): 83.

37. Title 11, U.S. Code.

38. John Maynard Keynes, *Essays in Persuasion* (London: Macmillan, 1972), p. 321.

Chapter 11. Global Issues and the New Security Agenda

1. Arms sales, particularly from developed to developing countries, are sometimes treated as being on the "new" security agenda. But in that they involve the transfer of military hardware, whether large (submarines, aircraft, nuclear materials) or small (hand-held weapons, mines), this is regarded here as a traditional security issue and not discussed.

2. For further discourse upon this theme, see Robert Chase, Emily Hill, and Paul Kennedy, eds., *The Pivotal States: A New Framework for U.S. Policy in the Developing World* (New York: Norton, 1998).

3. For a wonderful treatment of this and related themes, see William H. McNeill, *The Pursuit of Power: Technology, Armed Forces, and Society Since 1000 A.D.* (Chicago: University of Chicago Press, 1983).

4. Paul M. Kennedy, *Preparing for the Twenty-first Century* (New York: Random House, 1993), pp. 3–13.

5. See McNeill, *The Pursuit of Power*, p. 187.

6. Allen Hammond, *Which World? Scenarios for the Twenty-first Century* (Washington, D.C.: Island 1998), chapter 14, and Thomas F. Homer-Dixon, "On the Threshold: Environmental Changes as Causes of Acute Conflict," *International Security* 16, no. 2 (Fall 1991): 76–116.

7. On these points, see the chapters on India and Pakistan in Chase, Hill, and Kennedy, eds., *The Pivotal States*.

8. Homer-Dixon, "On the Threshold"; Kennedy, *Preparing for the Twenty-first Century*, pp. 101–3.

9. For an early, classic statement, see Jessica Tuchman Matthews, "Redefining Security," *Foreign Affairs* 68 (Spring 1989): 162–77.

10. Halford J. Mackinder, *Democratic Ideals and Reality* (1919; reprint, New York: Henry Holt, 1962), p. 23.

11. One thinks in this connection of the debates between Paul Ehrlich and Julian Simon over global resource depletion, or between Denis Avery and Lester Brown over future food supplies, in which all the advocates had a wealth of data to support quite contradictory positions. See John Tierney, "Betting the Planet," *New York Times Magazine,* December 2, 1990, pp. 52–53; David Berreby, *Discover* 11 (April 1990): 42–43; and Dennis T. Avery, "Feast or Famine?" *Far Eastern Economic Review* 157 (December 1, 1994): 40.

12. A case in point: In the December 1994 issue of the *Atlantic Monthly,* I and my co-author Matthew Connelly attempted to discuss this issue through the lens of a very racist novel, Jean Raspail's *The Camp of the Saints,* and ended with an appeal for international understanding and cooperation between North and South on population and migration. But the article was retitled "Must It Be the West Against the Rest?"

and the imaginative front cover showed a mild-mannered (white) American cooking a barbecue in his back yard while a vast sea of colored faces peered over the stockade fence. Unsurprisingly, as the authors we received many a letter from individuals who presumed from that cover alone that we were calling for efforts to prevent the demise of the white race.

13. See, for example, the proposals described in *Our Global Neighborhood,* the report of the Commission on Global Governance (Oxford: Oxford University Press, 1995); and *The United Nations in Its Second Half-Century* (New York: Yale University/Ford Foundation, 1995).

14. Best articulated in a UNDP publication, Inge Kaul, Isabelle Grunberg, and Marc Stern, eds., *Global Public Goods: International Cooperation in the Twenty-first Century* (New York: Oxford University Press, 1999).

15. See the nuanced arguments to this effect in the essays by Dan Esty and Charles Norchi in Chase, Hill, and Kennedy, eds., *The Pivotal States.*

Contributors

CAROLE FINK, professor of European international history at Ohio State University, is the author of *The Genoa Conference* (1984) and *Marc Bloch: A Life* (1989), co-editor of *1968: The World Transformed* (1999) and *The Establishment of European Frontiers After World Wars I and II* (1996), and has written several articles and essays on the international protection of minorities after the First World War.

GREGORY FLYNN is associate professor of international affairs and director of the M.A. program in German and European studies, School of Foreign Service, Georgetown University. He has written extensively on European security and international relations and is currently completing a book on European order after the collapse of bipolarity.

WILLIAM I. HITCHCOCK teaches history at Wellesley College. From 1996 to 1999 he was assistant professor of history and associate director of International Security Studies at Yale University. He is the author of *France Restored: Cold War Diplomacy and the Quest for Leadership in Europe* (1998).

MICHAEL HOWARD was Robert A. Lovett Professor of History at Yale University and Regius Professor of History at Oxford University. His many books include *The Lessons of History* (1991), *The Causes of Wars* (1983), and *War and the Liberal Conscience* (1978). He is the co-editor of *The Laws of War: Constraints on Warfare in the Western World* (1994).

PAUL KENNEDY is J. Richardson Dilworth Professor of History and director of International Security Studies at Yale University. He is the author of *The Rise and Fall of the Great Powers* (1987) and *Preparing for the Twenty-first Century* (1993).

DIANE B. KUNZ is adjunct professor of international relations at Columbia University. Her most recent book is *Butter and Guns: America's Cold War Economic Diplomacy* (1997).

MELVYN P. LEFFLER is Edward Stettinius Professor of American History at the University of Virginia. He is the author of *The Specter of Communism* (1994) and *A Preponderance of Power* (1992). The latter volume won the Bancroft, Hoover, and Ferrell prizes.

CHARLES S. MAIER is director of the Minda de Gunzburg Center for European Studies and a member of the history department at Harvard University. He is the author most recently of *Dissolution: The Crisis of Communism and the End of East Germany* (1997).

TONY SMITH is the Cornelia M. Jackson Professor of Political Science at Tufts University. He is the author of four books, two edited volumes, and some forty essays on international relations. He is currently completing a book on ethnic groups in U.S. foreign policy.

MARC TRACHTENBERG is professor of history at the University of Pennsylvania. He is the author most recently of *A Constructed Peace: The Making of the European Settlement, 1945–1963* (1999).

RANDALL B. WOODS is John A. Cooper, Sr., Distinguished Professor of History at the University of Arkansas. His books include *Fulbright: A Biography* (1995), which won the Ferrell Award. He is also the co-author, with Howard Jones, of *The Dawning of the Cold War: The United States' Quest for Security, 1944–1950* (1991), and *A Changing of the Guard: Anglo-American Relations, 1941–1946* (1990).

PHILIP ZELIKOW is White Burkett Miller Professor of History and director of the Miller Center of Public Affairs at the University of Virginia. A former official at the State Department and the White House, he is the co-author of *Essence of Decision* (second edition, 1999), *The Kennedy Tapes* (1997), and *Germany Unified and Europe Transformed* (1995).

Index